Smithsonian Folklife Cookbook

With appreciation for your support as
a Contributing Member of the Smithsonian National Associate Program

Katherine S. Kirlin and Thomas M. Kirlin

Smithsonian Institution Press · Washington and London

Smithsonian
Folklife Cookbook

Contents

✳ · ✳ · ✳ · ✳

* · * · * · *

Foreword

✳ · ✳ · ✳ · ✳

Ralph Rinzler

Food plays a unique role in human communication around the world. And if we look back, thousands of years, to the myths of early Greek and Roman civilization, the tale of Baucis and Philemon teaches us that when humble people share food at their table with traveling strangers of modest means, they are rewarded for their unstinting generosity. In this case, the gods Zeus and Hermes had disguised themselves as impoverished travelers.

The New Year's feast days of early Greco-Roman civilization, the Kalends, were marked with the leveling of caste differences and the sharing of ceremonially prepared dishes. In the countless tribal, village, and urban communities of today's world, commensality — sharing food with others — remains inseparable from celebratory and honoring occasions.

In my own fieldwork experience, which began in the late 1950s, I was warmly welcomed with special meals at the tables of musicians and craftspeople in Europe, Asia, and throughout the United States. The noted southern ballad singer Texas Gladden once remarked over a meal that she had just prepared, "I never met a stranger." On another occasion in the South, a hefty six-foot-four craftsman took me by surprise when we were seated at a veritable groaning board in his house. I asked him if he ate this way all the time. He replied, "Hell no, son, only three times a day."

The fact is, food is still one of the important ways in which people indicate that a guest is welcome in their home. In the Appalachians, Ozarks, Cajun country, Native American communities, and inner-city cultural enclaves, carefully prepared food invariably reaffirms the other assurances that you truly are welcome.

Food traditions were incorporated into the Festival of American Folklife in 1968. In each year's planning, we invariably went to community leaders to discuss how they would like to design this component of their cultural program. This question always provoked thought and often involved com-

Previous pages: A communal meal follows a wrist-tying ceremony by Khmer refugees from California at the Smithsonian's 1985 Festival of American Folklife. (Eric Long)

✳ · ✳ · ✳ · ✳

plex problem solving: Can we roast, on the National Mall, enough full-sized lambs and pigs to feed the public as well as our community participants? Can we build a beehive oven large enough and cure it quickly enough to bake our festival bread for all who attend the festival? The exercise always carried with it a special element of excitement, deep pleasure, and surprise, because the cooks, unlike the musicians, dancers, and other craftspeople, were seldom invited to "perform" their unique skills at events held outside the community. It is through their generous spirit of cooperation and adventure that cooks have enabled us to design relocated community celebrations for the festival. These attempts, on the Smithsonian's part, to establish community reaffirmation projects have benefited from the unique dimension that traditional food preparation and shared tasting contribute to celebrations.

In sum, the deep pleasure of new tastes and shared experience increases our understanding and affection for the genius and generosity of human cultural variety.

"She rubbed the table down with some sweet-smelling herbs. Upon it, she set some of chaste Minerva's olives, some cornel berries preserved in vinegar, and added radishes and cheese, with eggs lightly cooked in the ashes. All were served in earthen dishes, and an earthenware pitcher, with wooden cups, stood beside them. When all was ready, the stew, smoking hot, was set on the table. Some wine, not of the oldest, was added; and for dessert, apples and wild honey; and over and above all, friendly faces, and simple but hearty welcome."

**Baucis and Philemon
Bulfinch's Mythology**

Introduction

✳ · ✳ · ✳ · ✳

Katherine S. Kirlin and Thomas M. Kirlin

Like humor and jazz, food defines much of the American character. To celebrate this fact, the Smithsonian Institution has included food demonstrations in its Festival of American Folklife, held for the past twenty-five years in Washington, D.C. Festival participants are everyday people. They have a knack for cooking and a habit of sharing with other cooks — and good eaters — the culinary wisdom of their cultures.

To the more than 275 recipes collected here, the *Smithsonian Folklife Cookbook* has added anecdotes, essays, photographs, and drawings. Together, recipes, illustrations, and essays paint a vivid picture of America's foods and people who enjoy it. Lean a little closer to the conversation, and you can almost touch this gaggle of cooks, passing across a wonderfully fertile New World landscape, eating as they go, or preparing to eat, or talking about the food they just ate, and in whose company.

Cooks are not the only ones who relish talking about food. Here's Rayna Green, an American Indian (Cherokee) folklorist: "I am a wild-onion eater, from a whole region of wild-onion eaters. To me, those stinky *Allium*-family members are home, where I'm from, where I belong. Poke, cochanna, conunchi, hominy, and hog — these things make me myself, a Cherokee. Their presence tells me, even when they are served in an apartment in Washington, D.C., that I'm in Tsalagí, the Cherokee homeland."

Regardless of our origins, food is a source of self-identification, a means of alliance, the primary bond between a land and its people. Food enables us to speak across generations and to demonstrate a group's proud heritage by literally nourishing the appetite of others.

For this reason, in June and early July, a sampling of America's best ethnic cooks join the best singers, dancers, craftspeople, and storytellers at the Festival of American Folklife. Held on the National Mall, the festival has become a "living museum," a celebration of our vast array of social and cul-

Previous pages: Carmen Ricard of New Orleans makes stuffed crabs during the 1985 festival's Louisiana program. (Kim Nielson)

tural traditions. During this two-week event, more than a million visitors wander along a fairway of tents and stages set between the Washington Monument and the U.S. Capitol — which rises like a Ferris wheel at one end of the Mall.

Seldom are cooks invited to deliver their own State of the Union messages, but they have been making savory statements at the Festival of American Folklife each year since the second festival in 1968. That year, the Texas delegation demonstrated foods of its state. The next year, North Carolina was the featured state, and Ora Watson, a quiltmaker and cousin of blues singer Doc Watson, fixed homemade biscuits, although without her favorite black iron stove. As quickly as butter melts on a hot biscuit, food programs became a hit, attracting not only fine cooks, but people who could also tell a tall tale or explain why their culture prepared a certain food on Christmas or Hanukkah or for christenings.

Food demonstrations have been good to the festival and its visitors. In 1985 the smell of Maude Ancelet's chicken and sausage gumbo no doubt made the Cajun musicians feel right at home on the Mall. The same was true — in other years for other festival participants — when Trinidadian Cecilia Ojoe fixed pelau, Dorothy Marcucci baked her grandmother's lasagne, Alberta Stanley prepared her blackberry delight, Nellie Jensen Doke brewed her chicken dumpling soup, and Louise Petersen Samuel made kallaloo and fungi. The list is nearly endless.

The festival has also been good to its cooks. Originally organized to give voice to folk, tribal, ethnic, and regional cultural expressions not otherwise likely to be heard in a national setting, the Festival of American Folklife has been credited with helping revitalize Cajun culture in Louisiana, various American Indian tribes, a broad range of African American communities, and numerous crafts, songs, dances, stories, and other expressions of America's cultural pluralism. No less important has been the festival's role in recognizing the significance of such everyday foods as Chippewa wild rice, Portuguese kale soup, steamed brown bread, Japanese obento, Finnish oven pancakes, Creole red snapper, and Alberta Higginbotham's rice pudding.

In the *Smithsonian Folklife Cookbook,* many participants discuss the origins of particular recipes or their importance to a culture and family. Most of the recipes were discovered during three years of research in the archives of the Smithsonian's Office of Folklife Programs, followed by more than a thousand phone calls and selected field visits. Such contacts usually resulted in additional leads and recipes. Sometimes, field workers would come up with a name and an address. Occasionally, a state folklorist would be the key to finding a lost recipe or participant. Newspapers also were reviewed for additional leads. A food club at the Library of Congress helped locate other par-

"The possibility of using a historical documentary museum as a theater of live performance where people actually show that the objects in the cases were made by human hands, and are still being made, practiced on, [and] worked with, is a very valuable asset for our role as a preserver and conservator of living cultural forms."

Secretary Emeritus S. Dillon Ripley, 1969

Borrowing from Friends Everywhere

ticipants, notably Lucy Mike King, who preserves the Sicilian tradition of elaborate food-filled altars honoring St. Joseph's Day (March 19) in her Italian community in Hammond, Louisiana. After dictating recipes over the phone for hours, she mailed the baked results — forty-five pounds of breads and cookies! — to show us how they should look.

We are grateful, too, to America's small-town post offices. Several of their postmasters helped us track down participants from ten and twenty years ago who had since moved away. Thanks in particular to the postmaster of Fitzgerald, Georgia, we found German-born Maria Agner. She contributed wine making, wild-mushroom gathering techniques, and desserts at the 1980 festival when Georgia was featured, but she now lives in California.

The first chapter focuses on Native American foods around the country. Thereafter, the book is divided into seven geographic sections: New England, Mid-Atlantic, South, Upper Great Lakes, Great Plains, West and Southwest, and the islands of Hawaii, Puerto Rico, and the U.S. Virgin Islands. However, the book you hold in your hands is not a typical regional cookbook. Wherever you browse, you are likely to find recipes that challenge traditional notions of regional cooking. Instead, what you will see is the ebb and flow of ethnic cuisines — regardless of region — across generations as Old World inhabitants adapt family or cultural recipes and food customs to the New World. A lot of borrowing goes on among cultures, as "secret" recipes are passed from generation to generation in a country as complex, socially and ethnically, as ours.

Nor can you ever be certain, as you turn the page, how many people the next recipe will feed. Some, such as Stella Hughes' chili con carne, which serves eighty people, may fill the refrigerator with leftovers for a week. Many of the recipes do not even indicate servings. For others, the quantities of ingredients are often left to the cook's knowledge or taste. Because this is a documentary work, no attempt has been made to standardize "taste." Expect to find on one page a recipe for cooking muskrat and, in the same region (the Upper Great Lakes), one for spritz cookies prepared by Barbara Swenson, a 1984 participant who observes that "a good Scandinavian cook can stake her reputation on the fragility of her cookies. In fact, when we took cookies to someone else's house for a holiday gathering, we would carefully place them in a box on top of a pillow in the car seat."

Savoring and Sharing

The documentary nature of this cookbook also explains why some regions, such as the Great Plains and Puerto Rico, contain fewer recipes than others (apparently, fewer cooks than farmers, craftspeople, musicians, and storytellers from this region were participants in the festival). Likewise, the chapter on island foods contains items foreign to the typical American palate. Cooks interested in preparing these or other dishes unfamiliar to their cul-

"The festival, like all Smithsonian museums, is free. No tickets or turnstiles to in-gather patrons and exclude the rest. The festival has always been free — by the original vision of the event's founders — because the festival is the Smithsonian's forum of living cultural ideas."

Secretary Robert McC. Adams, 1989

ture may want to refer to other cookbooks to find more details or explanations for certain ingredients. Among the most helpful may be Irma S. Rombauer and Marion Rombauer Becker's *Joy of Cooking* (Bobbs-Merrill Company, 1975), Jeff Smith's *The Frugal Gourmet on Our Immigrant Ancestors* (William Morrow and Company, 1990), and Betty Fussell's *I Hear America Cooking* (Viking Penguin, 1986).

Chapters open with essays as varied as the recipes. Some are personal accounts in which the author savors every game bird and berry served at a wedding feast. Others portray ethnic family gatherings and foods typically served when the neighbors stop by. Still others take a folklore or historical view of a region, then trace the impact of various immigrant groups on recipes typical of the region. Regardless of their focus, each of these essays is intended to help ease your way into another culture and to enlarge your appreciation of your own food traditions.

Certainly, assembling the recipes, anecdotes, essays, and photographs that make up the *Smithsonian Folklife Cookbook* has enriched our lives. During its preparation over three years, complete strangers have been generous for no reason other than that they wished to share with others what they have loved. We have tried to do the same through this book. We hope that you may be as surprised and delighted by these American friends and foods as we are.

✳ · ✳ · ✳ · ✳

Acknowledgments

✳ · ✳ · ✳ · ✳

The authors wish to thank the many wonderful cooks who kindly shared their family recipes to make this book possible. We are grateful also for the hospitality of our Louisiana friends Maude and Elmo Ancelet, Louise and Irvan Perez, Loretta Harrison, and Carmen Ricard. In Philadelphia we were treated to delicious homecooked meals by Pat and Bill Carson and Dorothy Marcucci.

The folklore scholars who had the unenviable task of fitting history, food customs, and cultural diversity into the brief essays also deserve a place at the head table. So do our many researchers, interns, friends, and volunteers who helped tremendously: Lee Barnes, Emily Botein, Dana Boyd, Gretchen Brotman, Shirley and Lisa Cherkasky, Denise Cronin, Daphne Cunningham, Ann Dentry, Phyllis Lesansky, Virginia McCauley, Peggy McNair, Joan Nathan, Louann Reed, Roberta Sabban, Beverly Simons, Jane Smith, and Michelle Smith. Thanks also to our professional and volunteer recipe testers, especially Joe Carper, Jennifer Cutting, Beverly Lang Pierce, Kathryn Powers, and Lorraine Ramsdell.

We also wish to thank the Smithsonian's Office of Folklife Programs, which gave us the opportunity to do the research and work for two years in its office. We are grateful to our colleagues Richard Kurin, Peter Seitel, Jeff Place, and Diana Parker, who lent support and professional guidance. And Katherine is indebted to her office mate and colleague, Betty Belanus, who saw her through all of the cookbook's trials and tribulations. Our appreciation goes also to the James Smithson Society, Office of Printing and Photography, and Office of Public Affairs, especially our friends Mary Combs, Madeleine Jacobs, and Linda St. Thomas.

We are very thankful to Amy Pastan, our editor at the Smithsonian Institution Press, for her help and guidance with this book.

Finally, sincere thanks to all of our friends and family, particularly our parents, who long ago inscribed in us a pride that certain things could be done.

Opposite: The fare of the day is corn for this young folklife festival visitor. (Smithsonian Institution)

The Folklife Festival

✳ · ✳ · ✳ · ✳

The Festival of American Folklife: A Timeline

The Festival of American Folklife celebrates and preserves the richness and diversity of folk culture. Held every year on the National Mall since 1967, the festival has brought together people from all over the United States and the world to share with the American public the skills, knowledge, personal experience, forms, and creative vitality of tradition-based cultures. They do so in craft and cooking demonstrations, concerts, dances, workshops, panel discussions, and especially in one-to-one exchanges with visitors. The festival was founded so that people can be heard — giving voice to individuals and cultures whose traditions too often are unknown outside their own communities. It also encourages practitioners to pass on their skills and, ultimately, symbolizes many aspects of our own culture and sense of community. Highlights of the festival appear on the following pages.

1967

Performances: American fife and drum groups, brass and string bands, gospels, shouts, jubilees, spirituals, Puerto Rican music, New Orleans jazz, Cajun music, ballads, Mesquakie Indian music, blues, country music, polkas, cowboy songs, clogging, Scottish dancing, Russian dancing, Irish dancing, Chinese New Year's pantomime, King Island Eskimo dancing, dance of Galicia
Crafts: American basket making, carving, doll making, needleworking, pottery, blacksmithing, silversmithing, spinning, weaving

1968

Featured State: Texas
Native American Program: Lummi Indians
City-Country Area: Blues, bluegrass, jazz, gospels, Cajun dancing, Basque dancing, Indian dancing, ballads
Crafts: Butter churning, sheep shearing, soap making, candy making, sorghum making, milling

Featured State: Pennsylvania

1969

Performances: French songs from New Hampshire and Louisiana, Grand Ole Opry, Turkish singing and dancing, Afro-Cuban singing and dancing, Greek singing and dancing, ballads, string bands, fife and drum groups, blues, shouts, jubilees, spirituals

Crafts: Sheep shearing and wool processing, corn culture, Seminole Indian crafts, carving, toy making, doll making, blacksmithing, basket making, pottery

Toby Show: Traditional touring tent theater

Featured State: Arkansas

1970

Native American Program: Southern Plains Indians

Performances: Spanish, Irish and Scottish bagpipers, country music, bluegrass, southern blues, sacred harp, Portuguese American Fado music, Chinese dragon dancing, shouts, spirituals, jubilees, string bands, eastern European folk songs

Crafts: Dairy traditions

Featured State: Ohio

1971

Native American Program: Northwest Coast Indians

Labor Program: Meat cutters and butchers, bakery and confectionery workers, glass-bottle blowers, bridge, structural, and ornamental iron workers

Performances: Puerto Rican music and dancing, Cajun music, country music, ragtime, shouts, jubilees, work songs, blues, Caribbean music and dancing, rock and roll, rhythm and blues, old-time banjo and fiddle music

Featured State: Maryland

1972

Native American Program: Southwest Indians

Labor Program: International Ladies Garment Workers Union, lithographers and photoengravers, carpenters and joiners, molders and allied workers

Performances: Chicago blues, old-time country blues, gospels, first annual fiddlers convention

Featured State: Kentucky

1973

Native American Program: Northern Plains Indians

Working Americans: Plumbers, carpenters, electricians, stone masons, lathers, bricklayers, plasterers, millwrights, operating engineers, pipe fitters, sheet-metal workers, steam fitters

Old Ways in the New World: Britain, Yugoslavia, Gundenci, Siskovci, Novi Sad

Featured State: Mississippi

1974

Native American Program: California tribes (Tolowa, Pomo, Hoopa, Yurok, Karok, Luiseno, Maidu, Cahuilla), basin and plateau tribes (Paiute, Shoshone, Kaibab, Northern Ute, Ute Mountain, Southern Ute, Nez Perce), Creek, Cherokee, Eskimo, Acoma, Athabaskan, Jemez, Laguna

Working Americans: Graphic artists, amateur and commercial radio operators

Old Ways in the New World: Sweden, Norway, Finland, Tunisia, Greece

African Diaspora: Ghana, Trinidad and Tobago, Nigeria, Caribbean

Children's Program

Family Folklore Performance: Evolution of American folk music

Regional America: Northern plains, California heartland

1975

Native American Program: Iroquois confederacy

Working Americans: Railroad workers, aircraft employees, truckers, seafarers

Old Ways in the New World: Germany, Italy, Lebanon, Japan, Mexico

African Diaspora: Jamaica, Ghana, Haiti

Children's Program

Family Folklore

Regional America: Northeast, Great Lakes, South, upland South, heartland, great West, Pacific Northwest, Pacific Southwest

1976

Native American Program: Tribes from the Northeast, Southeast, southern plains, prairie, northern plains, Northwest Coast, Southwest, plateau, basin, northern California, Arctic

Working Americans: Workers who feed us, workers who extract and shape, workers who build, workers in technical and professional skills, workers who clothe us, workers in communications, arts, and recreation

Old Ways in the New World: Germany, Pakistan, Mexico, South America, Ireland, Yugoslavia, Belgium, Egypt, Greece, Japan, Austria, India, France, Poland, Britain, Portugal, Israel, Romania, Denmark, Norway, Finland, Sweden, Hungary, Switzerland, Italy

African Diaspora: Ghana, Jamaica, Haiti, Liberia, Trinidad and Tobago, Nigeria, Brazil, Puerto Rico, Zaire, Surinam, Senegal

Children's Program

Family Folklore

Featured State: Virginia

1977

Native American Program: Ojibway, Tolowa, San Juan Pueblo (New Mexico), Navajo, Seneca

Working Americans: Folklore in your community (Washington, D.C., cab drivers, bartenders, vendors, Capitol building workers)

Energy and Community: America's appetite (for energy)
Nation of Nations: Dunham School, Ellis Island and immigrant lore, baseball bat turning, ethnic foods
Crafts: Painting on wood, crafts with natural fibers

1978

Native American Community: San Juan Pueblo (New Mexico)
Occupational Community: Organ builders, sleeping car porters, sharecroppers
Energy and Community: Oil and coal industry workers
Ethnic Community: Ellis Island and American immigration
Regional Community: Chesapeake Bay, Smith Island
Mexican Communities

1979

Energy and Community: Native American architecture
Folklore in Your Community: Baseball players, citizens-band radio operators, fire fighters, gospel singers, market vendors, neighborhood store owners, stone carvers, street hawkers, cab drivers, Vietnamese community
Children's Program
Medicine Show

1980

Old Ways in the New World: Caribbean Americans, Southeast Asian Americans, Finnish Americans
Energy and Community: Folk housing and energy efficiency, community activities and food preservation
American Talkers: Auctioneers, pitchmen, street criers

1981

Regional America: Southeastern music and crafts, northeastern music and dance
Native American Program: Ojibway
Old Ways in the New World: South Slavic Americans
Energy and Community: Adobe architecture
Children's Program
Folklore of the Deaf
American Tent Show
National Endowment for the Arts Program

1982

Featured State: Oklahoma
Featured Country: Korea
Children's Program
National Endowment for the Arts Program

1983

Featured State: New Jersey
Featured Country: France
Occupational Folklife: Flight
National Endowment for the Arts Program

1984

Featured State: Alaska
The Grand Generation: Folklore and aging
Black Urban Expressive Culture from Philadelphia
Traditional Foodways

1985

Featured State: Louisiana
Featured Country: India (Mela! An Indian Fair)
Cultural Conservation: Makah and Puerto Rican mask makers, African American corn rowers, Kmhmu craftspeople, Seneca basket makers, Appalachian ballads, Cajun music, cowboy music, song and poetry, Irish music, Mayan marimba music, Mayan Indian weaving
Traditional Foodways
Dance Parties

1986

Featured State: Tennessee
Featured Country: Japan (Rice in Japanese Folk Culture)
Cultural Conservation (Traditional Crafts in a Post-industrial Age): Cherokee and split-oak basket making, Hispanic weaving and wood carving, Hmong embroidery, African American quilting, Italian American stone carving, Zuni and southern pottery, rag-rug weaving
American Trial Lawyers
Twentieth-Anniversary Music Stage
Dance Parties

1987

Featured State: Michigan
Cultural Conservation (Cultural Conservation and Languages: America's Many Voices): Appalachian community, Chinese American community, Lao-American community, Mexican American community
Metropolitan Washington: Music from the area
Dance Parties

1988

Featured State: Massachusetts
Cultural Conservation: American Folklore Society centennial
Migration to Metropolitan Washington: Making a New Place Home
Music from the Peoples of the Soviet Union: Russia, Georgia, Uzbekistan, Azerbaijan, Estonia, Lithuania, the Ukraine, Tuva, Yakutsk
Festival Music Stage: Bluegrass, Piedmont blues, Cajun and Puerto Rican

music, American Indian performance, double-dutch jump roping
Dance Parties

1989

Featured State: Hawaii
Cultural Conservation: Problems of access and cultural continuity among the Iroquois nation, Yaqui, Washoe, Paiute, Shoshone, Ojibway, northern plains tribes
"Les Fêtes Chez Nous:" France and North America
The Caribbean: Cultural Encounters in the New World: Musicians, dancers, and cooks from Puerto Rico, Haiti, Jamaica, and Cuba

1990

Featured Territory: U.S. Virgin Islands
Featured Country: Senegal
Musics of Struggle: U.S. civil rights movement, Gallaudet University's "Deaf President Now" campaign, Appalachian coal miners, farm workers' movement, Quichua Indians from Ecuador, South African antiapartheid movement, struggles of Israelis, Palestinians, Kurds, and Irish

1991

Featured Program: Family Farming in the Heartland
Featured Country: Indonesia
Land in Native American Cultures: Tlingit, Haida, and Tsimshian people from Alaska; Aymara and Quechua people from the Andean highlands of Bolivia and Peru; Mayans from Chiapas and Zapotecs and Ikoods from Oaxaca, Mexico; Canelos Quichua, Shuar, and Achuar people from Ecuador; and Hopis from Arizona.
Roots of Rhythm and Blues: The Robert Johnson era
Traditional Foodways
Dance Parties

Photograph on pages 2–3: Tepees rise in front of the Smithsonian's Castle for the Festival of American Folklife. (Laurie Minor)

Photograph on page 6: The festival takes place on the National Mall in Washington, D.C., each summer. (Jim Pickerell)

Photograph on page 9: A Louisiana Mardi Gras float passes the Castle during the 1985 festival. (Smithsonian Institution)

Native American

▲ · ▲ · ▲ · ▲

Rayna Green

I am a wild-onion eater, from a whole region of wild-onion eaters. To me, those stinky *Allium*-family members are home, where I'm from, where I belong. Poke, cochanna, conunchi, hominy, and hog — these things make me myself, a Cherokee. Their presence tells me, even when they are served in an apartment in Washington, D.C., that I'm in Tsalagí, the Cherokee homeland. For other Native American people, these foods announce who they are, wherever they are, whether at a feast day on a New Mexico pueblo, at home on an ordinary day in that same pueblo, or when a relative comes back from a job firefighting in Idaho. Or at the annual Cherokee Homecoming, Otoe Powwow or Crow Fair; at the local Catholic church basement; at a political fund raiser for a Native American candidate; at a stomp dance in eastern Oklahoma or a potlatch in Canada; when the boats come in from whale hunting in southeast Alaska; when special friends come to visit anywhere; or a memorial feast for a dead relative or a baby-naming feast for a new one.

To talk of Native American cookery is to talk of the oldest foods and the oldest cooking methods in North America. It is to talk of food and cooking traditions based solely in the natural universe, of things gathered from the ground, from trees and bushes, from plants, from fresh and salt waters, from desert sands and mountain forests, from animals as old and older than the people who took food from them. And to talk of Native American food and cooking is to talk of dynamic change, movement, acceptance of the new and strange, and creative adaptation, like Native American people themselves.

Once, long ago, as now, there was bear and buffalo, seal, salmon and oyster, cactus fruit and wild rice, hickory nut and prairie turnip; now and for a while, there has been pig and cow, wheat flour and sugar, watermelon and black pepper, even gelatin. In between what was gathered and hunted long ago and now, there was corn — Corn Mother, which, together with beans and squash, became what the Iroquois call the Three Sisters. People learned to cultivate corn until it became central to and even emblematic of life itself.

Previous pages: Bread is baked the Native American way, in a clay horno (oven), during the Smithsonian's folklife festival. (Robert Yellin)

Once, there was food eaten raw, smoked, dried, and boiled; now too, foods are fried, baked, even microwaved. The people still hunt; they grow things; they gather, but they also get commodity surplus cheese and beans from the federal agency; they, too, like other Americans, hunt and gather at the grocery store.

The native foods and foodstuffs that were once associated with ceremonial life remain so. Every morning in the Southwest, someone throws corn pollen into the wind and prays for the renewal of life. In the Northwest, someone fills with tobacco the hole made when the bitterroot is dug up — and offers a prayer and thanks for its gift. Certain things are still eaten in certain seasons only by certain people. To all things, a season, a time. Nothing — not even Jell-O salad — is eaten without prayer. Everything is shared with family, with neighbors, with new friends.

Now, as in the past, how much food there might be is less important than sharing it, as the Lakota prayer says, with "all our relations." All our relations in Native American traditions include other humans, plants, animals, the spirits in the universe. Thus, what we eat is central to being native, even as, with all people, it is central to the sustenance of life. The center of each native food tradition is still based in the oldest things; what characterizes the traditions now is what characterized them a hundred, five hundred, probably several thousand years ago. For subsistence-based peoples, the animals they hunt and the things they find in the lands they inhabit remain the significant foods. Those animals and plants also provide clothing, tools, fuel, cosmetics, medicines — the many substances necessary for life and "culture" to go on.

What we eat is central to being native, even as, with all people, it is central to the sustenance of life.

In the Southwest, the Southeast, and the Northeast as well, corn is the primary food. Life centers around corn in one form or another; songs, dances, stories, ceremonies, and many, many foods are built on the extraordinary grain that revolutionized world agriculture — whole corn kernels, corn on the cob, cornmeal, hominy. Combined with the preservation and cooking processes of fermentation, toasting, baking, lye and ash soaking, corn produced literally hundreds of dishes and the world's most substantial agricultural form next to rice and wheat. Prayers are made with cornmeal; prayers are made to the corn spirits; dances and prayers for healing take place around corn; art everywhere centers around corn. In the Southeast, the Green Corn Ceremony reconciles all ill, all bad feelings among people. For the Southwest's pueblo people, other occasions, such as a baby's name ceremony, are accompanied by a wash of corn pollen over the ground, thrown into the air, rubbed in the hair. There, too, corn ears are given by friends and family to dancers who, in dancing with them and returning them after the dance, ensure good fortune, good health, good will for those who receive them.

Corn Mother

Prayers for rain are prayers for the growth of corn — indeed, for the persistence of life.

In the Northeast and Southwest, archaeological evidence exists that native people stored enough corn to feed thousands of people for more than a year. Tribes went to war when the British and Spanish destroyed or confiscated corn stores. And everyone knows the original American myth, the story of how Squanto, a Wampanoag, saved the starving immigrant and British settlers, the Pilgrims, by teaching them how to grow corn in the Wampanoag way. "Indian corn" was, in the seventeenth and eighteenth centuries, one of the major export crops of North America, and today it remains one of the leading grains of world commerce and consumption. Even now, ecologists and agronomists insist that we may have much to learn from the way native people grew and preserved so many varieties of corn. Blue, red, white, yellow, and black, corn varieties mirror the sacred colors of the universe, the possibility of diversity and survival among the beings, plants, and animals of the universe — all relatives.

Hunting, Fishing, Gathering

In the Northwest, salmon and the other fish that traverse the big rivers are the source of life. Life revolves around fishing, whether in fresh or salt water. Heat smoking and drying are the major form of preservation, while shallow-pit and direct-fire baking provide the cooking source. As with corn, ceremony, song, dance, and prayer bring back the salmon each year to spawn and make their run for preservation of their species. Killer whale, salmon, and the other inhabitants of the water appear everywhere in artistic material form, as clan and family spirits that guide and define people's relationships with each other.

And in the Great Lakes, hunting and fishing, combined with the long-held traditions of gathering that marvelous grass species known in the vernacular as wild rice, form the staple of social activity and subsistence living. For the plains people, buffalo, deer, elk — the four-leggeds — were the primary animal relatives, the source of life, supplemented, as in the Northwest, by the abundance of gathered plants — berries, nuts, tubers.

In many cases, however, events, intrusions, ecosystem failures and pressures, and, in some instances, actual assaults on the primary foods of native people caused them to lose those foods. Some supplies have been considerably diminished and have had to be replaced by others; in other cases, the primary food is so scarce that it has been reduced to ceremonial or special use, rather than as an everyday staple. The building of giant dams, shifting of rivers, pollution of streams, and overfishing brought considerable change to fish resources in the Northwest and Great Lakes. Where some rivers once ran with five varieties of salmon and other fish in the Northwest, now one variety is common. Sport fishing and fishermen, even claims by Japanese

Opposite: A Native American clambake is recreated on the Mall for the 1977 festival. (Smithsonian Institution)

industrial interests on fishing resources, have reduced the number of salmon available for native people. Legal disputes challenging rights to take fish from once-tribal waterways and to take them by traditional practices such as gill netting and spearfishing have eroded native spiritual and valid claims to those resources.

Buffalo are the most dramatic example of lives altered by assault. Once so numerous that plains tribes planned their whole existence around them — providers of food, clothing, housing, trade — buffalo were the true lords of the plains. But the increased pressures for hides and meat brought by whites, with highly efficient rifle hunting, and their wanton extermination of herds, brought the buffalo population regrowth to an end. Once the plains tribes were sent to reservations and the cattle industry reaped huge profits from cheap or freed Native American land and the sale of cattle to the government to feed then-starving tribes, the buffalo all but disappeared. Still, meat-eating native people continued to eat meat, delivered by government wagons, and then by trains.

Cattle could not replace ceremony, however, and so the story survived that told of White Buffalo Calf Woman, who brought the way of the pipe and truth to the Sioux people. It was she they remembered and it was she who, it was said by them, would return when the tribes once again would drive out the whites and the old ways would return. Wovoka, the prophet, who brought the Ghost Dance to the people, said that the buffalo would return when the native tribes restored the plains to the people. But while the people were not able to restore the plains, they never forgot the buffalo; they shifted their attentions to beef for everyday food, deer meat, and deer skins when they could get them.

But buffalo remained the figure of symbolic importance. Today, it has come back on the plains; tribes everywhere have a few hundred, and at ceremonial times, for remembrance, buffalo is the ceremonial food. Buffalo imagery continues to dominate the art. But the preference for red meat remained as well, and the plains diet, while altered radically in so many ways, stayed a meat-based diet. Stewed, baked, and fried, beef is the centerpiece of meals.

Opposite: Pieces of salmon on handcut sticks roast slowly over an open fire during the 1975 folk-life festival. (Smithsonian Institution)

New Foods Now Old

Some foods now deeply identified with Native American people, such as frybread, come totally from substances — wheat and lard — imported from European sources. Bannock, a wheat-based breadstuff eaten by Canadian Indians, is Scottish in origin but was adapted by native people when they were colonized by Scottish immigrants. In the plains, stew made of beef and commodity rice, American grown and Asian in origin, is a staple of everyday Sioux life. In the Southeast and Northeast, the Spanish-introduced pig and in the Southwest the Spanish-introduced sheep — with its wool for weaving and its meat for eating — brought a new staple into the native economy and diet in the sixteenth century.

These and other dietary introductions such as sugar and dairy products have been welcomed and widely used, but they have not come without serious consequences. Nutritional problems and dietary diseases, such as diabetes, dental health deterioration, and lactose intolerance-induced illnesses, are very much a result of the encounter between native and European people and a major problem for native people everywhere. Of these, diabetes- and alcohol-related illness and death constitute the most deadly assaults on Indians. Loss of traditional food resources, many of them precisely those touted as nutritionally perfect, and the increasing contamination by environmental and industrial pollutants, such as mercury contamination of fish, have created a second tier of hazards.

Many relatively new foods, however, for various reasons, fit well into the seasonal round of ceremony and daily life. Some, such as frybread, have become so associated with Indians everywhere that even native people think of it as an "Indian" dish. Thus, throughout the country a Southwest version of frybread, the Indian or Navajo taco, is common fare at fairs, festivals, feast days, church suppers, and powwows. Everything on this taco, including its name, comes from Mexican and European sources — wheat flour, lard, beef, lettuce, and tomatoes; there is nothing Navajo about it except the inventiveness of combining a primary pan-Indian food, frybread, with the toppings — spiced ground meat, tomatoes, onions, lettuce, salsa, cheese, sour cream — so characteristic of the taco as it is known and understood in northern Mexico and El Norte, the United States. Frybread recipes, shapes, and desired tastes vary from region to region. In the Southwest, Indians make it large, thin, and crispy; in the Great Lakes and southern plains, they make it smaller, doughier, puffier. But everywhere, frybread jokes abound. At an education conference in Alaska, native people from Arizona once sold T-shirts modeled after the famous Hard Rock Cafe logo, but with the logo "Frybread Cafe" printed on a big, round piece of frybread.

Like all people, Native Americans joke about their favorite foods.

Laughing Matters

Like all people, Native Americans joke about their favorite foods, especially if those foods are strange or forbidden to other people. The largest group of jokes center around Sioux, other plains people, and dog eating. Many tribal people all over the world eat dog, and, in fact, many such as the plains tribes ate it only ceremonially or used other animals specially raised for ceremonial consumption. However, because the dog also enjoys the status among Europeans of being a domestic pet, a certain ambivalence about dog eating spread among native people that taints the practice. For Native Americans, teasing Sioux about dog eating amounts to a national sport. A typical example: two Sioux men go to the city on a bus and stop at a hot dog stand, an unfamiliar institution. When one opens his wax-paper wrapped hot dog, he is quite startled and asks the other which part he got. When their Chippewa-enemy neighbors sing "How Much Is That Doggie in the Window?" to them, the Sioux retaliate with "Here Comes Peter Cottontail," to tease the rabbit-loving Chippewa.

Another joking cycle centers around Navajos and their culinary passion for mutton. The specialty of the McDonald's in Window Rock, Arizona, is described as "Egg McMutton." And in Oklahoma, the Comanche appetite for entrails, known in Comanche as "bote," spawns an entire joke cycle in which the Comanches are described as the original "bote people." A bumper sticker boasts of "Bote, Breakfast of Champions."

Crops for Cash

Many tribal people for centuries have created commercial enterprises out of the special foods they catch or prepare. Of course, buffalo and deer, meat and skins, were a major commodity for trade among native people before the coming of Europeans, and they became a significant trade item when Europeans arrived. Besides meat, corn came to be the cash crop for Native Americans, even as it was the source of warfare when their stores were taken or destroyed by the same Europeans. But other crops and resources — fish in the Great Lakes and Northwest, wild rice in the Great Lakes, ginseng in the Southeast, mutton in the Southwest, sea mammals in Alaska and Canada — all were and still are resources used by Indians for cash income as well as for food.

Today, wild rice remains a staple of the diet, and Native Americans in rice-growing areas have turned some of their ricing into cash crops. However, commercial ricing and domesticated wild rice, along with environmental degradation of the ricing fields everywhere, seriously undermined both traditional subsistence gathering and cash-barter usage for tribes. Some pueblos turned to blue corn harvesting and product manufacture in the 1980s to cash in on nouvelle cuisine hunting among the urbanized affluent, much as Southwest ranchers have turned to harvesting mesquite for charcoal and flavoring. And the Northwest tribes process some fish for the gourmet market. By and large, however, tribal peoples have rarely been able to capitalize on those markets; inevitably, they are exploited by nonnative interests.

Preserving Food Traditions

However, for the restoration and preservation of ceremonial foods — indeed, for the restoration and preservation of the ways of life centered around traditional agriculture and subsistence — native people everywhere are trying to save or support traditional foods as well as traditional forms of gathering, preserving, and growing. In the Southwest, Northwest, and Great Lakes in particular, enormous efforts are being undertaken to prevent further economic, environmental, and sociocultural assaults on traditional foods and food-gathering or growing lands. Whether it is through the reacquisition of alienated lands, the recovery and teaching of old and environmentally sound, productive agricultural methods, the cleanup of contaminated land and water resources, attempts to halt development or further erosion and alienation of water and land resources, or the reintroduction or increase of traditional animal or plant resource use, tribal people have shown concern about their way of life. With the assistance of specialists such as plant ecologists, hydrologists, ethnobotanists, fisheries biologists, foresters, agronomists — some of whom are now Native American — tribes have begun to undertake the process of protecting their resources.

Gooooood Grease for Celebration

As with all people, you are what you eat. Native people everywhere want to be Indian, to eat Indian. To preserve a way of life means, in part, to preserve those things that connect one to who you are and who you belong to. Even the intertribal joking identifies the subject of the joke as one of "those" people to whom it is good to belong. After all, food is more than nourishment, so we all share the sentiments of Mary Tallmountain, an Athabaskan writer, who tells us in a poem about the hunters who came back to camp with caribou:

By the fires that night
we feasted...grease was beautiful
oozing
dripping and running down our chins
brown hands shining and running with grease.
We talk of it when we see each other far from home.
Remember the marrow
sweet in the bones
we grabbed for them like candy.
Good
Gooooood
Good Grease.

In the recipes that follow can be found the good grease with which native people celebrate our endurance.

▲ · ▲ · ▲ · ▲

Recipes

Wampanoag Clambake

Smoked Salmon

Roast Salmon on Sticks

Alaskan Fish Chowder

Alaskan Fish Soufflé

Tamales

Chile Stew

Manoomin (Wild Rice Side Dish)

Venison and Wild Rice Stew

Wild Rice Stuffing

Squash with Sweet Corn

Corn Soup

Ta Kwa a Wi (Corn Mush)

Blue Corn Tortillas

Pashofa (Hominy and Pork Stew)

Tolowa Indian Sand Bread

Plains Indian Frybread

Seneca Frybread

Oven Bread

Blue Dumplings

Biscochitos (Sugar Cookies)

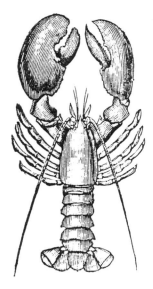

Wampanoag Clambake

½ bushel clams
6 whole live lobsters
3 pounds cod fillets
6 ears corn
6 onions

6 sweet potatoes
6 white potatoes
butter, for topping
sausage (or hot dogs)
 (optional)

mussels (optional)
oysters (optional)

"The Wampanoag clambake developed over many centuries, originating long before the first European settlers came to New England and learned to eat foods prepared this way. And yet very little has really changed. The flavors of fresh seafoods and garden vegetables, steamed slowly over hot rocks and nestled on a bed of seaweed, remain an unmistakable delight, well worth the long day's toil to prepare.

As with many traditional recipes, we don't use measuring cups or spoons, and I cannot tell you to add a dash of this or that. We don't have a recommended oven temperature or a precise cooking time. The main ingredient is hard work, usually shared by all who partake in the feast.

While traditionally the clambake has been a meal for many — a hundred or more — the recipe here is for six people. If your guest list exceeds this, just add rocks, add seaweed, add food."

1. Begin a day in advance by digging a shallow pit, a few inches deep and about 6 × 6 feet, in an open site. Fill the pit with stones as big as a football or larger than a softball. If you live near the ocean, beaches are a good place to find such rocks. Pile the rocks 2 or 3 deep in the pit. Have plenty of dry wood nearby for the fire.

2. Gather 2 or 3 garbage-size bags of seaweed. Seal tightly to keep the seaweed moist; store in a cool, dark location.

3. On the day of the clambake, check the local tide schedule and dig a half bushel of clams or buy them fresh from the market. Set aside clams and lobsters (and mussels and oysters if you are using them), preferably on ice in a cool, dark place.

4. To prepare the food, teamwork is suggested. First, cut cod into individual portions and wrap it in aluminum foil. Then cut cheesecloth into squares, each large enough to hold a portion of fish, ear of corn, onion, sweet and regular potatoes, and any optional ingredients. Next, tie ingredients tightly in the cheesecloth and store in the refrigerator until ready to bake them. Finally, wrap and tie clams in cheesecloth, which will save them from getting lost in the seaweed during the bake.

5. Meanwhile, take turns tending the fire. Build it right over the rocks, and let it burn strongly for at least 1 to 2 hours. The rocks are ready when they glow bright red. When they are hot, use a rake or broom to remove whatever wood and cinders are left. The ones that nestle between the rocks can stay.

6. Now you must act quickly, for while the rocks are amazingly good at holding the original heat of the fire, left uncovered they will cool quickly. To prevent heat loss, cover the rocks with another layer of seaweed. It will crackle, and a heavenly steam will rise.

7. In the middle of the seaweed bed, lay the live lobsters and clams and quickly surround them with the sacks of food. Cover them with another layer of seaweed, and cover the entire pit with a large sheet of polyurethane plastic. The plastic will immediately fill with steam. Seal the edges, using whatever is handy — logs or stones — and use leftover seaweed to close any gaps. Keep the plastic from touching the rocks. A hole in the covering lets valuable steam escape.

8. Now wait, put your feet up, and relax. You have worked hard; you must be tired, and you certainly are hungry. It takes about 1 hour for the clams, mussels, lobsters, and corn to cook, but the only way to know for sure that the clambake is done is to open a corner and poke a potato. If it is tender, the meal is done, so uncover the clambake and serve. Don't forget the butter! Serves 6.

Paula and Russell Peters, Wampanoag Tribe, Plymouth, Massachusetts.
Native American Program, 1977

Smoked Salmon

1 fresh salmon

Brine:
1 cup salt
1 gallon cold water
1 cup brown sugar

1. Cut salmon from the backbone, then cut in strips 1 inch wide the length of the fish.

2. Make brine and soak salmon in it for 30 minutes. Remove salmon from brine, hang it in a smokehouse, and let the water drip off.

3. Make a fire of alder wood or wood chips. Place salmon over the fire, making certain that the smoke rather than high heat is used. (You want the smoke, not the fire, under the fish.) Let the fish smoke for 2 days.

4. Can or freeze the smoked salmon. (It keeps better when canned.)

Deborah Ann Dalton, Hoonah, Alaska. Alaska Program, 1984

Roast Salmon on Sticks

fresh salmon
salt
pepper

1. Dig a pit about 5 × 3 feet and 6 inches deep. Loosen the soil around the edges, which lets the sticks penetrate deep enough into the ground so that the sticks and the fish on them stay upright.

2. Build a fire in the pit, using seasoned maple, apple, oak, or another wood that does not contain pitch.

3. While the coals are heating up, which takes about 2 hours, fillet the salmon. Allow about ½ to ¾ pound per person. Once it is filleted into slabs, cut each slab into pieces about 3 inches wide.

4. For roasting sticks, we use redwood, which is whittled out of seasoned straight-grained redwood, each about 3 feet long and ½ inch thick and wide. I sharpen my sticks to a point on both ends to allow me to pierce each piece of fish between the fleshy meat and skin. Then I slide the first piece down the stick until it is about 10 inches up from the bottom. Each stick should hold 3 or 4 pieces.

5. Once all the fish is on the sticks, season with salt and pepper. Push the stick into the ground around the edges of the pit. Always face the fleshy part of the fish toward the fire, because this part should cook first. It takes about 1 hour to cook the entire stick, but start by cooking each side for about 15 minutes or until whitish streaks can be seen in the fleshy part of the fish.

Agnes E. Pilgrim, Yurok Tribe, Crescent City, California. Native American Program, 1977

Alaskan Fish Chowder

2 medium potatoes, sliced	2 to 3 pounds fish (salmon, halibut, snapper, etc.), cut up	½ cup evaporated milk
2 medium onions, diced		salt
2 to 3 cups water	2 to 3 pieces bacon	pepper
	1 tablespoon bacon fat	butter

1. Boil potatoes and onions in water until almost cooked.

2. Add fish to the pot when potatoes are almost done. (I add the bones for flavor, but this is optional.) Do not overcook the fish.

3. Fry bacon until crisp and add to mixture along with bacon fat.

4. Add milk and salt, pepper, and butter to taste. Serves 6.

Charlene Nelson, Ketchikan, Alaska. Alaska Program, 1984

"I'm a Shore Water Bay Tribe native originally from Washington State. My father was a logger, and we moved to Alaska when I was three and a half years old. My husband is a Haida native and has fished for fifty-five years. We took our three children out on the fishing boat all the time, and we made this basic fish chowder."

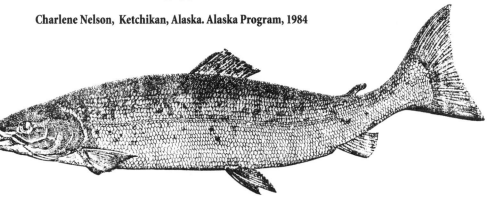

Alaskan Fish Soufflé

8 slices bread, diced or torn into small pieces
6 eggs
3 cups milk
salt
pepper
2 cups cooked salmon (or shrimp or crab meat)
1 cup chopped onion
1 cup chopped celery
1 cup chopped green pepper
1 can mushroom soup
grated cheese
paprika, for garnish

1. Cover bottom of a well-greased 9 × 13-inch pan with half of diced bread.

2. Beat eggs and add milk. Season with salt and pepper if desired; set aside.

3. Mix fish, onion, celery, and pepper, and spread over bread. Top with remaining bread.

4. Pour egg mixture over fish. Set overnight in the refrigerator, or make in the morning for an evening meal.

5. Bake at 325°F for 15 minutes. Remove from oven and top with mushroom soup and grated cheese. Return to oven and bake for 1 hour.

Charlene Nelson

Tamales

1 medium pork roast
1 clove garlic
dash of salt
4 tablespoons red
  chili powder
30 to 40 cornhusks

Dough:
4 cups masa harina
2 tablespoons lard
1 teaspoon salt
1 cup hot water

1. Boil pork roast with garlic and salt until cooked. Shred meat and mix with chili powder; set aside.

2. For dough, mix masa harina, lard, and salt. After lard is worked in well, add hot water; use more water if needed to make a thick dough.

3. Spread dough on each wet cornhusk. Put a strip of meat mix in the middle of the dough, wrap husk around it, and tie husk with thin strips of cornhusk.

4. Steam for 45 to 60 minutes. Yields 30 to 40.

Reycita Garcia, San Juan Pueblo, San Juan, New Mexico. Native American Program, 1978

Chile Stew

4 cups water
4 to 6 chile caribes
  (or ancho chiles),
  stems and seeds
  removed
1 clove garlic,
  chopped
  (or 1 teaspoon
  garlic powder)
1 teaspoon oregano
2 tablespoons oil
3 medium potatoes,
  cubed
1 onion, chopped
2 pounds stewing
  meat
1 teaspoon saffron
  (or cumin)
  (optional)
salt (optional)

1. In a large pot, boil 4 cups water. Add chiles, garlic, and oregano. Simmer for about 1 hour.

2. Remove chiles from pot and save liquid. Place chile in blender and blend until fine. The water used to boil it may be added to chiles if it is too dry to blend.

3. In a frying pan, add oil and fry potatoes, onion, and meat. When almost done, add chiles and cook for 10 minutes.

4. In a deep saucepan, add chile mixture and saffron or cumin to reserved liquid reheated to boiling; add more water if necessary to make 4 cups. Cook until meat is tender, about 45 minutes. Salt to taste. Serves 4 to 6.

Tigua Tribe, El Paso, Texas. Native American Program, 1968

Manoomin (Wild Rice Side Dish)

1 cup uncooked wild
rice
1 pound bacon
salt
pepper

1. Cook rice with enough water to cover until it comes to a boil for 10 minutes. Drain.

2. Cook the same way again until rice is fluffy and done. Drain and keep warm.

3. Fry bacon until crisp and remove from pan. Break into small pieces and mix bacon and drippings with rice, until moist. Add salt and pepper to taste. Yields 4 cups.

Julia Nyholm, Keweemaw Bay Band of Ojibway, Crystal Falls, Michigan. American Indian Program, 1987

Venison and Wild Rice Stew

2½ pounds venison
(or beef), cut into
small pieces
2½ quarts water
3 large onions, diced
1½ cups uncooked
wild rice, washed
and rinsed
2 teaspoons salt
1 teaspoon pepper

1. In a large kettle, simmer meat, water, and onions on low heat until meat is done or tender.

2. Add rice, salt, and pepper, cover, and simmer stew for about 30 minutes.

3. Uncover and cook on low heat for another 30 to 40 minutes, until rice is done.

Julia Nyholm

"The Chippewa (Ojibway) of long ago named this grain 'manoomin,' now known as wild rice. In the olden times, long before the European came upon this great island of the Indian, the native people ate a natural variety of foods, with wild rice being of the uppermost importance.

It was the women who would embark in canoes to harvest the rice in vast sloughs. Upon their return to the rice camps, the rice would be parched, and then the young men would thresh the harvest in dance.

The process of winnowing took place with special birch-bark trays. When all of the rice was free of hulls and cleaned, it was stored away in basket containers to be consumed during the long winter season.

The people of long ago would always conduct a ceremony before eating the first harvested wild rice."

Wild Rice Stuffing

"The Chippewa always boiled everything they ate — never fried food — just boiled or roasted over fire. When my mother, Maude Kegg, was at the Smithsonian Folklife Festival, she helped parch rice, and they boiled some of it. This is what we do at home, even now, to get the true taste of wild rice."

Betty Kegg, Chippewa Tribe, Anamia, Minnesota. Native American Program, 1976

1 cup uncooked wild rice
1 loaf white bread, cubed
1 pound bacon, fried and broken
1 large onion, diced
1 teaspoon salt
½ teaspoon pepper
1 teaspoon sage
¼ teaspoon thyme
2 cups chicken broth

1. Cook rice twice as described in previous recipe for manoomin.

2. Drain rice and add remaining ingredients. Stir in chicken broth to moisten as needed.

3. Put stuffing in a fowl or bake in a casserole at 350°F for 30 to 40 minutes. Yields 4 cups.

Julia Nyholm, Keweemaw Bay Band of Ojibway, Crystal Falls, Michigan. American Indian Program, 1987

Squash with Sweet Corn

1 to 2 cups dried yellow or white corn
4 medium acorn squash
4 cups water
white or brown sugar (or honey)

1. Bring water to a boil and add corn. Cook for about 1½ hours or until corn is tender.

2. Peel squash and cut into ¼-inch slices. Add to boiled mixture and cook until squash is tender but not falling apart.

3. Add white sugar, brown sugar, or honey to taste. Serves 4 to 6.

Florence Tiger, Sac and Fox Tribe, Cushing, Oklahoma. Native American Program, 1976

Corn Soup

1 pound stewing
   meat, cubed
oil, for frying
1 cup dried corn
4 to 6 cups water
salt
pepper

1. Sear meat in oil in a frying pan.

2. In a large pot, cook meat in 4 cups water on medium heat for about 1 hour or until tender.

3. Add corn and cook for 1 hour longer. Season to taste with salt and pepper. Add additional water if the soup gets too thick. Serves 6.

Lilly Nahwooksy, Kiowa Tribe, Walters, Oklahoma. Native American Program, 1970

Ta Kwa a Wi (Corn Mush)

1 cup dried corn
4 cups water
1 tablespoon
   shortening
sugar (or salt)

1. Grind corn in a grinder. Keep the coarse corn separate from the fine grounds.

2. Boil water and shortening in a pot. Stir in coarse corn grounds and cook until tender; then add fine corn grounds.

3. Stir mixture until it becomes mushy. Serve ta kwa a wi (pronounced ta qua hawn) with sugar or salt to taste.

Rose Allen, Sac and Fox Tribe, Cushing, Oklahoma. Native American Program, 1976

Blue Corn Tortillas

4 cups water
1 tablespoon lard
pinch of salt
4 to 5 cups blue
   cornmeal (or masa
   harina)

1. Boil water and add a little lard and dash of salt.

2. Add boiling water to cornmeal. Stir with a spoon, mixing well.

3. Grease a flat griddle. Moisten hands with water, and make flat patties about 6 inches in diameter. Fry tortillas on griddle. Yields 12.

Reycita Garcia, San Juan Pueblo, San Juan, New Mexico. Native American Program, 1978

Pashofa (Hominy and Pork Stew)

"The Pashofa Dance was used in curing the sick. The family called the medicine man, who performed rituals three or four times a day for three days; a fire was kept burning in front of the front door of the house, facing the east. It is believed that the illness left the sick person through the smoke from the fire. On the afternoon of the third day, all the family feasted on the pashofa, with the men on one side and the women on the other. In later times, pashofa became the national dish to us."

2 to 3 quarts water
1 pound pearl
  hominy (cracked
  corn), washed and
  cleaned
1 to 1½ pounds lean
  pork meat
salt

1. Put water in a large pot and bring to a boil. Add corn and meat.

2. Cook mixture on low to medium heat for about 4 hours or until done. Add more water if needed. Do not salt until ready to serve individual portions.

Glenda A. Galvan, Chickasaw Tribe, Ada, Oklahoma. Native American Program, 1976

Tolowa Indian Sand Bread

7 cups flour
3 cups water
1 teaspoon salt
2 teaspoons baking powder

"In our culture we have fish camps on the beach where we catch and dry fish. We either cooked on or under the fire. This was how we cooked our bread."

1. Three hours before baking bread, build a good-size fire on coarse-textured sand. Use wood with no pitch — alder is best because the ashes burn clean. Let the fire burn down to hot coals; then the sand beneath the fire should be hot enough to bake the bread.

2. Mix flour, water, salt, and baking powder. Knead the dough, then shape it into 5 loaves, about ½ inch thick and 8 inches in diameter. Pat flour around the loaves.

3. Scrape away the fire with a wooden paddle, and scoop out a flat pit in the hot sand. To test for the correct temperature, put a pinch of flour on the sand — if it burns, the sand is too hot, and if it browns slowly, the sand is just right.

4. Lay the loaves in the pit and cover with warm sand. Build a small fire off to the side to keep more sand warm in which to rotate the loaves. After about 25 minutes, remove the sand on top of the loaves, turn them over, and cover with hot sand from the nearby fire. Continue cooking for another 25 minutes until bread is done. Brush off the sand before eating. Yields 5 loaves.

Viola Richards, Tolowa Tribe, Smith River, California. Native American Program, 1974

Plains Indian Frybread

2 cups flour
3 teaspoons baking
    powder
1 teaspoon salt
¾ cup milk
oil, for frying

1. Mix dry ingredients well. Stir in milk, adding more if needed to make a smooth dough when it is formed into a ball.

2. Divide dough into small balls, about 1 cup each, and roll out rounds ½ to ¾ inch thick. Cut each circle into 4 pieces.

3. Drop a few at a time into about 2 inches of hot oil in a cast-iron frying pan. The oil should be hot enough for frying doughnuts, about 365°F.

4. Fry until golden brown, turning once. The bread will puff up immediately if the oil is the right temperature. Drain on paper towels.

Lilly Nahwooksy, Kiowa Tribe, Walters, Oklahoma. Native American Program, 1970

"Frybread is a staple among Plains Indians. Because of their nomadic lifestyle, Plains Indians did not have ovens, so they learned to use flour in creative ways. One of the easiest ways is to fry it."

Seneca Frybread

4 cups flour
2 teaspoons baking
 powder
½ teaspoon salt
3 cups milk
2 cups oil

1. Fill a large bowl with flour, and make a well in the center of the flour.

2. Add baking powder, salt, and milk. Using a large spoon, slowly stir flour into milk until dough follows spoon. Scrape off spoon, and knead dough until firm.

3. Break off a ball of dough about the size of a lemon and flatten. Slowly add to hot oil and fry for 2 to 3 minutes on each side. The bread will puff up and turn golden brown.

Edith R. John, Seneca Tribe, Lawtons, New York.
Native American Program, 1975

Oven Bread

1 package dry yeast
5 pounds white flour
1 cup whole-wheat
 flour

2 tablespoons salt
1 cup dry powdered
 milk
2 tablespoons sugar

1 cup lard
 (or shortening)

1. In a 4-quart bowl, dissolve yeast in 4 cups warm water.

2. Mix in dry ingredients. Add lard and more water if necessary.

3. Knead dough until smooth and elastic. Put in an oiled bowl and cover with a cloth for about 4 hours so dough will rise until double in size.

4. Form dough into loaves about ½ inch thick and 8 inches in diameter. Place in bread pans or pie plates and let rise until double in size, about 1½ hours.

5. Bake at 375°F until golden brown, about 45 minutes. Yields 8 to 10 loaves.

Lorencita C. Lujan and Crucita C. Mondragon, Taos Pueblo, Taos, New Mexico. Native American Program, 1981

Blue Dumplings

¼ teaspoon baking powder
½ teaspoon salt
2 tablespoons oil
½ cup water
1½ to 2 cups flour
1 quart unsweetened grape juice (or other juices such as blackberry or blueberry)
2 cups sugar

1. Mix baking powder, salt, oil, and water. Add flour, a little at a time, until a thick ball of dough forms, rather rubbery in consistency. Roll out onto a floured surface like a pie crust, until it is elastic and ⅛ inch thick.

2. Boil juice and sugar on high heat for about 4 minutes, until the mixture begins to get sticky and almost jellylike; stir occasionally.

3. Slice dough into narrow strips about ½ inch wide and 4 to 6 inches long.

4. Rapidly drop dough into boiling juice all at once, keeping dumplings apart. Boil for 2 to 3 minutes. Cover and set aside for about 30 minutes to cool and thicken. Serve hot or cold with ice cream or whipped cream.

Clydia Nahwoosky, Cherokee Tribe, Norman, Oklahoma. Native American Program, 1970

Biscochitos (Sugar Cookies)

2 cups sugar
2 cups lard (or shortening)
4 teaspoons anise flavoring
2 teaspoons vanilla extract (or rum flavoring)
8 cups flour
8 teaspoons baking powder
4 eggs
1 cup milk
2 teaspoons anise seeds

1. Preheat oven to 400°F.

2. Cream sugar, lard, anise flavoring, and vanilla in a large bowl.

3. In a separate bowl, mix flour and baking powder. Add half to sugar mixture. Stir in eggs, milk, and anise seeds. Mix well, then add remaining flour mixture.

4. Knead until smooth. Divide dough in half and roll out each piece ¼ inch thick on a lightly floured surface. Cut into favorite shapes.

5. Place on a cookie sheet and bake until bottoms are light brown, about 10 to 12 minutes. Yields 5 dozen.

Lorencita C. Lujan and Crucita C. Mondragon

"These are the cookies we bake for our annual feast days, Christmas, and New Year's. At the folklife festival, after we finished building the horno (clay oven), we baked the oven bread and biscochitos as part of our demonstration."

New England

★ · ★ · ★ · ★

Kathy Neustadt

My first association of food with New England was a poster that appeared, as if by magic, each November in my grade-school classrooms. In it, solemn-looking Pilgrims wearing high hats, their blunderbusses leaning against nearby trees, sat around a rough-hewn table beside noble-looking Indians and celebrated the first Thanksgiving. In the midst of this natural scene, rendered in faded earth tones, was the nearly sacred meal of wild turkey, cranberries, assorted other toothsome treats, and — is it possible? — pumpkin pie for dessert. This Thanksgiving portrait pulsed with significance, representing the American spirit at the very moment of its inception, the beginning of a new national identity, the product of a new kind of pilgrim spirit in a brand-new England. And at the unmistakable center of this patriotic myth was food. The first American meal belonged to New England, and, the message seemed to say, Yankee food and the Yankee spirit were one and the same thing: simple and nourishing, born of adversity yet given to celebration, a symbol of the natural resources of the nation's rich future.

It may not always be so broadly drawn, but I think that most people associate this idiomatic Thanksgiving with the phrase New England food. Add to it some Boston baked beans, a New England boiled dinner, lobster and clambakes on the beach, various chowders, johnnycakes and brown bread, pies, maple sugar and maple syrup from the north, and maybe some hearty meals using potatoes or blueberries, and the popular conception of the region's cuisine is nearly complete.

Of course, there is much more to New England food — and the complex of activities surrounding it, called foodways — than the landing of the Pilgrims and the much later invention of the pumpkin pie, however grateful for both we may be. Indeed, thanks to developments in technology since the 1600s, virtually all of the world's foodstuffs have become available in New

Previous pages: Brown bread awaits guests at the annual clambake held in Allen's Neck, Massachusetts. (Betty Belanus)

England while its own regional bounty has become increasingly accessible throughout the world.

New England cooking has neither stalled in the seventeenth century nor been confined to a Yankee milieu. When entering a New England kitchen today, one is just as likely to encounter yalanchi, basdek, ferlouche, and golabki as to find a boiled dinner or lobster pie — don't even bother to look for pit-baked beans or johnnycakes! And let's face it, Thanksgiving itself is more about microwaves and football coverage these days than it is about the celebration of a region's cultural, spiritual, and culinary ecology.

This is not to say that I am altogether ready to abandon my grade-school training. Food really does figure prominently in our national story, and the foods of New England played an essential role in the early years of colonization. When the Pilgrim fathers quoted passages from the Bible concerning God's care of the faithful, they were as much concerned with the tangible feeding of the body as they were with the nourishment of the soul.

Where Yankees Got Their Salt

In 1630 Frances Higginson, reporting on the settlement at Salem, wrote that "the aboundance of Sea-Fish was almost beyond beleeving, and sure I would scarce have beleeved it except I had scene it with mine owne Eyes." This early wealth of seafood affected not only the form and content of New England culture and diet, but it also shaped its occupational traditions, industrial developments, the regional economy, and a host of more subtle symbolic systems. People have suggested, for example, that the dependence of their forebears on dried fish — the result of both Native American and British preservative traditions — correlates somehow with the development of a "salty" Yankee character.

In 1602 the prevalence of cod caused English explorer Bartholomew Gosnold to confer the name "Cape of Cod" on the fishhooked peninsula in the southeast corner of Massachusetts, an area that has survived and flourished long after its aquatic namesake lost its place of privilege on New England's tables. The early prosperity of the commonwealth was so directly attributable to this fish that since the 1700s it has been identified as a symbol of Massachusetts. Even today, a carved wooden replica of the "sacred cod" hangs in the statehouse in Boston.

Thriving on the Three Sisters

In addition to the bounty of the sea, the English settlers found an abundance of game, grains, and plants on the land. Trained as cobblers and theologians, the Pilgrims-turned-farmers survived in the New World largely because of its natural fertility and the generosity of their native hosts. As wheat crops failed and peas refused to grow in sandy soil, the "Indian triad" — corn, beans, and squash, what native people call the Three Sisters — saved the early settlers from complete annihilation. Native Americans not

only shared their available goods, they also taught the settlers to cultivate new crops and introduced them to new ways of eating and preserving the foodstuffs they did produce.

The recipes prepared during the past twenty-five Festivals of American Folklife clearly demonstrate that the "old ways" constantly engage in an inventive dialogue with necessity to produce change. It was no different in the 1600s — the food traditions of the English settlers collided with native foods and the requirements of an unfamiliar environment. Sometimes the old ways prevailed, sometimes the new, but in most cases the two combined to produce a hybrid such as "Indian pudding," a uniting of corn (a new grain) and pudding (an old recipe).

The religious convictions of New England's early settlers also affected the development of its cuisine. The Puritans judged all aspects of daily life by standards that favored simplicity, rejected luxury, and viewed food as a moral matter. For example, in Boston in the 1600s, Puritan authorities banned mincemeat pies because they believed the dish to be idolatrous. Days for fasting were as common during the early colonial period as days for feasting, and the strict Puritan ban against working on the Sabbath led to such adaptations as the slow baking of brown bread and beans, which had been prepared the day before.

But it would be a mistake to conclude that New Englanders confined themselves to an austere diet. For one thing, New England's role as a trading center made it a marketplace for international goods and influences. Spices were imported from the Orient (Salem was known as the pepper port); rum, molasses, and chocolate came from the West Indies; and coffee arrived from Brazil. Increasingly, these foods were absorbed into the culinary repertoire of the region, and imported wines and rich foods, however simply presented, were to be found even on Puritan tables.

In addition, the early colonial population was far from homogeneous. Even among the self-avowed Puritans, considerable cultural and theological differences existed, and subsequent waves of immigration introduced even greater diversity into the region. By the early eighteenth century, all the arenas of English life in which food was publicly and recreationally consumed — from sporting events to agrarian festivals to tavern life — had reappeared in colonial New England, despite, or perhaps because of, Puritan disapproval.

After the colonies broke with England and established a federal government, concern with national identity refocused attention on America's Puritan heritage and on what could be considered distinctly American foods. Forefathers' Day celebrations, usually centered around a special meal, began to be held in New England during the eighteenth century, and patriotic feast-

Puritan Simplicity, with Spice

Opposite: A fisherman shows festival visitors in 1988 how lobster traps are used. (Smithsonian Institution)

ing events were held increasingly throughout the nineteenth century. The foods most often highlighted were those considered to have been native to the North American continent and its original inhabitants, the Indians, who were rapidly being transformed into America's own version of the Noble Savage of European romanticism.

Shaping America's Cuisine

Food and national politics came together more and more in rugged, outdoor eating events attended largely by men. As early as 1840, William Henry Harrison attempted to woo 10,000 Rhode Island voters at a presidential reelection clambake held on the Fourth of July — a date that was also popular for barbecues and salmon dinners. During this same period, transportation improved and leisure time increased in industrial America, making tourism an increasingly viable industry. New England's distinctive foodways became a marketable commodity.

An especially literate region, New England reflected and shaped the emerging American cuisine. While the earliest cookbooks in the American colonies were British in origin, by the end of the eighteenth century indigenous American adaptations and even a few original cookbooks began to appear. Recipes included such local specialties as cranberry tarts, Indian pudding, maple sugar, and pumpkin pie. By the 1870s the regional New England diet was making its way to a national audience as general circulation periodicals, imitating the women's magazines of the 1840s, carried recipes and menus. Farmers throughout the country, for example, could learn in their farm journals how New Englanders prepared their pumpkins or what side dishes they served with their salt cod.

The Boston Cooking School, founded in the 1880s, also played a major role in disseminating New England gastronomy. Through its publications and graduates, additional information about New England cookery spread across the nation. Perhaps more important was the broadcasting of Yankee notions about housewifery as both a moral and an increasingly complex and scientific undertaking. These ideas were to have lasting significance in the social history of women, in particular, and contributed to such organizational developments as domestic science (now known as home economics) and the settlement house movement, an early form of social welfare service.

By the latter part of the nineteenth century, the Industrial Revolution had affected every aspect of American life and had changed the profile of the human community. As cities expanded and factory towns were born, the nation needed different food preparation, storage, and distribution methods. The scientific and technological advances in safer canning techniques, more elaborate transportation systems, and the development of refrigeration made possible greater quantity and availability of foodstuffs that, in turn, affected the tastes of the nation.

Opposite: Anahid Kazazian of Lexington, Massachusetts, demonstrates the correct way to twist Armenian string cheese. (Nijdeh Havopian Havan)

Melting Pots

New England is no longer the homogeneous cultural cluster of stalwart Pilgrims and salty old Yankees, if such a portrait were ever adequate.

Before the 1800s the population of New England consisted almost exclusively of Native Americans, English immigrants and African slaves. By the middle of the nineteenth century, Irish families and Acadians from French Canada began arriving in large numbers and were followed by an influx of Scandinavians, Central European Jews, Eastern Europeans, and Mediterraneans. At the turn of the century, in the Yankee stronghold of Boston, approximately one-third of the city's population was foreign born.

Immigrants pursued occupational opportunities throughout New England. In southeastern Massachusetts, for example, Portuguese sailors — and, subsequently, their families — came to New Bedford because of its whaling industry. Many of these sailors accumulated wealth, left the city, and started farming the land that had been abandoned by the old Yankees. Polish immigrants followed a similar pattern in the Connecticut River valley. Acadians came to work in the textile mills, while Italians, Poles, and Finns were attracted to the cranberry bogs of Cape Cod. Later, these groups were replaced on the bogs by Cape Verdeans and, more recently, by Puerto Ricans.

The influx of each new immigrant group has brought with it new gastronomic traditions, new tastes, and even new foods. And the same dynamic that characterized the Pilgrim experience has remained in effect throughout the decades: people have conserved, adapted, adopted, and exchanged food and food-related customs with one another. At the same time that technology has been producing the means for greater uniformity across the country, new populations consistently have redefined regional and cultural boundaries.

Food traditions are often the most tangible evidence of such assertions of distinct identity, expressed, as they are, in the aromas that exude from neighborhoods, the produce presented in local market stalls, and the ethnic dishes available only in certain restaurants. The continuing presence of Italians in Connecticut and Rhode Island, or the Irish, French, and native populations in Vermont, New Hampshire, and Maine, have quite literally affected the flavor of these regions. In time, the same will undoubtedly be true for today's Southeast Asian, Latin, and Caribbean newcomers.

New England is no longer the homogeneous cultural cluster of stalwart Pilgrims and salty old Yankees, if such a portrait were ever adequate. The summer that Massachusetts was featured at the Festival of American Folklife, we put on a Yankee clambake, attended a Puerto Rican pig roast, and enjoyed the processionals honoring Italian and Portuguese saints — all major food events in the community life of multiethnic New England. We cooked with cranberries, talked about maple syrup, sampled chicken cacciatore, demonstrated lobster pots, made Irish bread, replicated urban ethnic gardens and rural greenhouses, consumed Armenian delicacies, baked some pies, stuffed grape leaves and cabbage rolls, and passed around the tripe. It was enough to make an old Pilgrim remove his high hat.

Recipes

Steak and Kidney Pie

Six Pâtés

Tourtière (Pork and Beef Pie)

Puerto Rican Pies with Pork

Ham and Rice with Pigeon Peas

Pork with Gandules
(Green Pigeon Peas)

White Cut Chicken with Dumpling Soup

Chicken and Spinach

Chicken Cacciatore

Alio and Olio with Anchovies

Portuguese Steamed Clams

Ryba Smazona (Fried Fish)

Oyster Stew for Two

White Perch Chowder

Caldo Verde
(Portugal's Famous Kale Soup)

Pierogi

Taishan Dumplings

Steamed Eggs with Bean Thread
and Oyster Sauce

Armenian Tel-Banir (String Cheese)

Yalanchi (Stuffed Grape Leaves)

Golabki (Cabbage Rolls)

Kapusta Smazona
(Sweet and Sour Cabbage)

Smothered Cabbage

Turnips with Dried Shrimp

Mushroom Cutlets

Irish Bread

Cranberry Nut Bread

Les Ployes (Buckwheat Cakes)

Steamed Brown Bread

Beignets in Maple Syrup

Puklavah (Armenian Pastry)

Chruscik (Polish Fried Pastry)

Ricotta Cookies

Lemon Raisin Pie

Squash Pie

Cranberry Raisin Pie

Spice and Rum Cake

Currant Cake

Arroz Doce (Rice Pudding)

Potato Fudge

Apple Basduk
(Armenian Fruit Leather)

Grape Rojik
(Fruit Leather with Walnuts)

"My grandmother, Faith Elizabeth Sharp, was born at The Gables, Garton-on-the-Wolds, Yorkshire, England, in 1848. With her sister Hope and her parents, she emigrated when she was three. Theirs was a poor farming family, and the cooking was frugal and plain. The aroma of steak and kidney pie and fresh baking powder biscuits, though certainly not a gourmet meal, was most welcome in the winter in a house heated by wood stoves."

Steak and Kidney Pie

1 beef kidney (or 6 lamb kidneys)	3 tablespoons flour	1 tablespoon Worcestershire sauce
1½ pounds round steak (or stewing meat)	1½ teaspoons salt	1 teaspoon mustard
	½ teaspoon ginger	3 onions, chopped
	3 cups water	1 pie crust
4 tablespoons oil		

1. Discard fat and membranes of kidneys and slice. Soak in salt water to cover for 30 minutes. Drain. If using beef kidney, cut into 1-inch pieces. Cut round steak also into 1-inch pieces.

2. Preheat oven to 425°F.

3. Mix flour, salt, and ginger in a bag, and shake kidneys and steak to coat. Brown in heated oil. Add water, Worcestershire sauce, mustard, and onions. Bring to a boil, then cover and simmer for 1 hour. If gravy is too thick, add more water.

4. Put mixture in a large casserole. Cover with pastry rolled to fit, press edges firmly against sides, and cut four slits near the center.

5. Bake for 45 minutes. Serve with mashed potatoes. Serves 6 to 8.

C. Eleanor Genovese, Wellesley, Massachusetts. Old Ways in the New World: British American, 1976

Six Pâtés

Pâte (crust):	such as wild duck or pheasant)	1 tablespoon salt
6 cups flour		1 pound fatback
dash of pepper	2 pounds venison	2 pounds onions
1 teaspoon salt	2 jack rabbits	10 pounds Maine potatoes
3 cups water (or chicken stock)	2 partridges	
	2 pounds beef (or veal or lamb)	1 teaspoon cinnamon
		½ teaspoon cloves
Filling:	2 pounds lean pork	1 tablespoon summer savory
2 pounds moose (or any game meat	½ turkey (or large chicken)	1 teaspoon pepper

1. To make pâte, combine flour, pepper, salt, and liquid to form a dough. Roll dough into a ball. Divide in half and roll out each half to ¼ inch thick or like a pie crust. Leave one round and cut the other into 2 × 4-inch strips, making sure to sprinkle plenty of flour before rolling. Set aside.

2. In 1 or 2 large roasting pans, cook all meats until well done. Allow to cool a bit, then remove bones, skin, fat, and unwanted parts. Tear meat into bite-size pieces, and place individual meats in separate bowls. Save drippings to replenish stock later.

3. Place strips of sliced fatback, ¼ × 2 × 4 inches, to line the bottom of a large, high pot; a 16-gallon canning pot works well.

4. Slice uncooked onions and potatoes for use as layers.

5. Put a tall, skinny bottle in the center of pot to keep layers from tumbling.

6. Start layering with pork first, followed by a layer of onions, potatoes, and pâte. The next layer should begin with a game meat, alternating with a domestic and a game meat until all meat, pâte, potatoes, and other ingredients have been used. When stacking is completed, remove bottle from pot. There should be 6 layers of potatoes, onions, and pâte and 7 layers of meat.

7. Place pâte on top of layers, leaving a hole in the center. Brush crust with milk or meat stock. Add water to the meat drippings and juices and pour in center hole, where bottle was, until stock reaches the same level as the top layer of meat. Keep enough stock to replenish while cooking.

8. Bake at 450°F until liquid begins to boil, then reduce heat to 275°F or 300°F and cook all day (5 to 6 hours). Add more stock or water as the liquid evaporates. Serves 30 to 40.

Claudette P. Beaulieu, Madawaska, Maine. French Program, 1983

> **"Six pâtés is traditionally served during the Christmas season and is a favorite among the St. John Valley Acadians. In my youth it was served at family reunions after midnight Mass on Christmas Eve."**

Tourtière (Pork and Beef Pie)

> "Tourtière was usually served after a family gathering called Reveilon, starting after midnight Mass with fiddle playing, jigging, singing, and dancing all night long to celebrate the birth of Christ and give thanks and rejoice and share with family and friends. It is a feast that is cherished from generation to generation. Of my childhood memories, this is the one I cherish the most, and my own children look back on this feast as the most loving and pleasurable of their time at home."

½ cup water
1 pound boneless pork, cubed
1 pound boneless beef, cubed
3 onions, diced
1 teaspoon salt
½ teaspoon pepper
6 medium potatoes
2 slices fresh bread
1 teaspoon fresh parsley, chopped
1 to 2 cups meat juice
double pie crust
butter (or cream of mushroom soup) (optional)

1. In water, cook meat, 1 onion, salt, and pepper for 2 to 3 hours or until meat is done.

2. When meat is about 45 minutes from being done, peel and slice potatoes and boil them. Drain and mash potatoes or run them through a grinder with meat and remaining onions.

3. Run bread through grinder last to clean it. Add to meat and potato mixture, with parsley, salt, and pepper. Mix well.

4. Pour in juice in which meat was cooked to make a thick filling, adding more water if necessary. Place mixture in double pie crust.

5. Bake in a preheated 350°F oven until crust is golden, about 45 minutes. To serve hot with butter or mushroom soup as a sauce, open wedges horizontally and top with small pieces of cold butter or mushroom soup. Serves 6.

Claudette P. Beaulieu, Madawaska, Maine. French Program, 1983

Puerto Rican Pies with Pork

Filling:
3 pounds pork, cut into small chunks
½ cup chopped onions
½ cup chopped green pepper
5 cloves garlic, chopped
6 green leaves recao, chopped
½ teaspoon pepper
Dough:
5 pounds purple yautías (Spanish root)
2 pounds pumpkin
2 green plaintains
4 pounds green bananas
1 cup meat broth
½ cup annatto oil
salt
olives
1 red bell pepper, thinly sliced

1. Prepare filling by sautéeing meat with other ingredients until well done.

2. To make dough, peel and slice yautías and pumpkin. Grind, with plaintains and bananass, in a food processor until soft. Add 1 cup meat broth, annatto oil, and salt to taste; mix well. If mixture is not soft enough, add more broth.

3. Form pies by cutting several pieces of aluminum foil into 6 × 8-inch squares. Spread ½ cup dough on piece of foil. Add 2 tablespoons meat mixture, 1 olive, and red pepper slice. Fold foil to cover meat mixture and secure so it will not fall out.

4. Cook pies covered in boiling water for about 20 minutes. Uneaten pies may be frozen; when ready to use, cook for about 30 minutes.

Bienvenida Figueroa, Lowell, Massachusetts. Ingenuity and Tradition: The Common Wealth of Massachusetts, 1988

Ham and Rice with Pigeon Peas

1 cup chopped ham
2 tablespoons oil
6 leaves green recao, chopped
½ cup chopped onions
3 cloves garlic, mashed
½ cup chopped green pepper
8 black peppercorns, ground
½ can tomato sauce
1 can green pigeon peas
½ cup annatto oil
3 cups water
2 tablespoons salt
3 cups medium-grain rice

1. Sauté ham in oil, stirring constantly for about 3 minutes. Add recao leaves, onions, garlic, green pepper, and black pepper, and sauté for a few minutes until tender.

2. Stir in tomato sauce, peas, and annato oil. Add water and salt to taste. Bring to a boil, add rice, and boil uncovered on medium heat until water evaporates.

3. Stir mixture, cover, and place on low heat for about 15 to 20 minutes, until rice is soft and completely cooked. Serves 6.

Bienvenida Figueroa

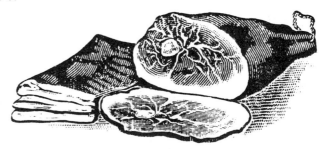

Pork with Gandules (Green Pigeon Peas)

"I started cooking in my native Puerto Rico when I was about thirteen years old and my mother went to work. She taught me a few basics, and I experimented from there. I learned some from other relatives, too, especially from my father's mother. I enjoyed cooking for my brother and sister. This recipe for gandules with pork is served at special occasions such as weddings, christenings, family reunions, and sweet-sixteen birthdays."

Marinade:

1 cup olive oil
2 large onions, chopped
3 teaspoons oregano
1 to 2 green peppers, chopped
3 cloves garlic, minced
2 teaspoons cumin
4 teaspoons Goya recaito
1 teaspoon freshly ground pepper
1 teaspoon salt

6 pounds lean pork, cut into oversize pieces

3 pounds long-grain rice
½ cup olive oil
1½ teaspoons achiote
2 cans gandules (green pigeon peas)
4 cups water
2 8-ounce cans tomato sauce

1. The night before cooking, make marinade and add pork. Refrigerate, stirring several times.

2. In a large covered cast-iron pot, cook pork and marinade ingredients on medium heat for at least 1 hour, stirring occasionally.

3. While pork is cooking, soak rice in water to cover for 20 minutes.

4. Heat olive oil and add achiote until oil turns red. Remove from heat and set aside.

5. After pork mixture has cooked for 35 to 40 minutes, add gandules with can liquid, water, tomato sauce, rice, and ½ cup olive oil mixture.

6. Cook, covered, on medium heat for about 10 minutes, stirring occasionally until rice looks like a "mountain." Uncover, stir, and cover again. This process should take about 30 minutes, allowing rice to absorb all liquid. Serves 12.

Miguel Almestica, Worcester, Massachusetts. Ingenuity and Tradition: The Common Wealth of Massachusetts, 1988

White Cut Chicken with Dumpling Soup

1 whole 5-pound
  chicken, cleaned
8 to 10 dried
  mushrooms
½ cup dried shrimp
2 pounds Chinese
  turnips

⅓ pound Chinese
  sausage

Dumplings:
1 pound glutinous
  flour
salt

Dipping sauce:
2 green onions
1 teaspoon fresh
  ginger
½ cup light soy sauce
½ cup corn oil,
  heated

1. Fill a large stock pot (8 to 10 quarts) halfway with water and bring to a boil.

2. Place chicken in boiling water for about 20 minutes, turning once. Turn off heat, and let chicken sit in hot water for another 20 minutes. Check to see if chicken is cooked by inserting a fork into the thickest part. It is ready if no red juice comes out; if chicken is not cooked, repeat cooking process.

3. While chicken is cooking, soak mushrooms and shrimp, peel turnips, and shred and slice sausage.

4. In a bowl, mix flour with enough water to make a thick paste. When dough is dry enough, knead and roll into marble-size pieces.

5. Boil another pot of water. Drop dumplings into boiling water; they are cooked when they rise to the surface. Remove each dumpling and place in a pot of cold water.

6. Remove chicken from stock. Add mushrooms, turnips, and sausage, and cook until the turnips are soft. Skim off fat from stock. When ready to serve, add drained dumplings. Salt to taste.

7. Slice chicken into serving pieces. Serve on the side and dip in sauce.

8. To make sauce, mince green onions and a few slices of ginger, add a little salt, and mix with soy sauce and heated oil. Serves 4 to 6.

Mary Ning and Stephen Ning, Cambridge, Massachusetts, and New York City. Cultural Conservation, 1985

Chicken and Spinach

"The response of festival visitors to my recipes was enthusiastic and heart-warming. People of all ages enjoyed the chicken and spinach. That didn't surprise me. This recipe has a long history in my family and a number of health benefits."

1 large clove garlic, minced
¼ cup olive oil
1 whole chicken, boiled and removed from bone

1 to 2 cups spinach, chopped (or 1 10-ounce package frozen spinach, chopped)
¼ cup fresh lemon juice

1 tablespoon salt
3 tablespoons coriander powder
1½ cups water

1. Sauté garlic in olive oil.

2. Add remaining ingredients. Let simmer for about 30 minutes. Serves 4 to 6.

Bertha McCrary, Boston, Massachusetts. Ingenuity and Tradition: The Common Wealth of Massachusetts — Urban Ethnic Gardens, 1988

Chicken Cacciatore

5 to 7 pounds chicken thighs, drumsticks, wings
3 tablespoons olive oil
2 tablespoons oregano
salt (optional)
pepper
1 large head garlic
1 cup wine vinegar
½ to ¾ cup red table wine

1. Preheat oven to 350°F.

2. Rinse chicken, pat dry, and coat in oil, making sure it is thoroughly coated; skin may be removed before oiling. Sprinkle with oregano, salt, and pepper, and mix well. Bake chicken, uncovered, for 30 minutes.

3. Break open head of garlic and smash a few to open. Rub garlic on chicken, add vinegar and wine to roasting pan, cover with aluminum foil, and bake for another 30 minutes. Remove foil and cook for an additional 7 to 10 minutes. Serves 8.

Joanne Saltamartini, North Adams, Massachusetts. Ingenuity and Tradition: The Common Wealth of Massachusetts, 1988

Alio and Olio with Anchovies

2 pounds spaghetti
¼ cup olive oil
¼ pound margarine
1 large clove garlic,
   minced
2 large onions,
   chopped
3 cans anchovies with
   capers, flat and
   rolled
grated Parmesan or
   Romano cheese

1. Fill a large pot with 5 quarts water and bring to a boil. Cook spaghetti according to directions and drain.

2. In a medium frying pan, heat olive oil and margarine. Sauté garlic and onions.

3. Reduce heat to medium, add anchovies, and cook for 10 minutes. Mix with cooked spaghetti.

4. Serve warm with grated cheese. Serves 8 to 10.

Joanne Saltamartini

"This recipe is usually made on Good Friday (without meat) and on Christmas Eve. When the church did not allow meat on the day or night of Christmas Eve, alio was served with other fish, including cod. This dish is a very important recipe as part of my Italian heritage and a tradition that has been handed down by my parents."

Portuguese Steamed Clams

1. Melt butter. Add onion, garlic, and linguiça. Fry until mixture is almost cooked.

2. Add wine and bay leaf, and cook until wine reduces by half.

3. Add water, corn, and clams. Cover and simmer to steam open clams. After 5 minutes, add parsley. Clams are done when they open and the belly turns from a watery sack and becomes a little dry, about 12 minutes.

4. Pour off broth into a container. Place clams in individual bowls, and put corn and linguiça in others. Serve broth on the side for dipping clams. Serves 1 to 2.

Note: Littleneck hard-shell clams may be substituted for soft-shell clams.

David P. Francis, Wellfleet, Massachusetts. Ingenuity and Tradition: The Common Wealth of Massachusetts — Maritime, 1988

2 tablespoons butter
¼ cup chopped
   onion (or shallots)
½ clove garlic,
   crushed
4 to 5 inches linguiça
   (Portuguese
   sausage), cut into
   ¼-inch slices
¼ cup white wine
½ bay leaf
1 cup water
1 ear corn, broken in
   half
1½ pounds soft-shell
   clams
1 tablespoon fresh
   parsley, chopped

Ryba Smazona (Fried Fish)

1 pound cod (or
   haddock)
1 large onion, sliced
salt
pepper
flour
1 egg, lightly beaten
   with 2 tablespoons
   water
1 cup bread crumbs
butter
parsley and lemon,
   for garnish

1. Slice fish into serving-size pieces. Layer in a dish with onion, salt, and pepper. Cover with aluminum foil and refrigerate for about 1 hour.

2. Preheat oven to 350°F.

3. Remove fish from refrigerator. Discard onion.

4. Dry fish and dredge in flour. Dip fish in egg and water mixture. Roll in bread crumbs. Fry in butter until brown on both sides. Place in a baking pan, and bake for about 30 minutes. Garnish with parsley and lemon. Serves 2 to 3.

Julia Gelowtsky, Cambridge, Massachusetts. Ingenuity and Tradition: The Common Wealth of Massachusetts — Urban Ethnic Gardens, 1988

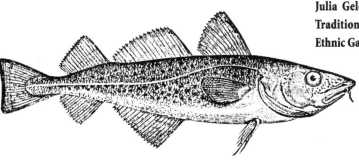

Oyster Stew for Two

"My father, a life-long oyster farmer in Wellfleet, would often make this oyster stew for us kids. Lunch was always preceded by a demonstration of his shucking technique and a few words about the stew's goodness. He performed this ritual with a secret pride. We knew how special this was to him."

2 tablespoons butter
16 mouth-size
   oysters, shucked
   (or larger ones cut
   to bite size)
pepper
2 cups milk

1. Melt butter in a saucepan. Sauté oysters until edges curl a bit. Add pepper to taste.

2. Pour in milk (more or less as desired), continue to stir, and heat until steam begins to rise from milk. Remove from heat and serve in shallow soup bowls. Divide fairly, of course.

David P. Francis, Wellfleet, Massachusetts. Ingenuity and Tradition: The Common Wealth of Massachusetts — Maritime, 1988

White Perch Chowder

2½ quarts white
    perch fillets
3 quarts water
12 cups diced
    potatoes
2 cups diced onions
¼ pound salt pork
6 cans evaporated
    milk

1. Cook fish in water until done. Remove fish, then cook potatoes and onions in same water.

2. Break up fish while potatoes are cooking. When potatoes are done, return fish to water.

3. Fry salt pork until crisp but not burned. Cut up pork and add, with grease, to fish.

4. Stir in evaporated milk and heat through. Serves 10 to 12.

Edna Worster, Springfield, Maine. Regional America: The Northeast, 1976

"My father worked in the mills and farmed to raise seven kids. He and my mother both worked hard, but we tried to eat well. She lived until she was sixty-two, and he lived until he was eighty-three. I've been married forty-three years, but long ago my brothers and sisters kind of developed this recipe."

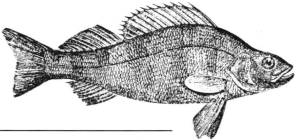

Caldo Verde (Portugal's Famous Kale Soup)

3 cups water
2 tablespoons olive
    oil
2 potatoes, sliced
1 pound kale
1 linguiça
    (Portuguese
    sausage), sliced
salt

1. Bring water to a boil and slowly add olive oil.

2. Add potatoes, cover, and cook until soft. Mash potatoes in water so liquid becomes creamy.

3. Tightly roll up kale leaves and cut into shreds. Drop kale and sausage into boiling potato water. Cook until kale and sausage are done, about 10 to 15 minutes. Add salt to taste. Serves 2 to 4.

Lurdes Rodrigues, Medford, Massachusetts. Ingenuity and Tradition: The Common Wealth of Massachusetts — Urban Ethnic Gardens, 1988

Pierogi

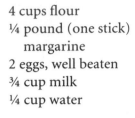

4 cups flour
¼ pound (one stick) margarine
2 eggs, well beaten
¾ cup milk
¼ cup water

Cheese filling:
1 cup cottage cheese
1 teaspoon butter, melted
1 egg, beaten

3 tablespoons sugar
3 tablespoons currants
¼ teaspoon cinnamon

Cabbage filling:
4 cans sauerkraut
½ pound butter
2 to 3 onions, finely chopped

Cheese and potato filling:
4 large potatoes, peeled and chopped
1 pound dry farmer's cheese
1 egg, beaten
1 teaspoon salt
4 tablespoons butter
1 onion, chopped
dried mint flakes

1. Put flour in a large bowl. Cut up margarine and work into flour with fingers as for a pie crust.

2. Add eggs, then stir in milk and water to make a stiff dough.

3. On a lightly floured surface, knead dough for about 5 minutes. Roll out very thin. Cut with a round cookie cutter or glass.

4. Prepare your choice of filling. For cheese, cream cottage cheese with melted butter. Add remaining ingredients and mix well. To make cabbage filling, boil sauerkraut for 5 minutes and drain. Boil again for 5 minutes and drain. Let sauerkraut cool. Squeeze out juice. Melt butter in a frying pan. Add onions, and fry until onions are soft and begin to color. For cheese and potato filling, cook potatoes in boiling water and drain. Mash with cheese, breaking up cheese into small pieces. Add egg and salt and blend well. Sauté onion in butter, then combine with potato mixture, add a sprinkle of mint leaves, and mix well.

5. Fill dough with choice of filling. Fold over one side, and press edges together.

6. Boil in lightly salted water for about 5 minutes. Remove and cool in cold water. Pierogi may be dipped in a sautéed onion and butter sauce or served with sour cream. Yields about 30.

Roberta Szala, Mary Szala, and Anastacia Swartz, Amherst, Massachusetts. Regional America: The Northeast, 1976

Taishan Dumplings

1 pound Chinese
    wheat flour
boiling water
⅓ pound tapioca
    flour (or minute
    tapioca)

Filling:
½ cup Chinese black
    mushrooms
½ cup bamboo shoots
½ cup Chinese ham
½ cup green onions

½ cup celery
½ cup water chestnuts
½ cup shrimp
    (optional)
1 pound pork,
    minced

1. Put wheat flour in a large mixing bowl. Slowly pour in boiling water while stirring with chopsticks. Quickly stir mixture until it looks glassy, meaning that flour is cooked. Cover bowl to keep in heat for about 30 minutes.

2. If using minute tapioca, soak in water until it feels soft. For tapioca flour, add water until mixture feels wet.

3. Knead wheat flour until mixture has a soft consistency. Slowly fold in tapioca, until dough feels elastic. If dough is too sticky, use some oil on your hands.

4. Roll dough into a long string, then cut into small pieces. Form each piece into a round ball. With a rolling pin, make a flat circle from each. Use some tapioca flour to help in rolling.

5. Finely dice mushrooms, bamboo shoots, ham, onions, celery, and water chestnuts for filling. Peel, clean, and mince shrimp. Combine all ingredients and mix well. Filling may be used cooked or raw, depending on personal preference. If filling is precooked, dumplings will be less juicy than if filled with raw ingredients.

6. Place filling on dough wrappers. Fold wrappers in half, and seal the edges by pressing them together.

7. Steam dumplings with precooked filling for about 10 minutes. Dumplings with raw ingredients will take a little longer, to ensure that the filling is cooked through.

Note: Dumpling wrappers, available from Asian markets, may be substituted for homemade dumplings.

Mary Ning and Stephen Ning, Cambridge, Massachusetts, and New York City. Cultural Conservation, 1985

Steamed Eggs with Bean Thread and Oyster Sauce

1 2-ounce package
   bean threads
6 eggs
1 to 2 tablespoons oil
oyster sauce

1. Soak bean threads in water until soft; drain.

2. Place a rack inside a large pot, and boil water for steaming.

3. Beat eggs with an equal amount of water. Add drained bean threads and mix in a 2-quart glass baking dish.

4. When water comes to a boil, place dish with eggs on rack, cover pot, and lower heat. Cook until eggs look like a custard. Remove egg dish from pot.

5. Add oil and oyster sauce to taste before serving. Serves 4 to 6.

Mary Ning and Stephen Ning, Cambridge, Massachusetts, and New York City. Cultural Conservation, 1985

Armenian Tel-Banir (String Cheese)

4 cups water
1 cup salt
½ pound unsalted
   curd cheese
mahleb (black
   currant kernel)
caraway seed

1. Mix water and salt. To determine if mixture is salty enough, measure the density by floating an egg in the water; add more salt if necessary. Stir in ice cubes and set aside.

2. Preheat oven to 350°F.

3. Slice cheese ½ inch thick. Put slices on a baking sheet and bake until cheese resembles cheese fondue. Empty melted cheese into a strainer.

4. Sprinkle cheese with mahleb and caraway seed. Knead quickly by hand or with a wooden spoon, making it like a ball of dough. Poke a hole with your thumb, and start to pull outward with both thumbs, as if making a skein. Repeat many times, overlapping the circle until the cheese hardens so that it cannot be pulled any more. Twist the cheese, and secure it at each end to give it the shape of string cheese.

5. Put cheese in salty water for 3 to 4 hours. Remove and place cheese in plastic lunch bags; store in the freezer. Cheese takes 1 hour to defrost. Serves 6.

Anahid Kazazian, Lexington, Massachusetts. Ingenuity and Tradition: The Common Wealth of Massachusetts — Foodways, 1988

Yalanchi (Stuffed Grape Leaves)

1 cup rice
1½ cups olive oil
5 cups chopped
   onions
¼ cup pine nuts
½ cup raisins
½ cup minced parsley
½ teaspoon allspice
¼ teaspoon
   cinnamon
pinch of red pepper
1 teaspoon chopped
   dill
salt
pepper
grape leaves, bottled
   or freshly blanched
1½ cups water
2 to 3 tablespoons
   lemon juice

1. Parboil rice and set aside.

2. Sauté onions in olive oil until golden, but not brown. Add pine nuts, raisins, parsley, and seasonings, and stir for a few minutes. Mix with rice. Cover and let stand for 15 minutes.

3. Place grape leaves on a board with vein side up. Place 1 tablespoon filling on each leaf at the top, near the stem. Fold sides and stem end over the stuffing, and roll into the shape of a small hot dog.

4. Place extra leaves on the bottom of a stove-top pan. Layer stuffed grape leaves side by side. Top with a heavy plate to keep them in place. Add water, lemon juice, and a pinch of salt.

5. Cover pan and simmer for 50 to 60 minutes, until rice is fully cooked. Let grape leaves rest until set. Serve warm or cold.

Rose Avadanian, Waltham, Massachusetts. The Grand Generation: Folklore and Aging, 1984

"What a delight to see men listening and asking questions about food! I told the parents in the audience not to be afraid of turning my Armenian string cheese recipe into a game with their children. And I told the women to get together and make a party out of it. Talk, laugh, gossip (why not?) about their husbands, in-laws, neighbors, the milkman, the mailman, the teachers, and the minister. And please, not to go to the psychiatrist. With that money, I told them, they could have cheese, family, and friendship."

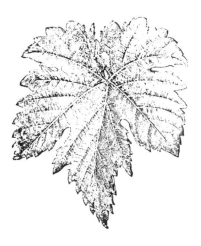

Golabki (Cabbage Rolls)

1 large head cabbage
½ cup rice
2 quarts water
1 large onion, diced
1 green pepper, diced
2 tablespoons butter
1 pound ground beef
salt
pepper
5 slices bacon
tomato sauce
    (optional)

1. Remove core from cabbage with a sharp knife. Scald cabbage in boiling water. Remove a few leaves at a time, as they wilt. Let leaves cool before using.

2. Wash rice in cold water and stir into 2 quarts rapidly boiling salted water. Boil 10 minutes. Strain by running cold water through rice in strainer. The rice will be only half-cooked.

3. Preheat oven to 300°F.

4. Sauté onion and green pepper in butter until onion becomes transparent. Fry ground beef, breaking it into pea-size pieces. Combine rice, beef, onion, and pepper in a large bowl. Season to taste.

5. Spread each cabbage leaf with meat, about ½ inch thick. Fold the two sides to the middle and roll up, starting with one of the open ends. Place cabbage rolls in a baking dish that has been lined with extra cabbage leaves, and cover rolls with bacon.

6. Bake with the cover partly off for 2 hours, basting occasionally. Golabki may be covered with tomato sauce for additional flavor. Yields 35 to 40.

Roberta Szala, Mary Szala, and Anastacia Swartz, Amherst, Massachusetts. Regional America: The Northeast, 1976

Kapusta Smazona (Sweet and Sour Cabbage)

1 medium head
  cabbage, shredded
½ cup oil
1 medium onion,
  chopped
salt
pepper
1 large can sauerkraut
¼ teaspoon caraway
  seed
½ teaspoon celery
  seed
1 bay leaf
1 tablespoon sugar

1. Cook shredded cabbage in boiling water until wilted. Drain and set aside.

2. Heat oil in a large frying pan. Add onion, salt, and pepper, and fry onion until soft.

3. Rinse sauerkraut and add to pan for 5 minutes. Mix in drained cabbage, caraway seed, celery seed, and bay leaf. Stir well, cover, and cook for 30 minutes, stirring frequently.

4. When browned, add sugar and stir. Cook for 10 more minutes.

Julia Gelowtsky, Cambridge, Massachusetts. Ingenuity and Tradition: The Common Wealth of Massachusetts — Urban Ethnic Gardens, 1988

"In a Polish home the traditional greeting, 'Gosc w dom, Bog w dom' ('Guest in the house, God in the house') is always followed by, 'Set another plate.' In many a household the father gave his stamp of approval for a daughter to be married when she could cook a good, hearty meal like cabbage and kielbasa."

Smothered Cabbage

4 chicken wings
4 beef bones
3 to 4 cups water
1 medium to large
  head cabbage
1 red bell pepper,
  finely chopped
2 teaspoons chicken
  bouillon
salt
pepper

1. Make stock by boiling chicken wings and beef bones in water for 1 hour. Remove wings and bones.

2. Separate green and white cabbage leaves. Chop green leaves and add to stock. Cook for about 30 minutes.

3. Chop white cabbage leaves. Add to stock with chopped pepper and bouillon. Continue cooking for 15 minutes. Season with salt and pepper to taste. Serves 4.

Bertha McCrary, Boston, Massachusetts. Ingenuity and Tradition: The Common Wealth of Massachusetts — Urban Ethnic Gardens, 1988

Turnips with Dried Shrimp

½ cup dried shrimp
2 pounds Chinese
  turnips (or cabbage
  or zucchini)
1 to 2 green onions
1 to 2 cloves garlic,
  smashed
oil, for frying
salt

1. Soak dried shrimp and clean. Peel, wash, slice, and shred turnips. Cut onions about 2 inches long.

2. Heat a wok until very hot, add oil, and cook garlic until browned.

3. If desired, remove garlic; add turnips, stir, cover pan, and cook until turnips are soft. Add water if dish appears too dry, but occasional stirring should produce enough water.

4. Add onions and shrimp; stir cook until done. Salt to taste. Serves 6.

Mary Ning and Stephen Ning, Cambridge, Massachusetts, and New York City. Cultural Conservation, 1985

Mushroom Cutlets

2 tablespoons butter
1 pound mushrooms,
  finely chopped
1 onion, finely
  chopped
1 tablespoon
  chopped parsley
6 hard rolls (or 1½
  cups mashed
  potatoes)
3 eggs, beaten
salt
pepper
1 tablespoon bread
  crumbs

1. In a large pan, fry mushrooms and onion in 1 tablespoon butter. Add parsley.

2. Moisten hard rolls and squeeze dry. Add eggs and bread (or mashed potatoes) to mushrooms. Season to taste with salt and pepper.

3. Form small cutlets by hand, dip in bread crumbs, and fry in remaining butter. Serves 4.

Marcessia Gelowtsky, Cambridge, Massachusetts. Ingenuity and Tradition: The Common Wealth of Massachusetts — Urban Ethnic Gardens, 1988

Irish Bread

3 cups flour
3½ teaspoons baking
    powder
½ teaspoon salt
3 tablespoons butter,
    melted
¼ cup sugar
raisins
1 egg, lightly beaten
1½ cups milk

1. Preheat oven to 350°F.

2. Sift flour with baking powder and salt. Cream butter and sugar. Add flour to butter mixture, with a few handfuls of raisins. Mix egg with milk and add to flour mixture. Let dough sit for 5 minutes.

3. Put in a greased 8-inch round or square pan. Bake for 1 hour or until knife comes out clean.

Ann Horkan, Watertown, Massachusetts. Ingenuity and Tradition: The Common Wealth of Massachusetts — Crafts, 1988

"This is my short-cut version of the bread my mom and grandma made. They used less milk and kneaded it to death, as we used to say. We could always tell if our mom was upset by the pounding she gave the bread as she kneaded it. Boy, when she was angry the bread got a beating, and we knew to stay out of her way. But when it came out of the oven she would cut us a big chunk and spread it with her own homemade butter, and you would think you were in heaven."

Cranberry Nut Bread

2 cups flour
1 cup sugar
1½ teaspoons baking
    powder
1 teaspoon salt
½ teaspoon baking
    soda
½ teaspoon nutmeg
½ teaspoon
    cinnamon
¼ cup shortening
1 teaspoon grated
    orange peel
¾ cup orange juice
1 egg, beaten
1 cup chopped
    cranberries
½ cup chopped nuts

1. Preheat oven to 350°F.

2. Sift dry ingredients. Cut in shortening.

3. Combine orange peel, juice, and egg. Add dry ingredients to egg mixture, stirring just enough to moisten. Fold in cranberries and nuts.

4. Pour batter into a greased 9 × 5 × 3-inch loaf pan. Bake for 60 minutes. Cool, then wrap and store overnight.

Dorothy Angley, Carver, Massachusetts. Ingenuity and Tradition: The Common Wealth of Massachusetts — Agriculture Fair Area, 1988

"My early memories include going with my mother to the bog outside the small town of Carver when she worked at the harvest. Other mothers were there with their children, and we played in the warm fall sunshine as our mothers gathered the berries. At noontime we ate our picnic lunches, seated beside the bog on cranberry harvest boxes."

Les Ployes (Buckwheat Cakes)

"When the Acadians settled in Madawaska County, they were so isolated that they had to travel forty miles by canoe and then forty miles on foot to reach Rivière du Laup to get supplies. Because the season was so short and buckwheat would grow almost anywhere, they planted buckwheat, harvested it, and took it to Caron Brook to be milled into flour.

Les ployes, pronounced 'plugs,' are eaten with all meals — plugging the hole in the stomachs of hardworking Acadians. Unlike pancakes, they are served like bread at each meal or as dessert, spread with maple syrup or molasses or rolled around fresh fruit. "

1 cup buckwheat flour
1 cup white flour
3 tablespoons baking powder
1 teaspoon salt
1½ cups cold water
½ cup very hot water

1. Combine all dry ingredients.

2. Add cold water and mix vigorously for 2 minutes. Add hot water and beat again for 1 minute.

3. Heat an ungreased griddle to 400°F. Pour out 6-inch rounds of mixture ⅛ inch thick. Cook for 1 minute on one side only. Keep warm by wrapping in aluminum foil until served. Yields 16.

Albina Martin, Gardner, Massachusetts. Ingenuity and Tradition: The Common Wealth of Massachusetts — Foodways, 1988

Steamed Brown Bread

"One lady from Maine told me that Saturday night baked bean dinners were not complete unless they included homemade brown bread. I still make this bread for all of the clambakes my husband puts on in the summer."

2½ cups bran cereal
2½ cups milk
1 cup dark raisins
2 tablespoons molasses
2½ cups flour
1 teaspoon salt
2 teaspoons baking soda
1¼ cups sugar

1. Soak cereal, milk, raisins, and molasses in a large bowl for 5 minutes.

2. Sift together flour, salt, baking soda, and sugar. Add dry ingredients and mix well.

3. Grease 3 12-ounce coffee cans. Divide batter evenly among the cans. Cover with a double thickness of aluminum foil, and secure with a wide rubber band. Set in a pot with a rack on the bottom. Add enough cold water to reach the middle of the cans. Bring to a boil, lower heat, and simmer for 2½ hours. Add additional boiling water to keep the water at the halfway level.

4. Remove cans from the pot and take off foil. Gently tap cans on their sides to loosen bread. Cool completely on a wire rack. This bread freezes well for later use.

Priscilla Davoll, Dartmouth, Massachusetts. Ingenuity and Tradition: The Common Wealth of Massachusetts — Clambake, 1988

Beignets in Maple Syrup

1 cup flour
2 tablespoons sugar
2 teaspoons baking
    powder
¼ teaspoon salt
1 tablespoon butter
    (or shortening)
¾ cup milk

Syrup:
2½ cups maple syrup
½ stick butter
    (or margarine)
pinch of salt
1 cup water
1 teaspoon vanilla
    extract

1. Mix flour, sugar, baking powder, and salt. Add butter or shortening and milk, and stir with a fork.

2. To make syrup, place maple syrup, butter, salt, water, and vanilla in a pot and slowly boil for 5 minutes.

3. With a tablespoon drop batter into boiling syrup. Cover and boil for 10 to 12 minutes. Remove and serve as is or with whipped cream.

Claudette P. Beaulieu, Madawaska, Maine. French Program, 1983

"The fact that my mother exhibited such pleasure and satisfaction preparing food (for thirteen people) was a source of inspiration to me as a child. I would sing with her and feel important because I was allowed to participate in such an important role. I had my own little pile of dough, flour, cookie cutter, and other things. And it was so special because she looked very contented when cooking and baking. She was very creative and made food look beautiful and colorful. To this day, I enjoy garnishing most of all."

Puklavah (Armenian Pastry)

"Puklavah was lovingly taught to me by my fraternal grandmother, with whom I spent many memorable summers. Arabs and Greeks prepare puklavah, a Middle Eastern pastry, differently. My grandmother was very strict. She taught me the Armenian way of making puklavah and sternly warned me not to change the recipe in any way. At the Smithsonian festival, the audience asked me many of the same questions I had asked her years ago. When I asked, 'Why is it done this way?,' my grandmother would always respond, 'Because this is the way it is done.' To the audience's amusement, I found myself repeating my grandmother's words."

1 pound walnuts, finely chopped
¾ cup sugar
1 teaspoon cinnamon
1 pound unsalted butter, melted
1 pound filo dough
¾ cup sugar
¾ cup water

1. Preheat oven to 325°F.

2. Prepare filling by mixing walnuts, sugar, and cinnamon.

3. Layer filo in a puklavah pan (15 × 18 × 2 inches), spreading butter on every other layer with a large spoon. Spread filling over middle layer.

4. Cut puklavah into diamond shapes. Top with butter. Bake for 35 to 40 minutes, until bottom is brown. Cool slightly.

5. While puklavah is baking, prepare syrup by mixing sugar and water. Heat for about 15 minutes, stirring often.

6. Pour syrup over puklavah, letting it settle for some time before cutting and serving.

Susan Lind-Sinanian, Watertown, Massachusetts. Ingenuity and Tradition: The Common Wealth of Massachusetts — Crafts, 1988

Chruscik (Polish Fried Pastry)

½ teaspoon salt
5 egg yolks
3 tablespoons sugar
1 tablespoon brandy
(or cognac)
5 tablespoons sour
cream
2½ cups flour
oil, for frying
powdered sugar

1. Mix salt with eggs. Beat until thick and lemon colored.

2. Add sugar and brandy, and continue to beat. Alternately add sour cream and flour, mixing well after each addition.

3. Knead on a floured surface until dough blisters. Divide dough in half, and roll each piece very thin. Cut dough into strips about 4 inches long. Slit each piece in the center and pull one end through the slit.

4. Fry chruscik in hot oil, turning them to brown lightly on both sides. Drain on absorbent paper, and sprinkle with powdered sugar.

Stefanie and Julianna Gelowtsky Falzone, Cambridge, Massachusetts. Ingenuity and Tradition: The Common Wealth of Massachusetts — Urban Ethnic Gardens, 1988

"There's a pecking order to preparing chruscik in a large family, and making it is a rite of passage for young women. The more mature young women are allowed to prepare the dough, the younger to pull the dough through the slits, the youngest to sprinkle the chruscik with powdered sugar. A girl comes of age in the kitchen when she's allowed to fry the dough in hot fat until it is done on both sides. At the Smithsonian Folklife Festival, Julianna came of age on stage — the next generation of chruscik chefs — to the applause of all the observers."

Ricotta Cookies

½ pound butter,
   room temperature
½ cup ricotta cheese
2 teaspoons vanilla
   extract
2 cups sugar
2 eggs
4 cups flour, sifted
1 teaspoon baking
   soda
1 teaspoon salt

1. Preheat oven to 350°F.

2. Blend butter with ricotta until creamy. Add vanilla, and stir thoroughly. Gradually add sugar, beating until well blended. Add eggs; mix well.

3. Combine flour, baking soda, and salt. Gradually add dry ingredients to butter mixture and blend well.

4. Drop batter from a teaspoon onto a greased baking sheet. Bake for 10 minutes. Using a spatula, transfer to a serving platter. The cookies may be stored for several weeks in a container.

Joanne Saltamartini, North Adams, Massachusetts. Ingenuity and Tradition: The Common Wealth of Massachusetts, 1988

Lemon Raisin Pie

1½ cups raisins
2 cups cold water
1 egg
¾ cup sugar
2 tablespoons flour
¼ teaspoon salt
2 tablespoons butter
1 lemon, juice and
   grated rind
1 baked pie crust

1. Preheat oven to 350°F.

2. Cook raisins in water for 10 minutes.

3. Beat together egg and dry ingredients. Add to raisins and cook until thick. Remove from stove. Add butter, lemon juice, and rind. Let mixture cool.

4. Pour into crust. Bake for about 45 minutes or until set.

Marjorie Macomber, Acushnet, Massachusetts. Ingenuity and Tradition: The Common Wealth of Massachusetts — Clambake, 1988

Squash Pie

2 cups acorn or but-
  ternut squash (or
  16-ounce can
  squash)
3 eggs
¾ cup sugar

1 tablespoon
  cornstarch
½ teaspoon
  cinnamon
½ teaspoon nutmeg
½ teaspoon ginger
½ teaspoon salt

2 tablespoons
  molasses
1½ cups milk, canned
  or whole
1½ tablespoons
  butter, melted
1 baked pie crust

1. Preheat oven to 350°F.

2. Cook, peel, and mash squash. Combine with other ingredients, except butter, and beat until smooth.

3. Add butter at the last moment.

4. Pour into crust. Bake for about 45 minutes.

Marjorie Macomber

Cranberry Raisin Pie

1 cup raisins
3 cups cranberries
1 cup sugar
2 tablespoons
  cornstarch
¼ teaspoon salt
¾ cup water
1¼ teaspoons vanilla
  extract
double 9-inch pie
  crust

1. Preheat oven to 425°F.

2. Grind or chop raisins and cranberries. Combine with sugar, cornstarch, salt, and water in a saucepan. Cook on low heat for 8 to 10 minutes. Add vanilla and cool.

3. Make pie crust. Pour in filling, cover with top crust or lattice. Bake for 30 minutes or until brown.

Dorothy Angley, Carver, Massachusetts. Ingenuity and Tradition: The Common Wealth of Massachusetts — Agriculture Fair Area, 1988

"Cranberry raisin pie is one that my husband's mother developed. It is a family favorite at harvest time and throughout the holidays. But remember: cranberries that are left whole will puff up and burst, leaving a hollow that is also without sweetening."

Spice and Rum Cake

1 pound margarine
2 cups sugar
1 cup eggs, whole
1 tablespoon vanilla
    extract
¼ teaspoon nutmeg
4 cups flour, sifted
4 teaspoons baking
    powder
1 cup evaporated
    milk

Syrup:
3 cups water
2 cups sugar
6 cloves
1 stick cinnamon
½ cup white rum

1. Preheat oven to 325°F.

2. Cream sugar and margarine in mixer for about 10 minutes. Add eggs, and mix until well beaten. Add vanilla and nutmeg.

3. Mix flour and baking powder. Gradually add dry ingredients to egg mixture, alternately adding milk in small amounts. Blend until all ingredients are well mixed.

4. Pour batter into a greased 12 × 18 × 2-inch pan. Bake until a toothpick comes out clean. Cool on a platter.

5. Make syrup by mixing water, sugar, and spices. Simmer for 10 minutes. Remove from heat; add rum. Moisten cake with 2 cups syrup. Frost cake, if desired. Serves 25 to 30.

Bienvenida Figueroa, Lowell, Massachusetts. Ingenuity and Tradition: The Common Wealth of Massachusetts, 1988

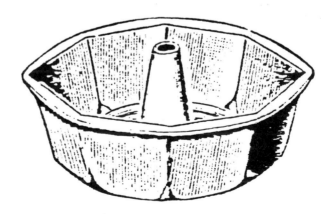

Currant Cake

½ pound butter (or margarine)
1 cup sugar
2 cups flour, sifted
¼ teaspoon cream of tartar
¼ teaspoon salt
¼ teaspoon mace
4 eggs
1 tablespoon brandy
½ teaspoon vanilla extract
½ package currants

1. Preheat oven to 350°F.

2. Beat butter and sugar until creamy.

3. Sift flour and dry ingredients.

4. Add eggs 1 at a time to butter mixture, alternating with flour mixture. Add brandy and vanilla, then mix in currants.

5. Pour into a greased and floured tube or bundt pan. Bake for 1 hour.

Ann Horkan, Watertown, Massachusetts. Ingenuity and Tradition: The Common Wealth of Massachusetts — Crafts, 1988

Arroz Doce (Rice Pudding)

1 cup rice
1 cup water
¼ teaspoon salt
1 cup milk
orange rind
sugar
2 egg yolks, beaten (optional)
cinnamon, for garnish

1. Wash rice and cook on low heat with water and salt, stirring constantly.

2. After water evaporates, slowly add milk, stirring constantly. When rice is almost cooked, add orange rind and sugar to taste, cooking until well done.

3. Remove rice from heat. Add egg yolks (if desired), stirring fast so that they do not curdle. Pour into a serving dish and sprinkle cinnamon on top.

Lurdes Rodrigues, Medford, Massachusetts. Ingenuity and Tradition: The Common Wealth of Massachusetts — Urban Ethnic Gardens, 1988

Potato Fudge

"Potatoes grow well in Maine, and for this reason potatoes are included in most of our recipes. The most popular recipe that I demonstrated in Washington, D.C. — to my great surprise — was potato fudge."

1 medium potato
1½ to 2 pounds
   powdered sugar
peanut butter

1. Peel and boil potato. Knead in sugar until moisture is absorbed.

2. Roll dough into a ball. Sprinkle a surface with sugar, and roll dough flat into a rectangle as thin as a pie crust. Spread with peanut butter. Roll up like a jellyroll.

3. Chill for 30 minutes to 1 hour. Cut into ¼-inch slices to form pinwheels.

Claudette P. Beaulieu, Madawaska, Maine. French Program, 1983

Apple Basduk (Armenian Fruit Leather)

⅔ to 1 cup cornstarch
1⅓ cups flour
2½ cups cold water
4 quarts apple juice
1 cup corn syrup
4 to 6 cups sugar

1. Mix cornstarch with flour in a pot. Add water gradually. Blend mixture with hands until well blended; pass it through a colander if lumpy. Set aside.

2. In a large pot, mix juice, corn syrup, and sugar to taste depending on the sweetness of the fruit juice. Bring to a boil.

3. Gradually add juice mixture to flour mixture, stirring constantly. Bring to a boil, stirring constantly. If the basduk is too thin, add more cornstarch; if it is too thick, mix in a little hot fruit juice, and bring to a boil again.

4. Pour hot basduk ⅛ inch thick onto clean cotton sheets, then spread evenly with a flat spoon or spatula. Cut into a size that is easy to handle. Dry on a flat surface. Hang partially dry basduk from a clothesline for a day or two until completely dry.

5. To peel off basduk, wet down the back of the sheet, soaking thoroughly with cold water. Let stand for a few minutes until the fruit has absorbed enough water to separate easily from the sheet. Peel it off, and sprinkle with cornstarch to avoid sticking. Store in tins in a cool place.

Rose Avadanian, Waltham, Massachusetts. The Grand Generation: Folklore and Aging, 1984

Grape Rojik (Fruit Leather with Walnuts)

1. Using medium to heavy cotton crochet thread, cut several 24-inch strings. Pass thread through walnut halves using a thin needle. Leave enough thread at top to hang on a stick to dry.

2. Blend flour, sugar to taste, cornstarch, and corn syrup. Add juice, and mix until smooth. Bring to a boil half of the juice and flour mixture, stirring constantly until thick. Remove from heat.

3. Working with a string of walnuts at a time, dip string into hot fruit leather several times. Hold over the pot, allowing the excess to drip back into the pan. Hang string on a rod and let dry overnight.

4. On the following day, boil remaining juice and flour mixture. Add excess leather from the day before, dissolving it through a strainer with a wooden spoon.

5. Repeat the dipping process. Hang the strings for several days in a cool, dry place. Pull out strings, then roll rojik in powdered sugar. Store in a covered jar or tin.

Rose Avadanian

3 cups flour
3 cups sugar
1 cup cornstarch
¾ cup corn syrup
3 quarts sweetened
  grape juice
walnut halves
powdered sugar

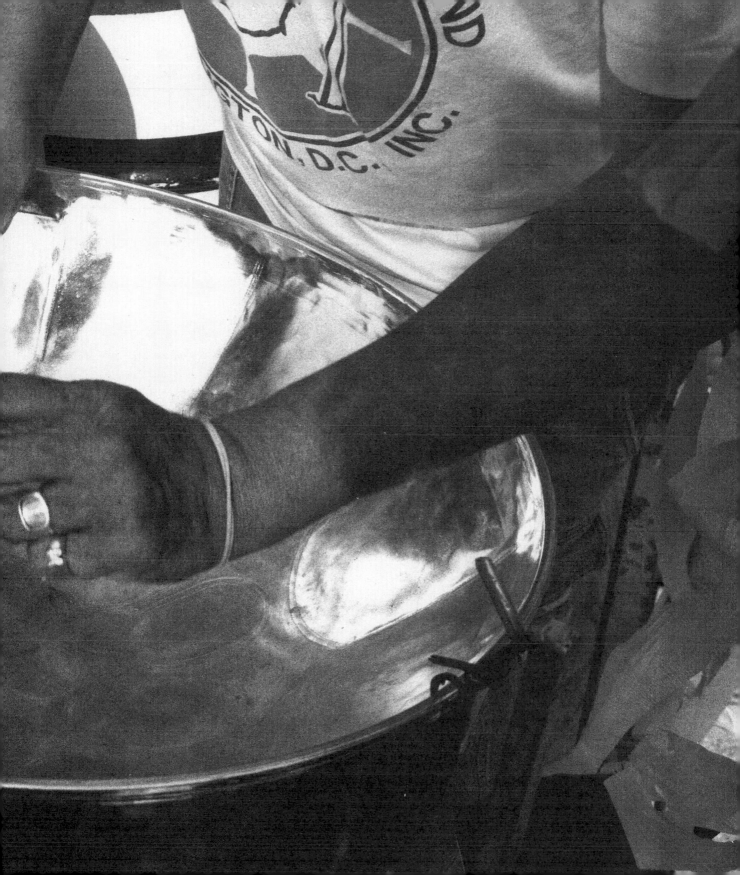

Mid-Atlantic

❧ · ❧ · ❧ · ❧

Charles Camp

Mid-Atlantic Meltdown

If America is a melting pot, then the meltdown begins in the Mid-Atlantic. Ties to old worlds and old ways historically have been shed in the region's port-of-entry cities, in a transition not unlike the molting of the Chesapeake Bay blue crab. The German-American culture characteristic of the Delaware and Ohio valleys is the product of the extended migration of a molted thing — a German culture that transformed itself in the Mid-Atlantic before heading south and west. Food traditions generally have displayed uncommon resistance to change, sheltered as they are within the family and home place. Customs related to food, as well as foods themselves, are under less immediate pressure to conform to practices in a new culture, unlike such public expressions of identity as language or music or the way in which people dress.

On closer inspection, however, two important aspects of this broad sketch appear different in this region, which includes New York, New Jersey, Pennsylvania, Maryland, Virginia, West Virginia, Delaware, and Washington, D.C. First, the transformations that have continued to take place with each wave of resettlement have been reciprocal: the places where these transformations have occurred have themselves been changed by the processes taking place in their midst. The cities of the Mid-Atlantic, in particular, have been loosened up by this experience — defined less by the traditions or intentions of their founders than by the way in which people have used them.

This helps explain a second detail, one that unravels the melting-pot theory. The Mid-Atlantic, more so than other American regions, displays ethnic and other cultural traditions in both variety and close proximity. This confounds the stereotypical view that folk culture flowers when undisturbed by alternatives or pressure to change. What I call close proximity — the cheek-by-jowl jostling of different cultures — astonishes people from other parts of the country, who find their notions of culture and space tested by the compression of communities in Mid-Atlantic cities. The idea that a traveler should leave one place and have a moment to catch his or her breath before entering another is foreign to the Mid-Atlantic; here, settlement patterns of the past century display a preference for proximity to kin and kindred over privacy, and culturally "neutral" areas or buffer zones between ethnic neighborhoods have long since been eroded by the wave action of continued immigration and community growth.

In fact, close quarters give rise to the very look and feel of urban life — the vibration that is created among dissimilar things close by each other. In a place where change, adaptation, and conversion are primary activities, the differences among people become more important than what they have in common. The high value of being different gives rise to racial and ethnic tension, gang violence, and seismic shifts in settlement and resettlement throughout the region. But it also gives rise to an inside-out expressiveness that lends shape and color to ethnic and cultural identities and several of their most prominent badges — music, costume, and food.

Inside Cooking, Outside Cooking

Home cooking is not the norm against which commercial food must be compared, but it is the source of notions about food and culture that are tested and changed outside the home. In this sense, the balance between food customs at home and in the public world is a more useful barometer of social change than an indicator of endangered traditions. For example, as two-wage-earner households become the norm, a wedding reception — rather than the supper table — may say more about ethnic traditions. A cake still made from scratch for such a special occasion has symbolic importance and shows that family, and community, traditions are still going strong.

The Mid-Atlantic, an oceanfront region with several large cities, should expect to be identified with seafood and ethnic restaurants. But people from other parts of the country who are perfectly sensible about the differences between homecooked and restaurant food that prevail in their home towns come to New York or Philadelphia and mistake accessibility for authenticity. In fact, the rules that govern consumer capitalism in Canton, Ohio, prevail in Hoboken, New Jersey. That foods confined to home kitchens in Bloomington, Indiana, are sold by pushcart vendors in lower Manhattan does not reveal a suspension of the social order. The best stuff is still under the counter and in the back room, as every small-town and big-city kid knows.

People who come to the Mid-Atlantic to eat can have it both ways. Some of the rarest and most regionally distinctive foodstuffs (crabs, oysters, cranberries, tomatoes) are grounded in this place, as is the cookery of conversion itself — foods prepared by people who are recently arrived and reluctant to change. And in an urban setting, competing suppliers of these foods — stores, stands, and restaurants — reinforce the importance of regional food-

stuffs by focusing their commercial struggle on them — the freshest fish, the hottest crabs, the biggest oysters, the thickest steaks.

But the Mid-Atlantic is neither exclusively nor definitively urban, and the competitive rules that apply to the region's big cities apply to Kansas City, New Orleans, and Los Angeles. Always, it is a region's particular foods or foodstuffs (the raw materials from which foods are prepared) that are the emblems of its identity, but their sustaining presence derives not from the foods themselves but the family and social events that revolve around them. You can export crab meat but not a crab feast.

They sell clams at the Eastside Market in Cleveland, but they don't have real New Jersey–style clambakes on the shores of Lake Erie. Does anyone really believe that the difference between Manhattan-style and New England–style clam chowder has anything to do with supplies of locally produced foodstuffs? That it isn't possible to buy tomatoes in Boston or milk in Manhattan?

A brief look at just one of the region's most popular food events may illustrate this point. Church suppers are among the most reliable indicators of appropriate and popular foods for sale in the Mid-Atlantic and elsewhere. But the tenure of many Maryland and Pennsylvania congregations and the social importance of these events have galvanized their menus with a degree of predictability formerly reserved for their liturgies. The fall social calendar in southern Maryland, for example, accords equal opportunity for churches to attract local people and Washingtonians to ham and oyster suppers. The dates for these events, based on the "second Saturday in October" counting method, are set in tablets of stone; one minister in Charles County, Maryland, told me that there were no prospects for evangelism in his community because there were no fall weekends that had not been spoken for.

The menus for these events are similarly fixed, but they are not always tied in an obvious way to traditional local foods. Spaghetti dinners sponsored by churches in rural Delaware and New Jersey do not feature quahog sauce. There is nothing — yet everything — about them that is particular to the place in which they occur each year. Nothing, because, after all, spaghetti is spaghetti. Everything, because the task of making the sauce is assigned according to ancient lineage; because church-supper spaghetti, cooked in huge quantities and served with sauce and noodles mixed, does taste different from homecooked; and because the social chemistry of the event — who comes, who does what, what happens after plates are cleared — is definitive of the particular community that produces it.

On the other hand, game suppers and clandestine terrapin feasts really do connect place and culture. However, they are not representative of general tastes in the Mid-Atlantic, where hunted game is usually eaten at home and

Fixed Events, Fixed Menus

Opposite: A child participates in one of the festival's craft activities. (Jim Pickerell)

terrapin has been elevated by its scarcity nearly beyond the ranks of the edible. Lingering bacterial diseases and shrinking supplies similarly threaten the oyster, which has enjoyed a region-specific popularity as great as any food for the past century. The varieties of oysters hauled each year from Mid-Atlantic waters fuel intraregional rivalries among devotees of bluepoints, Chincoteagues, and more than a dozen other kinds. So much is the oyster the product of its surroundings and so variable is the mixture of salt and fresh water in the Chesapeake Bay that educated palates can distinguish among oysters taken from beds a few miles apart.

Marketing Food, Transporting Culture

One of the most characteristic and enduring aspects of Mid-Atlantic food customs is the multifaceted system that delivers foodstuffs to the region's consumers. In an area whose history is shaped by patterns of transportation and commerce, food marketing is culturally complex and aesthetically evolved. The complexity derives from constant growth at both ends of the market world — the proliferation of ever-more inclusive supermarkets and the steady expansion of informal market systems.

The latter holds considerable interest for folklorists and other students of folk culture because the channels for distributing recently hunted geese in Delaware or home-cured hams in Maryland are the same ones used for the passage of other forms of culture. The social network that is the marketplace for this "underground" economy recapitulates and reinforces existing ties within communities throughout the region. The goose that makes its way from friend to cousin to coworker each year is the means for an annual system check of the region's food traditions and social ties. More formal markets flourish at all levels, including roadside produce stands and urban stall marketplaces, where vending cries or "hollers" and intricately stacked displays of fruit give evidence of culture amid commerce.

Recent immigrations to Mid-Atlantic cities, particularly from Southeast Asia and Central and South America, have provided new challenges and opportunities in a field already recognized as amenable to creative entrepreneurs. Specialty food stores established a generation ago to meet the needs of Philadelphia's Chinese communities now stock groceries favored by Vietnamese and Cambodian consumers. Where the needs of the recently immigrated are not quickly filled by existing businesses, new ones emerge, often built on family and community ties to the Old World. The Adams-Morgan neighborhood of Washington, D.C., has emerged as a center for Salvadoran émigrés in part because of the neighborhood's concentration of Hispanic businesses, but also because old patterns of daily and weekly food shopping are accommodated in a New World marketplace that provides comforting elements of tradition — the foods being sold and the way in which they are sold, from displays to language.

ᘒ • ᘒ • ᘒ • ᘒ

The goose that makes its way from friend to cousin to coworker each year is the means for an annual system check of the region's food traditions and social ties.

ᘒ • ᘒ • ᘒ • ᘒ

Cities such as Philadelphia, Trenton, and Baltimore were built around marketplaces and have maintained viable stall markets with historical continuity as well as contemporary utility. Many market stalls at Philadelphia's Reading Terminal Market and Baltimore's Lexington Market have remained family businesses for more than a century, and the practice of buying an Easter ham or the spring's first watercress at a favored stall maintains ties between vendors and customers that span generations. At the same time, markets provide new immigrants and the entrepreneurs who serve them with a place to stand and be seen within the community.

Baltimore's arabbers (produce vendors who hawk their wares from horse-drawn carts) are practitioners of a trade that was once more common throughout the region and more varied in the goods and services provided. The arabbers are more than itinerant hucksters; they serve as the fingertips of an elaborate urban market system that reaches deep into city neighborhoods as well as a counterbalance to the prevalent practice of separating residential and commercial life.

After World War II, the wagon trade became an almost exclusively black occupation because it offered two elements largely lacking for African Americans — economic opportunity and independence. In the first half of the century, the Mid-Atlantic drew successive waves of black migration from the rural southern coast and Piedmont in search of similar opportunities. These migrations have created — and as migrations persist, continue to create — a black culture in the Mid-Atlantic that is both self-sustaining and enormously influential.

There is no better measure of the strength and influence of this culture than its food customs, which have redefined the meaning of the South in the North. General attitudes about the South, and particularly the rural South, have been continually undercut by black contributions to Mid-Atlantic food traditions, which have moved from the Carolinas and Virginia and found acceptance first in the region's existing black communities, then in the Mid-Atlantic as a whole.

Much of the "home cooking" served in the region's diners and hole-in-the-wall eateries was called "soul food" or "country" twenty years ago. Stewed vegetables, greens with smoked pork, dirty rice — these staples of Mid-Atlantic cookery are recognized by blacks more recently resettled from the South as a taste of home, but within the region their acceptance has been so prompt and widespread that they are seldom acknowledged as black, southern, or rural.

In Washington, D.C., where white migrations from the rural South have matched black resettlement in numbers and impact, foods are an especially important note of familiarity, bridging racial distinctions. Throughout the

Markets and Carts

The South Moves North

Opposite: Dorothy Marcucci of Philadelphia makes homemade Italian pasta. (Courtesy Dorothy Marcucci)

region, recent immigrations of West Indian people have challenged notions of black cookery and reinvigorated its African-Caribbean synthesis.

Customs Well Seasoned

A final, and less frequently noted, way in which the Mid-Atlantic proclaims itself as a cultural region is in its celebration of local foods and the people who gather them. This is particularly true for the fishermen who work the region's waterways, whose occupational culture is oddly disassociated in the public mind from the fish, clams, oysters, and crabs they bring to market. The seasonal runs of shad, bluefish, and crabs are noted by many people within the region as markers of a new natural year.

Similarly, people who can buy almost anything in a supermarket almost any time of the year take note of the changing of the seasons with purchases of strawberries from stands set up on street corners or sweet corn sold from the trunk of a parked car. It seems too obvious to mention, but the rotation of four distinct seasons is a fact of life in the Mid-Atlantic and one that is repeatedly observed in the region's food customs.

The Mid-Atlantic is a region that tests our notion of common culture and its gravitation toward a recognizable center. Clearly, foods have always been the stuff of stereotyped regionalism — the popular characterizations that fuel tourist economies yet overlook local community traditions. But in the Mid-Atlantic, where change — the unsatisfied appetite for it and historical accommodation of it — is an essential cultural feature, how people produce, prepare, share, and consume food draws otherwise unobserved connections within a community that is both local and international.

꩜ • ꩜ • ꩜ • ꩜

Recipes

Pitt's Pork Barbecue

Carson's Barbecue Sauce

Cevapcici (Serbian Grilled Sausage)

Rouladen (Rolled Steaks)

Sukiyaki

Pupusas de Chicharrón (Salvadoran Pies)

Pimientos Rellenos Vizkainos
(Meat-stuffed Peppers)

Mafe (Ground Nut Stew)

Pelau (Stew)

Fried Chicken

Curried Chicken

Poulet Yassa
(Senegalese Chicken Casserole)

Pulpo Mugardesa
(Octopus)

Creole Red Snapper

Oyster Puffs

Crab Cakes

Clam Fritters

Calamari Salad

Linguine with Calamari

Sagne Chine di mia Nonna Annamaria
Venezia (Lasagne)

Ragù di mia Cognata (Tomato Sauce)

Pasta Fatta in Casa

Boora Shenkel (Filled Noodles)

Patatas Salsa Verde al Caseria
(Potatoes Country Style)

Nalysnyky (Ukrainian Blintzes)

Spanish Omelet

Obento (Japanese Boxed Lunch)

Cha-Gio (Vietnamese Spring Rolls)

Collard Greens

Hoppin' John

German Potato Salad

Slovenian Potato Salad

Chutney

Zucchini Pickles

Curtido (Pickled Coleslaw)

Mochi (Rice Cakes)

Corn Bubble Ring

Buttermilk Corn Bread

Zucchini Nut Bread

Serbian Walnut Roll

Potica (Yeast Nut Roll)

Rice Pudding

Corn Pudding

Steamed Sweet Rice and Banana

Egg Cheese

Blackberry Delight

Bourma (Strudel)

Gibanica (Cheese Pastries)

Flancati (Bowknots)

Taralles (Iced Cookies)

Shoo Fly Wet Bottom

Schwenkfelder Saffron Cake

Hardtack Candy

Fresco de Ensalada (Fruit Drink)

Apple Cider

Sow (Milk Drink)

"My family comes from Parmele, North Carolina, where I grew up on a farm. Hogs, chickens, peanuts, corn, cotton, tobacco, collard greens, and squash were raised. I now live in Washington, where my cousins and uncle and I grow many vegetables, especially collard greens. We all cook and freeze the collard greens a little different. On holidays, we eat barbecued pork, greens, and potato salad."

Pitt's Pork Barbecue

3 slabs (about 20 pounds) meaty pork ribs
1 small bottle hickory seasoning

Sauce:
½ cup oil
2 hot cherry peppers, chopped

1 medium onion, chopped
2 stalks celery, chopped
1 teaspoon dry mustard
1 teaspoon chili powder
2 teaspoons oregano
1 no. 10 can ketchup

2 no. 5 cans tomato juice
1 12-ounce bottle dark beer
3 lemons
2 tablespoons Worcestershire sauce
½ cup wine vinegar
1 cup brown sugar

1. In a large canning pot, cover ribs with water. Parboil with hickory seasoning, simmering for about 30 minutes. Cool.

2. To make sauce, heat oil in a heavy-bottom pot. Add chopped vegetables and sauté for several minutes until onions are transparent. Add spices and remaining ingredients. Simmer for about 30 minutes.

3. Put ribs on a grill over smoldering charcoal briquets, then smother in barbecue sauce. Grill 2 to 3 minutes on each side, basting continually and turning for about 10 minutes until done. Serves 20.

John Henry Pitt, Washington, D.C. Migration to Metropolitan Washington: Making a New Place Home, 1988

Carson's Barbecue Sauce

1 teaspoon salt
1 teaspoon chili powder
1 teaspoon celery seed (or 3 stalks celery)
¼ cup brown sugar
¼ cup vinegar

¼ cup Worcestershire sauce
1 cup ketchup
1 small can tomato paste
1 small can tomato sauce

2 cups water
½ teaspoon hot sauce
2 onions, chopped
1 small bottle hickory seasoning (optional)

1. Combine all ingredients, except celery (if used) and onions, and simmer for 1 hour.

2. To thicken sauce, put celery stalks and onions in a blender, then pour into sauce.

3. For a hotter sauce add more hot sauce; for a smoky flavor add hickory seasoning.

William and Patricia Carson, Philadelphia, Pennsylvania. Black Urban Expressive Culture from Philadelphia, 1984

"This recipe is from William Carson's mom. It has been in the family for years. The thickening step was added later by her son."

Cevapcici (Serbian Grilled Sausage)

1½ pounds ground
  beef
½ pound ground
  pork
2 teaspoons salt
½ teaspoon coriander
1 teaspoon pepper
½ teaspoon baking
  soda
½ cup water

1. Mix ingredients well. Shape into small sausages about 1 inch in diameter and 3 inches long.

2. Grill over charcoal for 6 to 8 minutes or until cooked through. Serve with minced onions, fresh sweet or hot peppers, fresh tomatoes, and a roll.

Olga Gurick, McLean, Virginia. South Slavic Cooking, 1976

Rouladen (Rolled Steaks)

"My mother was born in the Schwaben region of Germany and taught me these recipes. Many Sunday dinners consisted of rouladen and spätzle (homemade noodles). My mom's potato salad has always been a favorite in the summer at picnics. I hope to teach the German traditions and culture to my two daughters so that they will pass them on to their children."

6 thin beef steaks from top round or shoulder
6 slices bacon, diced
2 medium onions, chopped
1 green pepper, chopped

1 red bell pepper, chopped (optional)
½ cup parsley, chopped
½ pound fresh mushrooms, thinly sliced (optional)
salt
pepper

margarine, for frying
1 cup beef stock (or water)

Gravy:
4 tablespoons flour
pan juices
½ cup sour cream

1. Pound steaks with a mallet until they are ⅛ inch thick.

2. Mix bacon and vegetables. Divide mixture into 6 portions, then spoon each onto the ends of the steaks. Roll up each steak and secure with toothpicks or skewers.

3. Melt margarine in a frying pan. Sauté steaks until brown. Transfer to a 4-quart casserole and add about 1 cup beef stock or water. Cover tightly and simmer for about 60 minutes. Remove steak rolls and discard toothpicks or skewers.

4. To make gravy, add flour to juices in casserole, along with more stock or water if necessary. Stir well until smooth. Add sour cream and heat gently, being careful not to boil. Serves 6.

Betty Bunger, Piscataway, New Jersey. New Jersey Program, 1983

Sukiyaki

1½ pounds tender boneless beef, thinly sliced
2 onions, sliced
2 bunches green onions, sliced into 2-inch lengths

½ pound mushrooms
1 pound fresh spinach
1 cup bamboo shoots, sliced
1 8-ounce can shirataki (yam noodles)

1 pound square tofu, cut into 1-inch squares
2 or 3 pieces beef suet
beaten eggs (optional)

Sauce:
½ cup soy sauce
3 tablespoons sugar
¼ cup mirin (or dry sherry)
¾ cup beef broth

1. Cut meat into 1 × 2-inch squares. Arrange meat, vegetables, and tofu neatly on a large platter.

2. Set a cooking pot such as an electric frying pan in the middle of the dining table. Place platter of raw ingredients in front of pan.

3. Make cooking sauce by combining all ingredients, stirring until sugar melts. Pour into a pitcher.

4. Heat frying pan and rub well with suet. Remove suet. Place a third of the meat in pan and cook until it loses its pinkness. Push meat into a corner of pan. Add a third of the vegetables, keeping individual items in their own places. Pour a third of cooking sauce into pan. Cook for 3 to 5 minutes, turning vegetables over as necessary.

5. Guests take turns cooking their own portions. After cooking, ingredients may be dipped in a beaten egg in individual bowls before being mixed with cooked rice.

6. Cook successive servings from the remaining ingredients. Serves 6.

Iddy Asada and Harumi Taniguchi, Bridgeton, New Jersey. New Jersey Program, 1983

"Traditionally, sukiyaki is cooked at the table, with all guests enjoying the meal to their preferred doneness. And you may use whichever vegetables you wish, not necessarily the ones given in the recipe."

Pupusas de Chicharrón (Salvadoran Pies)

1 pork shoulder or
   roast, cut into 1½-
   inch pieces
salt
3 medium onions
3 green peppers
6 tomatoes
masa harina

1. Partially cover meat in a frying pan with water, add salt, and simmer until all fat is rendered. Continue frying in fat until meat turns golden brown, about 1 hour. Remove meat from pan and grind.

2. Grind vegetables, salt, and pan fat and add to ground meat.

3. To prepare pupusas, moisten masa harina with water until it has the consistency of pliable dough. Pat out into a large tortilla 15 inches in diameter. Place filling in center and fold over dough.

4. Gently shape and cook slowly on an ungreased griddle until done. Serve with curtido (see recipe, page 110).

Rita Torres Gonzalez, Washington, D.C. Cultural Conservation, 1985

Pimientos Rellenos Vizkainos (Meat-stuffed Peppers)

8 green peppers
2½ cups olive oil
8 cloves garlic,
    chopped
2 cups onions,
    chopped
chopped parsley
3 pounds ground beef
1 chicken bouillon
    cube

1 cup red wine
1 can plain bread
    crumbs
6 eggs
2 cups flour

Sauce:
1 cup olive oil
2 cups onions,
    chopped
4 cloves garlic,
    chopped
4 carrots, chopped
1 tablespoon flour
1 16-ounce can
    tomato sauce

½ cup white wine
½ cup water

1. Keeping peppers whole, remove stem and seeds and clean. In a large frying pan on high heat, fry peppers in olive oil until the skin is almost brown. Remove peppers, place on a large plate, and cover immediately with a cloth towel. Remove skins from peppers.

2. In a separate frying pan, sauté garlic, onions, and parsley in a moderate amount of olive oil until onions are translucent. Add ground beef and brown thoroughly. Add chicken bouillon and wine, then bread crumbs. Mixture should be firm but moist. Stuff peppers with meat mixture.

3. Beat eggs in a shallow mixing bowl. Place flour in a flat dish. Roll the stuffed peppers in flour, then dip in eggs. Fry peppers in cooking oil, top side down.

4. To make sauce, sauté onions, garlic, and carrots in olive oil until tender. Add flour to thicken. Add tomato sauce, wine, and water; stir and simmer for ½ hour.

5. Place peppers in a casserole. Strain sauce over peppers and cook on top of the stove for 15 minutes on medium heat. Serves 8.

Maria Luisa Vidasolo de Lamikiz, Brooklyn, New York. Old Ways in the New World: Basque, 1976

"My mother and grandmother taught me these recipes when I was a child living in Acorda, which is in Baskaia, the Basque region of Spain. I plan to pass these recipes on to my American-born children and grandchildren to keep our Basque heritage alive."

Mafe (Ground Nut Stew)

2 chickens, cut up (or
5 pounds lamb)
¾ cup peanut oil
3 large onions,
chopped
2 to 3 pounds toma-
toes, chopped
4 8-ounce cans
tomato paste,
thinned with water
4 to 5 cups hot water

1 tablespoon salt
8 ounces natural
peanut butter
6 carrots, whole
1 pound okra, whole
frozen cassava
(optional)
2 small cabbages, cut
into eighths
3 to 4 sweet potatoes,
cut into chunks

small red chile
peppers
dried red pepper
flakes
½ teaspoon cayenne
pepper

1. Brown chicken in oil. Reserve ½ cup onions, then add remaining onions and stir until brown. Stir in tomatoes and thinned tomato paste, hot water, and salt.

2. When mixture comes to a boil, gradually add peanut butter.

3. Simmer for 30 minutes, then add vegetables. Cook until vegetables and chicken are tender.

4. Before serving, crush peppers and spices and add with reserved onions. Serve with rice. Serves 10 to 12.

Anta Diop, New York, New York. Senegal Program, 1990

Pelau (Stew)

"In Trinidad and Tobago, pelau is made from the leftovers of our Sunday meal. It consists of stewing beef, chicken, pigeon peas, and bits of carrot. Traditionally, it is served on a Monday, making it much like the American 'pot luck' Monday."

1 pound chicken
   parts
½ pound salt pork
1 pound stewing beef,
   cut into chunks
2 cloves garlic,
   chopped
1 medium onion,
   chopped
1 tablespoon fresh
   chives

3 tablespoons oil
1 tablespoon butter
2 tablespoons sugar
4 cups fresh coconut
   milk
2 cups long-grain
   white rice
1 pound pigeon peas,
   dried (or canned
   green pigeon peas)
2 carrots, chopped

1 hot green pepper,
   whole
½ teaspoon black
   pepper

1. Season chicken and meat with garlic, onions, and chives.

2. Heat oil and butter on medium heat in a heavy-bottom pot or deep, cast-iron frying pan. Brown the sugar and add meat, cooking for about 20 minutes or until tender.

3. Add chicken parts and continue cooking for another 20 minutes, stirring occasionally.

4. Mix in coconut milk, rice, pigeon peas, carrots, and pepper. Simmer for 30 or 40 minutes until no water remains.

Cecilia Ojoe, Bethesda, Maryland. Migration to Metropolitan Washington: Making a New Place Home, 1988

Fried Chicken

1 2½- to 3-pound
   frying chicken
¼ cup lemon juice
onion powder
garlic powder
salt
pepper

paprika
cayenne pepper
   (optional)
flour
shortening (or oil),
   for frying

1. Rinse chicken and cut into quarters or smaller parts. Place in a large bowl filled with lemon juice and water to cover and soak for 1 hour.

2. Remove chicken and season with spices. Place in a plastic bag or covered container and season overnight in the refrigerator. If in a hurry, let chicken season for at least 2 hours; seasoned chicken also may be frozen until ready to cook.

3. To fry, mix flour with a little salt and place in a plastic or paper bag. Put chicken in bag and shake well, coating each piece thoroughly. Fry in ½ to 1 inch shortening or oil (oil must be hot). Cook, covered, for 30 to 40 minutes, turning the pieces so that both sides are golden brown. For crispier chicken, remove lid after the first side is browned.

William and Patricia Carson, Philadelphia, Pennsylvania. Black Urban Expressive Culture from Philadelphia, 1984

Curried Chicken

3 3- to 4-pound chickens
juice of 1 lemon (or lime)
1 medium onion, thinly sliced
3 green onions, chopped
1 medium tomato, thinly sliced
3 cloves garlic, chopped
salt
pepper
cayenne pepper
½ cup oil
3 tablespoons curry powder
½ cup water

1. Cut chickens into serving-size pieces and remove skin and fat.

2. In a large mixing bowl, mix lemon or lime juice with enough cool tap water to cover chicken. Add chicken and let stand for a few minutes. Drain well.

3. Reserve half of the sliced onion. Mix the other half with green onions, tomato, garlic, salt, and peppers. Use mixture to season chicken and marinate for several minutes.

4. Heat oil in a large, heavy-bottom pot on medium heat. Add reserved onion and sauté for a few minutes. Mix curry powder with water and add to pot. Cover and cook until water is almost evaporated. Add marinated chicken all at once and stir to coat each piece well. Cover pot tightly and simmer on low heat for about 1 hour. Serve with dal purée (lentils), roti, and rice. Serves 10 to 12.

Irab Juman, Alexandria, Virginia. Migration to Metropolitan Washington: Making a New Place Home, 1988

Poulet Yassa (Senegalese Chicken Casserole)

Marinade:
juice of 12 lemons
Dijon mustard
cayenne pepper (or 2 to 3 hot red peppers, whole)
salt
pepper
2 beef bouillon cubes dissolved in ½ cup water

12 to 15 (about 5 pounds) chicken breasts, thighs, and legs
8 to 10 onions, chopped
¾ cup lemon juice
¾ cup oil
1 jar Dijon mustard
2 or 3 bay leaves
garlic powder

salt
pepper
red pepper
6 beef bouillon cubes
1 cup hot water
2 6-ounce jars pitted green olives

1. Mix all marinade ingredients and marinate chicken for 1 to 2 days.

2. Remove chicken from marinade.

3. Prebake chicken at 325°F for 30 minutes.

4. Heat oil in a large, heavy pot. Sauté onions until soft. Add chicken, lemon juice, mustard, spices, and bouillon cubes dissolved in water. Cook on medium heat for about 1 hour.

5. Add olives when chicken is almost done. Serve over rice. Serves 10 to 12.

Anta Diop, New York, New York. Senegal Program, 1990

Pulpo Mugardesa (Octopus)

5 pounds fresh or
  frozen octopus
¼ cup salt
5 to 7 bay leaves

Sauce:
1 cup olive oil
1 large red bell
  pepper, sliced
1 large onion, diced
1 tablespoon paprika

¼ teaspoon hot red
  pepper powder
  (optional)
½ cup water
1 teaspoon salt

1. Wash octopus well and remove the eyes and mouth.

2. To a large pot filled with water, add salt and bay leaves and bring to a boil. When water is boiling, dip octopus in and out 3 times so the skin will not peel off. Cook octopus for 45 to 60 minutes or until it feels soft when poked with a fork. Remove to a plate and cool. Slice into ½-inch pieces.

3. To prepare the sauce, sauté pepper in oil until tender. Add onion and cook until soft. Lower heat and let oil cool. Add paprika and water at the same time to keep paprika from burning. This will bring oil to a boil. Add salt and hot pepper powder to taste.

4. Add octopus to sauce and simmer for about 5 to 10 minutes. Served either hot or cold, with white rice or diced boiled potatoes. It is even better the next day.

Julia Lara, Kearny, New Jersey. New Jersey Program, 1983

"I came to the United States from Spain in 1966 with my parents and two sisters. We came from a beautiful town called Betanzos, province of La Coruna, in the northwest of Spain, the region called Galicia. I was thirteen years old and the youngest of the family. It was a big change, but we adjusted well.

This octopus recipe was passed on to me by my in-laws. They come from a fishing village called Mugardo, El Ferrol, and people there use all kinds of seafood. Octopus is one dish always cooked for special occasions. The fishermen of this town are called 'pulpeiros' because they know all the tricks of catching pulpo, or octopus, by hand."

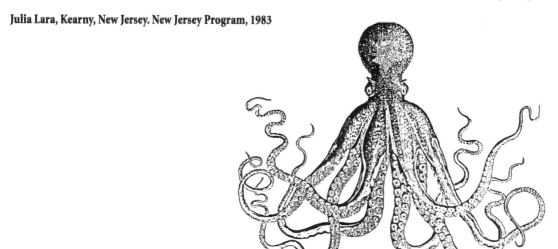

Creole Red Snapper

"In our Trinidad and Tobago culture, there's nothing like coming home to the aroma of red snapper, whether it's being broiled, fried, curried, or made into fish broth. For the male ego, fish broth is very essential — it makes men (and women) strong and healthy."

1 whole red snapper,
   about 4 pounds (or
   2 pounds fillets)
3 limes
salt
pepper
¼ cup oil
3 large onions, diced
2 stalks celery,
   chopped
4 cloves garlic,
   minced
1 green pepper,
   chopped
2 tomatoes, diced
1 cup water (or
   tomato juice)
1 teaspoon curry
   powder

1. Clean fish, leaving on the head if whole. Rub fish inside and outside with juice of 1 lime; sprinkle with salt and pepper and set aside.

2. In a heavy pan, heat oil and sauté onions, celery, garlic, and green pepper. Cook for 3 or 4 minutes on medium heat until onions are transparent. Add tomatoes, water, and curry powder.

3. Bring sauce to a boil and lower the heat to simmer. After 5 minutes, add fish. Cover and simmer for another 15 or 20 minutes until the fish flakes easily when tested with a fork.

4. Just before serving, stir in juice of remaining limes. Serve with rice.

Cecilia Ojoe, Bethesda, Maryland. Migration to Metropolitan Washington: Making a New Place Home, 1988

Oyster Puffs

"I've been serving people meals for thirty years in my one-room place. We're from a long line of fishermen on Smith Island, and I learned to cook by helping my grandmother prepare food for her family of thirteen. I guess I was the privileged one."

1 pint oysters,
   drained
1 teaspoon salt
dash of pepper
½ cup evaporated
   milk
¾ cup quick biscuit
   mix
1 teaspoon baking
   powder
oil, for frying

1. Mix all ingredients.

2. Drop small portions into hot oil with fork.

3. Fry until golden brown.

Frances Kitching, Smith Island, Maryland. Chesapeake Bay Program, 1978

Crab Cakes

1 pound crab meat,
    picked clean
1 teaspoon parsley
    flakes
3 tablespoons quick
    biscuit mix
1 egg
7 shakes Worcester-
    shire sauce
1½ tablespoons
    mustard
2 tablespoons
    mayonnaise
oil, for frying

1. Mix ingredients with a spoon; do not use hands.

2. Form cakes with an ice cream dipper.

3. Cook in 1 inch hot oil until golden brown.

Frances Kitching

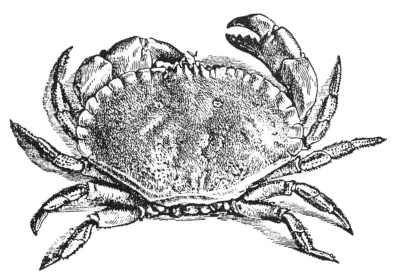

Clam Fritters

12 clams, blended
    with juice
¼ teaspoon pepper
1 egg, beaten
¼ cup milk
4 tablespoons quick
    biscuit mix
salt
oil, for frying

1. Mix all ingredients.

2. Fry fritters in hot oil in frying pan or on grill.

Frances Kitching

Calamari Salad

1 to 2 pounds squid
1 teaspoon salt
1 teaspoon pepper

2 teaspoons parsley, chopped
1 teaspoon oregano
1 to 2 tablespoons olive oil

1 tablespoon vinegar
black or green olives (optional)

1. Clean squid. Boil in 1 to 2 cups water until tender. Drain and cool.

2. Add remaining ingredients. Let stand 2 to 3 hours, or overnight for better flavor. Serves 2.

Rose Notoris, Ambler, Pennsylvania. Cultural Conservation, 1985

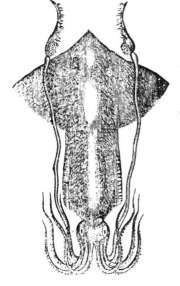

Linguine with Calamari

Sauce:
¼ cup light oil
3 pounds squid, cleaned and minced
1 large clove garlic, minced
2 cups tomatoes, coarsely chopped
1 pound tomato paste

¼ cup chopped flat-leaf Italian parsley
½ teaspoon oregano
1 bay leaf
¼ teaspoon crushed red pepper
salt
pepper

8 quarts water
2 teaspoons salt
3 tablespoons oil
2 pounds linguine, uncooked
¼ cup grated Locatelli or Romano cheese

1. Heat light oil in a large saucepan. Sauté minced squid and garlic for approximately 5 minutes. Add tomatoes, tomato paste, herbs, and spices. Bring to a boil, reduce heat, and simmer on very low heat for 1½ to 2 hours. Adjust seasonings.

2. Bring water to a boil in a large pot. Add 2 teaspoons salt and 3 tablespoons oil. Cook linguine until al dente.

3. To serve, place grated cheese on the bottom of a large bowl. Cover cheese with half of the sauce, then with the cooked linguine. Top with remaining sauce and toss gently. Serves 8.

Rose Notoris

Sagne Chine di mia Nonna Annamaria Venezia (Lasagne)

½ cup olive oil
1 small onion, diced
1 carrot, diced
1 celery stalk, diced
½ pound mush-
  rooms, chopped

1 recipe ragù di mia
  cognata
  (see below)
1 pound cooked
  lasagne, al dente

4 hard-boiled eggs,
  sliced
½ pound mozzarella,
  cubed
1 pound ricotta

½ cup grated
  Pecorino or
  Romano cheese
4 canned artichoke
  hearts, quartered

1. Preheat oven to 350°F. Grease a 12 × 8-inch baking dish.

2. Sauté onion, carrot, celery, and mushrooms in oil for 10 minutes.

3. Place a few spoonfuls of ragù in bottom of baking dish. Layer cooked lasagne with eggs, cheeses, artichokes, and vegetable mix. Use some sauce sparingly between layers. Top with more sauce and cheeses.

4. Bake at 350°F for 30 to 45 minutes. May be frozen. Serves 6 to 8.

Dorothy Marcucci, Philadelphia, Pennsylvania. Cultural Conservation, 1985

"This is my grand-mother's recipe. I received it later in life from my mother — who did not teach me to cook — but who gave me Calabrese recipes."

Ragù di mia Cognata (Tomato Sauce)

¾ pound pork, cut
  into 1-inch pieces
¾ pound beef, cut
  into 1-inch pieces
4 tablespoons olive
  oil
3 onions, chopped
2 cloves garlic,
  crushed
4 tablespoons flat-leaf
  parsley, chopped
1 6-ounce can tomato
  paste

1 32-ounce can
  tomatoes with basil
1 cup water
1 cup dry red wine
pinch of sugar
pinch of dried
  oregano
dash of salt
pepper

1. Brown meat in oil.

2. Add remaining in-gredients and simmer, covered, on low heat for 1 to 2 hours. Serves 6 to 8.

Dorothy Marcucci

"This was the first tomato sauce I learned from my husband's fam-ily, from Abruzzi (my mother's family was from Calabria.) It is customary for mothers-in-law to teach the new wives how to cook so that the son will adjust well to his new life. This makes for a happy marriage in which, as we say, 'The husband is the head of the family; the wife is the heart.' So, con-trary to society's under-standing of Italian Americans, we do have equal roles in the family."

Pasta Fatta in Casa

"My great grandmother used to make pasta noodles (dedrini) on a chitarra, a stringed implement resembling a guitar. My aunt inherited the chitarra, but my mother taught me how to make dedrini. It is a family favorite."

Rose Notoris

2 cups unbleached
  flour
2 to 3 eggs
2 tablespoons olive
  oil
½ teaspoon salt

1. Place flour in a bowl and make a well in the center. Add eggs, oil, and salt. Mix well.

2. Turn dough onto a floured surface and form into a ball. Knead dough for 15 to 20 minutes, until smooth. Let rest for 30 minutes or longer.

3. Divide dough in half and roll out each half until very thin. Roll up sheet of pasta and cut into desired thickness. Spread on floured surface and allow to dry for about 2 hours. The pasta may be frozen until used.

Dorothy Marcucci, Philadelphia, Pennsylvania. Cultural Conservation, 1985

Boora Shenkel (Filled Noodles)

2 cups flour
½ teaspoon baking
  powder
½ teaspoon salt
2 tablespoons
  shortening
1 egg
½ cup water

Filling:
4 potatoes, boiled
1 onion, minced
½ cup chopped celery
1 tablespoon minced
  parsley
2 eggs, beaten
1 slice bread,
  crumbled

2 tablespoons butter
½ teaspoon salt
dash of pepper

1. To make dough, combine dry ingredients, cut in shortening, and add egg and water, mixing to bind ingredients into a soft dough. Roll into 6 8-inch circles.

2. To make filling, mash potatoes. Add remaining ingredients, using potato water to moisten; do not make filling too thin.

3. Put filling on half of each dough circle, fold over the other side, and seal edges to look like half moons.

4. Drop noodles into boiling salted water or beef broth. Boil for 30 minutes, not too fast. Lift from broth.

5. Brown lightly in butter or margarine.

Sadie Kriebel, Hereford, Pennsylvania. Regional America: The Northeast, 1976

Patatas Salsa Verde al Caseria (Potatoes Country Style)

1. In a medium saucepan, approximately 4 inches deep, sauté onion and garlic in oil until garlic is golden brown. Add potatoes and parsley and cook for 15 minutes.

2. Add white wine, stirring continuously, and just enough water to cover. Place peas on top.

3. Gently break eggs on top of peas. Do not mix. Cover pan for 5 minutes. Remove cover and cook for an additional 5 minutes. Serves 8.

Maria Luisa Vidasolo de Lamikiz, Brooklyn, New York. Old Ways in the New World: Basque, 1976

1 cup olive oil
1 large onion, chopped
3 cloves garlic, chopped
2 pounds Idaho potatoes, thinly sliced
½ cup chopped parsley
1 cup white wine
1 package frozen peas
8 eggs
salt
pepper

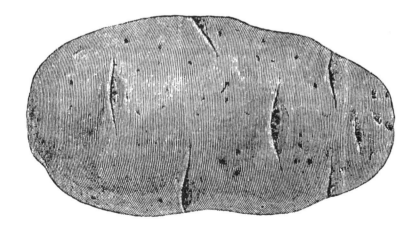

Nalysnyky (Ukrainian Blintzes)

"It was very turbulent in Washington, D.C., in 1970 when my grandmother made her Ukrainian blintzes. A marijuana smoke-in and a Bob Hope concert were held during the folklife festival. One day, the police tear-gassed the smoke-in, and we all got swept up in the chase down the Mall. Even the cows ran with us."

Beti Horvath

4 eggs
1 quart milk
2½ to 3 cups flour
butter

Cheese filling:
2 pounds dry farmer's
  (or cottage) cheese
2 eggs, beaten
sugar
2 tablespoons butter,
  melted
cinnamon
vanilla extract
raisins and lemon
  peel (optional)

1. Thoroughly beat eggs, then stir in milk. Slowly add flour while beating to make a very thin batter.

2. Grease a 9- to 10-inch nonstick frying pan with butter. Pour in just enough batter to cover pan surface. The thinner the pancake, the better the results.

3. When the top looks thoroughly cooked but not dry, flip pancake onto a clean towel or large bread board. Continue making pancakes, stacking them on towel. Cover to keep moist. Set aside while preparing filling.

4. To prepare filling, put cheese through a sieve until it is very fine. If using farmer's cheese, stir vigorously until the mixture is smooth. Add thoroughly beaten eggs, sugar, butter, cinnamon, and, if desired, raisins and lemon peel. Mix well.

5. Spoon mixture on the browned side of pancake, to within 2 inches of the edge. Gently fold closest edge over the mixture, then tuck in each side and roll up. Do not overfill pancakes, or they will burn when fried again.

6. Fry blintzes in a buttered frying pan on moderate heat until cheese is hot and each side is a delicate brown. Serve with sour cream, jam, or jelly. Serves 5.

Note: Leftover pork, veal, or beef may be mixed with a beaten egg to make a meat paste instead of the cheese filling.

Jaroslawa Tkach, Bloomingburg, New York. Foodways, 1970.

Spanish Omelet

6 eggs
5 to 6 large potatoes,
    peeled and sliced
½ red bell pepper,
    thinly sliced
1 small onion,
    minced
1 chorizo sausage,
    chopped small
1½ cups olive oil

1. In a medium frying pan, heat oil and add potatoes, pepper, onion, and sausage. Turn potatoes every 10 minutes to prevent burning. Once potatoes are soft with a golden color on the edges, drain and reserve oil.

2. In a large bowl, beat eggs well. Add fried ingredients and mix slowly so that eggs blend well with potatoes.

3. Heat ¼ cup remaining oil. Pour in egg mixture. When it turns golden, cover with a large plate. Turn over pan when omelet is done on one side, unmold onto plate, and slide omelet back into pan. Cook the other side for 10 minutes more, then turn over omelet on plate again. If a drier omelet is preferred, keep turning omelet every 5 minutes until it is cooked the way you like it. Serve hot or cold.

Julia Lara, Kearny, New Jersey. New Jersey Program, 1983

"Throughout Spain, omelets are prepared using many different ingredients, but the most common is potatoes. In my town, farmers going out to plant or harvest a field would take their lunches with them — often an omelet with fried tomato sauce and a lettuce and tomato salad. Eaten cold, an omelet is a very tasty and inexpensive meal."

Obento (Japanese Boxed Lunch)

The following foods typically are found in an obento:

Fried Chicken
Rolled Omelet
Fish Misozuke
Acorn Squash
Carrot Flowers
Flowered Turnip
Blanched Snow Peas
Rice

Tatsuta-age (Fried Chicken)

1 spring chicken
2 tablespoons sake
3 tablespoons soy sauce
2 tablespoons ginger juice
1 tablespoon oil
1 egg
3 tablespoons cornstarch
oil, for frying

1. Debone chicken and cut into bite-size pieces.

2. Marinate in mixture of sake, soy sauce, juice of grated ginger, and oil for about 1 hour.

3. Mix with egg and cornstarch. Deep fry in oil. Serves 5.

Tamago Yaki (Rolled Omelet)

4 tablespoons dashi (soup stock)
½ teaspoon soy sauce
⅓ teaspoon salt
2 tablespoons sugar
½ tablespoon mirin (sweet sake)
4 eggs, lightly beaten
3 to 4 tablespoons oil
3 tablespoons green peas

1. Mix dashi, soy sauce, salt, sugar, and mirin. Add beaten eggs and stir.

2. Lightly brush a tamagoyaki frying pan with oil and place on medium heat. Pour in a third of egg mixture. Sprinkle green peas on top. When egg begins to set, roll omelet into thirds. Slide to far end of pan.

3. Lightly oil pan again. Pour in half of remaining egg mixture, letting some run under the completed rolled egg. In several seconds, roll over the new layer of egg as before. Repeat with remaining egg mixture.

Fish Misozuke

½ pound miso
¼ cup mirin (sweet sake)
½ pound white fish fillet

1. Mix miso and mirin. Marinate fish in mixture overnight. Drain of most liquid.

2. Broil each side of fish for several minutes.

Acorn Squash

1 small acorn squash	(sweet sake)
1½ cups dashi (soup stock)	2 tablespoons soy sauce
7 tablespoons mirin	¼ teaspoon salt

1. Cut squash into bite-size pieces.

2. Cut off parts of skin, making a design with the green skin against the orange flesh.

3. Boil in dashi, mirin, soy sauce, and salt until tender.

Carrot Flowers

1 carrot, peeled	3 tablespoons sugar
dashi (soup stock)	

1. Thinly slice carrot crosswise.

2. Cut wedges in edges of slices to make flowers.

3. Cook in dashi with sugar until soft. Drain.

Kikka Kabu (Flowered Turnips)

5 small turnips	salmon roe, for garnish
½ teaspoon salt	chrysanthemum
3 tablespoons vinegar	leaves, for garnish
1½ tablespoons sugar	

1. Cut stems and tops of turnips. Place stem side down on a cutting board, resting on a pair of chopsticks to limit the depth of the subsequent cut. Slice thinly down to chopsticks, then repeat at right angles.

2. Put turnips in a small bowl and sprinkle with salt. When soft, wash and place in a dry bowl.

3. Mix vinegar and sugar and pour over turnips. Let stand for 2 hours. Drain.

4. Spread open turnips. Put a few salmon roe in the center of each turnip. Garnish with chrysanthemum leaves for a flowerlike effect.

Etsuko Y. Smith, Bethesda, Maryland. Japanese American Program, 1986

"A Japanese school child's favorite time comes when he or she opens a lunch box to see what mother has fixed. Their teacher might ask, 'What color do you see in your Obento? Is there something from the ocean? The mountain? The plain?' The variety of nutritious foods and the pleasing colors remind the children of their mother's smile."

Cha-Gio (Vietnamese Spring Rolls)

2 pounds ground fresh pork butt (half crab meat or fresh shrimp optional), finely chopped
2 tablespoons nuoc man (Vietnamese fish sauce)
1 teaspoon salt
½ teaspoon white pepper

1 large egg
½ pound onions (or green and white onions), finely chopped
½ pound carrots, finely chopped or grated
1 bunch (2 ounces) bean thread (or Chinese vermicelli softened in water, drained, and cut into 3-inch lengths)

½ ounce Chinese dried fungus (or Chinese mushrooms, softened in water, cleaned, drained, and sliced)
1 teaspoon sugar
2 cups water
rice papers
corn oil, for frying
lettuce, for garnish
fresh mint, for garnish

Sauce:
½ cup nuoc man (Vietnamese fish sauce)
½ cup water
¼ cup white vinegar
1 clove garlic, pounded
2 tablespoons sugar
1 small red hot pepper, crushed (optional)

1. Mix meat, or meat and fish mixture, with seasonings and egg. Cover and refrigerate.

2. Chop onions, carrots, bean thread, and Chinese fungus. Mix with meat.

3. To moisten rice papers (1 at a time), stir sugar into water and pour into a large plate. Dip whole rice paper into water, then quickly remove; drain excess water. Place paper flat on a large cutting board.

4. Put 1 heaping tablespoon of meat mixture on rice paper. Begin to roll gently; when half rolled, tuck under both ends, and then continue to roll up. As soon as several rolls are made, put them on a rack in the refrigerator to let rice paper dry.

5. To fry rolls, preheat oil in a frying pan on medium heat. When oil is hot enough, put in fresh rolls. Allow meat to cook well, for about 3 to 5 minutes.

6. Mix ingredients for sauce. Cha-gio is best when served crisp and warm, with sauce, lettuce, and fresh mint.

Phan Hoang, Bowie, Maryland. Folklore in Your Community: Vietnamese Community, 1979

Collard Greens

2 pounds collard
    greens
2-inch piece (about ¾
    pound) fatback
2 cups water
1 tablespoon salt
½ teaspoon sugar
dash of salt
pepper

1. Wash greens well, leaf by leaf, in cold water. Cut by gathering leaves into bunches and slicing crosswise in strips. Soak in water to cover with 1 tablespoon salt, then drain.

2. Cook fatback in water to cover on medium heat until tender, for about 30 minutes. Add drained greens and sprinkle with sugar, salt, and pepper.

3. Cover and cook on medium heat for about 30 minutes or until tender.

Anna Gilliard, Forestville, Maryland. Migration to Metropolitan Washington: Making a New Place Home, 1988

Hoppin' John

1 pound dried field
    peas (or black-eyed
    peas)
2-inch piece (about
    ¾ pound) fatback
1½ quarts water
1 medium onion,
    whole
2½ cups long-grain
    white rice
salt
pepper

1. Wash peas in cold water.

2. Boil fatback in a large pot of water on medium heat for about 30 minutes or until water is low and well seasoned with fatback flavor.

3. Add peas and onion and enough water to cover peas. Cook on low to medium heat for about 1 hour.

4. When peas are soft, season with salt and pepper, remove onion, and add rice. Add more water if necessary to cook rice (about 5 cups is needed). Cook for another 30 minutes and adjust seasonings. Serves 10

Anna Gilliard

"Hoppin' John, hot collard greens, candied sweet potatoes, and eggnog make a traditional New Year's Eve supper."

German Potato Salad

10 medium potatoes,
    well scrubbed
1 large onion,
    chopped
½ cup cider vinegar
¼ to ⅓ cup water
3 to 4 tablespoons
    olive oil
4 slices bacon, cooked
    and crumbled
parsley, chopped
salt
pepper

1. Cook potatoes in water until tender. While hot, remove skins and set potatoes aside until cool enough to handle comfortably. Slice into a large bowl.

2. Simmer onion in a saucepan with vinegar and water until tender. Pour over potatoes and allow to stand until cold. Do not mix or disturb the potatoes, or they will crumble and become mushy.

3. When potatoes are cool, add oil, bacon, parsley, salt, and pepper. Toss gently to blend flavors. Serve at room temperature. The potato salad is better if made early in the day to allow flavors to meld. Serves 6.

Betty Bunger, Piscataway, New Jersey. New Jersey Program, 1983

Slovenian Potato Salad

"Slovenian cooking is marked by a combination of Austrian, Germanic, and Romance influences. It is hearty and nourishing, using the abundance of food available — fresh vegetables, fruits, grains of all types, beef, veal, pork, smoked meats, and sausages. With most meals, a green salad of lettuce, endive, or dandelion greens is served with a dressing of plain vinegar and oil."

5 medium potatoes
1 medium onion,
    thinly sliced
pepper
garlic powder
salt
⅓ cup oil
⅔ cup diluted cider
    vinegar

1. Cook potatoes in skins; then peel and cool. In a large bowl, slice thinly and add onion. Sprinkle in pepper, garlic powder, and salt to taste.

2. Dilute cider vinegar with water to taste and combine with oil. Pour over potatoes and onions. Mix gently.

3. Serve warm or cold. It is especially good when served lukewarm immediately after preparation and is excellent with ham, sausages, or meatloaf. Serves 4.

Slovenian Women's Union, Rockville, Maryland. South Slavic American Program, 1981

Chutney

½ pound peeled
    tamarind fruit,
    refrigerated or
    frozen
1 tablespoon sugar
dash of salt
pepper
1 clove garlic, stone
    ground or crushed

1. Put fruit in warm water to cover, and soak overnight at room temperature.

2. Add other ingredients, mixing thoroughly to combine the flavors.

Note: Tart green apples or very firm green pears may be grated and used in place of the tamarind fruit. For a less sweet chutney, decrease the amount of sugar according to taste.

Irab Juman, Alexandria, Virginia. Migration to Metropolitan Washington: Making a New Place Home, 1988

Zucchini Pickles

2 medium onions,
    peeled
2 pounds small
    zucchini, washed
¼ cup salt
2 cups white vinegar
1 cup sugar
1 teaspoon celery
    seed
1 teaspoon mustard
    seed
1 teaspoon tumeric
½ teaspoon dry
    mustard

1. Cut onions and unpeeled zucchini in very thin slices and place in a bowl. Cover with water and add salt. Let stand one hour.

2. Transfer to a saucepan and bring to a boil. Let stand one hour, then bring to a boil again and cook for 3 minutes.

3. Pack in 3 hot sterilized pint jars. Seal according to directions. May be stored in refrigerator without processing for up to 3 weeks. Yields 6 cups.

Mary Sorbello, Mullica Hill, New Jersey. New Jersey Program, 1983

"Our parents couldn't own land in Sicily, so owning land here was the most precious asset they could have. Today, our extended family farms 600 acres that produce apples, peaches, tomatoes, soybeans, melons, and zucchini. I swap zucchini recipes with customers and probably have more than a hundred ways to cook it."

Curtido (Pickled Coleslaw)

1 head cabbage, finely
    sliced
3 carrots, grated
1 radish, grated
1 small hot pepper
    (optional)
oil, for frying
1 onion, thinly sliced
1 green pepper, finely
    chopped
pinch of oregano
salt

Pineapple vinegar:
1 pineapple
grapes (optional)
1 peach, sliced
    (optional)
pinch of oregano
    (optional)
water

1. Cover cabbage, carrots, and radish with hot water, and let sit for 30 minutes. Drain.

2. Heat oil and sauté onion, pepper, oregano, and salt. Combine with cabbage mixture. Add pineapple vinegar.

3. To make pineapple vinegar, use one of the following two methods:

Method no. 1: Remove peel of pineapple. Let peel dry in the sun or over a radiator for several days. Put in a jar with water and let sit for several weeks. Remove peel. Use liquid as vinegar.

Method no. 2: Cut pineapple in chunks, including rind. Combine in a jar with a handful of grapes, peach, oregano, and cover with water. Let sit for several days. Use liquid as vinegar.

Rita Torres Gonzalez, Washington, D.C. Cultural Conservation, 1985

Mochi (Rice Cakes)

"Rice cakes were eaten on New Year's Day, but only after they were first offered to the gods and deities as an expression of gratitude for our daily existence."

1 pound sweet rice
½ cup rice flour

1. Wash and soak rice for 3 hours. Steam for 30 minutes until cooked.

2. Put rice into a mortar. Pound with mallets until soft and pliable, turning and wetting dough, but keeping hot.

3. Flour dough and a surface with rice flour, then mold into 3-inch round rice cakes.

4. Mochi may be eaten in a variety of ways: roll in a mixture of 1 tablespoon soybean flour and 1 tablespoon sugar, coating evenly; or use corn syrup as a dipping sauce; or make a dipping sauce of 1 teaspoon soy sauce and 1 teaspoon sugar; or put into soups for soft dumplings.

Iddy Asada, Bridgeton, New Jersey. Old Ways in the New World: Japanese American, 1976

Corn Bubble Ring

4½ to 5½ cups flour
1½ cups yellow
   cornmeal
1 tablespoon salt
2 envelopes dry yeast
1¾ cups milk
½ cup water
3 tablespoons
   margarine
1½ tablespoons
   honey
oil
margarine

1. Combine 1¼ cups flour, cornmeal, salt, and yeast.

2. Heat milk, water, margarine, and honey until warm. Add to dry ingredients and beat for 2 minutes. Add ½ cup flour and beat with a mixer at high speed for 2 minutes. Stir in enough flour to make a soft dough.

3. Knead for 8 to 10 minutes. Cover with plastic wrap and a towel. Let rest for 20 minutes.

4. Punch down dough; divide into 32 equal balls and arrange in a greased 10-inch tube pan, making 2 layers. Brush with oil, cover with plastic wrap, and refrigerate for 2 to 24 hours.

5. Uncover and let stand at room temperature for 10 minutes. Bake at 375°F for about 55 to 60 minutes. Remove from pan and cool on a rack. Brush with melted margarine.

Mary Beth Lind, Harman, West Virginia. America's Appetite (for Energy), 1977

Buttermilk Corn Bread

1 cup self-rising flour
1 cup self-rising
　cornmeal
1 tablespoon sugar
2 tablespoons mar-
　garine, melted
1 egg
1 cup buttermilk

1. Mix all ingredients in a large bowl. Stir until smooth.

2. Pour into an 8-inch greased baking dish. Bake at 450°F until golden brown. Let stand for 5 minutes before serving. Serves 8.

Note: For a different taste, onion or peanut butter may be added to the batter.

Alberta Stanley, Appalachia, Virginia. Regional America: The Upland South, 1976

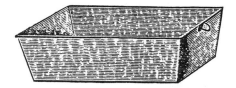

Zucchini Nut Bread

3 eggs
1 cup oil
2 cups sugar
2½ cups grated
　zucchini
2 teaspoons vanilla
　extract
3 cups flour
1 teaspoon baking
　powder
1 teaspoon baking
　soda
1 teaspoon salt
2½ teaspoons
　cinnamon
½ cup nuts, chopped

1. Beat eggs until light and foamy. Add oil, sugar, zucchini, and vanilla.

2. Combine dry ingredients. Add to egg mixture and mix just until blended. Stir in nuts.

3. Pour into 2 greased and floured loaf pans and bake at 325°F for 1 hour or until a toothpick inserted in the middle comes out clean. May be served plain or with cream cheese. Yields 2 loaves.

Mary Sorbello, Mullica Hill, New Jersey. New Jersey Program, 1983

Serbian Walnut Roll

7 cups flour
4 tablespoons sugar
2 packages dry yeast
1 teaspoon salt
1 cup sour cream
½ cup water
1 cup butter
4 eggs
1 egg, beaten with
   water

Filling:
2 pounds ground
   walnuts
1½ cups sugar
8 tablespoons butter,
   softened
½ to 1 cup warm
   milk
1 teaspoon vanilla
   extract

1. Combine 2 cups flour, sugar, salt, and yeast.

2. Mix sour cream, water, and butter. Heat until very warm (120°F) and add to dry ingredients. Beat well. Stir in remaining flour and beaten eggs.

3. Knead into a ball. Cover and let stand for 10 minutes, then divide into 5 rolls. Roll out into 12 × 14-inch rectangles.

4. Make filling by combining ingredients until they are of spreading consistency.

5. Spread filling on dough and roll up jellyroll fashion. Pinch ends and put on greased baking sheets.

6. Cover rolls and let rise in a warm place for 1½ hours. Brush tops with egg beaten with a little water. Bake at 350°F for 30 to 35 minutes. Cool on a wire rack and slice into ½-inch thick portions.

Olga Gurick, McLean, Virginia. South Slavic Cooking, 1976

Potica (Yeast Nut Roll)

"Slovenian desserts can be the heavy, sugared doughnuts (krofi) or the flaky flancati. Among the best known of our pastries is the Slovenian nut roll (potica) and a wide variety of strudel. Potica is central to Slovenian cuisine. Literally, it means 'something rolled in.' At social occasions it is served, unbuttered, either as a bread with the main course or as dessert with coffee."

1 2-ounce cake yeast
¾ cup lukewarm milk
2 tablespoons sugar
2 tablespoons flour
7 cups sifted flour
1 tablespoon salt
½ cup sugar
1 lemon rind
1 cup butter, softened

1 cup warm milk
6 egg yolks, beaten

Filling:
1 cup golden raisins
1 ounce rum
¼ cup milk (or cream)
½ cup honey

½ cup butter
1 pound walnuts, finely ground
1 teaspoon cinnamon
6 egg whites
1½ cups sugar

½ beaten egg, for glaze

1. In a small bowl, crumble yeast into ¾ cup lukewarm milk. Add 2 tablespoons each sugar and flour. Mix and let stand to proof, for about 10 minutes.

2. In another bowl, combine flour, salt, sugar, and lemon rind. Work in butter with fingers until absorbed. Make a well in the center and add milk, eggs, and yeast mixture. Mix and knead for a few minutes until smooth. Oil top of dough, cover well, and refrigerate for at least 6 hours or overnight.

3. Soak raisins in hot water for at least 10 minutes. Drain on paper towel. Put raisins in a small bowl, add rum, and let stand overnight.

4. Remove dough from the refrigerator. Let warm at room temperature for at least 1 hour. Grease 4 bread pans. Preheat oven to 350°F (325°F for glass pans).

5. While dough warms, heat milk or cream, honey, and butter on low heat, stirring until butter melts. Pour over walnuts and mix. Add cinnamon and set aside.

6. Roll out dough on a lightly floured surface, rolling from the center outward; turn it over occasionally and reflour surface if necessary. Roll into a rectangular shape about 26 × 40 inches.

7. Beat egg whites until stiff, gradually adding 1 cup sugar. Combine with nut mixture. Spread filling smoothly over entire dough and sprinkle with remaining sugar and raisins.

8. On long side of dough, start rolling to the middle, stretching back slightly to make a tight roll; repeat on the other side. Cut the double roll into 4 sections to fit pans. Cover with cloth and let rise in a warm place for 2 hours or until double in size.

9. Brush tops with ½ beaten egg for a shiny crust. Bake for 1 hour. Cool in pans before removing. Separate the rolls by cutting the loaf lengthwise, then slice for serving. Potica may be frozen once completely cool.

Slovenian Women's Union, Rockville, Maryland. South Slavic American Program, 1981

Rice Pudding

1. Put rice and water in a saucepan with a tight-fitting lid. Bring quickly to a boil on medium-high heat. Cover and simmer gently on low heat for about 15 minutes, until light and fluffy.

2. Add sugar (adjust to taste), eggs, and butter and mix well. Stir in milk, vanilla, nutmeg, and baking powder.

3. Mix rice once again and pour into a greased casserole. Bake at 350°F for about 1 hour. Cool and serve.

Alberta Higginbotham, Washington, D.C. Migration to Metropolitan Washington: Making a New Place Home, 1988

1 cup long-grain white rice
2 cups cold water
½ cup sugar
2 eggs and 1 egg yolk, beaten
2 tablespoons butter
1 can evaporated milk
1 teaspoon vanilla extract
dash of nutmeg
½ teaspoon baking powder

Corn Pudding

1. Remove corn kernels from cob.

2. Cook corn and coconut milk on medium-high heat for 20 minutes, stirring occasionally.

3. Add salt, sugar, and tapioca pearls. Cook for 3 more minutes, or until corn and tapioca are done. Serve warm or cool.

Phouang Phaka Khamvongsa, Springfield, Virginia. Cultural Conservation: America's Many Voices — Lao-Americans, 1987

10 ears corn
4½ cups coconut milk
½ teaspoon salt
1 cup sugar
1 cup small tapioca pearls, washed in warm water and drained (optional)

Steamed Sweet Rice and Banana

3 cups sweet rice,
   washed
4 cups coconut milk
½ cup sugar
¾ teaspoon salt
1 cup diced taro
   (or 1 can black
   beans) (optional)
8 ripe bananas
banana leaves
   (or aluminum foil)

1. Soak rice in water for 3 hours. Rinse and put in a strainer to drain.

2. Pour coconut milk in a deep pot. Boil on medium-high heat for 15 minutes, stirring occasionally to prevent overflowing.

3. Pour rice into coconut milk and stir. Add sugar and salt. Cook on medium-high heat for 5 minutes, stirring constantly to keep rice from sticking to the pot. If desired, add taro or drained black beans.

4. Cut bananas in half lengthwise, then into 6 or 8 pieces. Tear banana leaves or aluminum foil into pieces about 5 to 6 inches wide. Put several tablespoons of rice on each leaf. Spread rice out a little, then add a piece of banana and another tablespoon of rice on top. Wrap it up, tucking one end of the leaf or foil underneath the other end.

5. Put packets in a steamer, and cook on medium-high heat for 20 minutes. Serve warm or cool.

Phouang Phaka Khamvongsa, Springfield, Virginia. Cultural Conservation: America's Many Voices — Lao-Americans, 1987

Egg Cheese

2 quarts whole milk
4 eggs
1 pint buttermilk
¼ cup sugar
honey (or molasses)

1. Heat milk to a boil in a double boiler. Thoroughly mix eggs, buttermilk, and sugar and add to hot milk; continue heating until mixture separates, about 30 minutes.

2. Pour into an egg cheese mold or strainer. Let set until cold, about 2 to 3 hours.

3. Unmold onto a plate and serve with honey or molasses.

Note: The recipe may be doubled or cut in half. The cheese will keep in the refrigerator for up to 2 weeks.

Paul Shenk, Lancaster, Pennsylvania. Dairy Industry Program, 1970

"This is a Pennsylvania Dutch food that is more like a dessert. My mother used to serve this delicacy on Easter Sunday."

Blackberry Delight

4 cups blackberries, fresh or frozen
2 cups self-rising flour
½ cup margarine, melted
1½ cups sugar
2 eggs
1⅓ cups milk
1 teaspoon vanilla extract
1 teaspoon cinnamon (optional)
1 teaspoon nutmeg (optional)

1. Spread thawed blackberries in the bottom of a 13 × 9-inch baking pan.

2. Combine remaining ingredients in a separate bowl and mix well. Pour over blackberries.

3. Bake at 350°F for 30 to 40 minutes or until topping springs back. Leave in pan until ready to serve. Cut into squares and serve with whipped cream.

Alberta Stanley, Appalachia, Virginia. Regional America: The Upland South, 1976

Bourma (Strudel)

"Bourma, along with its famous cousin, baklava, came into the food world during the time of the Ottoman Empire. The recipe came to my family via two routes. The Sephardic members of my Jewish family carried their treasured recipes during their diaspora from the Middle East to the Iberian peninsula and after the fourteenth century to North Africa. The Ashkenazi members of my family settled throughout Middle Europe. They filled this light, delicate dough with fruits, cheese, and nuts and called it strudel."

1 pound filo dough
1½ pounds almonds (or walnuts), ground
⅔ cup sugar

2 teaspoons cinnamon
1 pound unsalted butter (or margarine), melted

8 ounces honey
1 tablespoon orange-blossom water

1. Place package of filo on sheet of wax paper. Cut leaves in half to form 8 × 10-inch sheets. Cover with a towel.

2. Combine nuts, sugar, and cinnamon.

3. Place a sheet of filo lengthwise on a work surface and brush with melted butter. Place 1 tablespoon nut mixture in the center of the sheet and spread evenly throughout center third of leaf. Fold a third over mixture and cover with the last third.

4. Preheat oven to 350°F. Brush the wooden handle of a kitchen spoon with melted butter or margarine. Roll dough from bottom to top over spoon handle like a jellyroll. Turn spoon on its end and gently push pastry off handle. Place on a lightly greased baking sheet. Repeat with remaining filo and filling.

5. Bake for about 20 minutes or until lightly browned. Combine honey and orange blossom water and pour over warm pastry. Yields 4 dozen.

Roberta Sabban, Bethesda, Maryland. Ethnic Foods: Jewish Cook, 1977

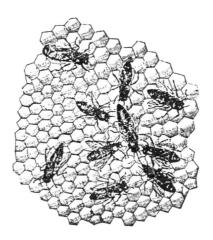

Gibanica (Cheese Pastries)

6 eggs
½ cup flour, sifted
1 teaspoon salt
1 pound filo
1 cup clarified butter
1 cup sour cream
2 pounds creamed
large-curd cottage
cheese

1. Beat eggs until fluffy. Stir in flour and salt, then add cheese and thoroughly fold in sour cream.

2. Grease with butter a 9 × 13 × 2-inch pan. Spread 3 sheets filo in pan and brush with clarified butter between sheets.

3. Spread 8 teaspoons cheese mixture on every third sheet. Alternate filo and filling, ending with filo.

4. Bake at 325°F for 1 hour, or until risen and brown. Cool slightly and cut in squares.

Olga Gurick, McLean, Virginia. South Slavic Cooking, 1976

"This recipe is one we still use today for our well-known bake sales twice a year at the St. Luke Serbian Eastern Orthodox Church in McLean, Virginia. We sell hundreds of nut rolls, strudels, and gibanica. The people line up outside the door to get in."

Flancati (Bowknots)

3 cups flour
6 teaspoons sugar
1 tablespoon butter
6 egg yolks
6 tablespoons white
wine
¼ teaspoon salt
1½ pounds
shortening, for
frying
powdered sugar

1. Sift flour into a bowl; set aside ½ cup for later use. Mix in sugar and butter. Add egg yolks, wine, and salt. Combine well with a fork.

2. Place dough on a floured surface. Knead by hand until hard and smooth and tiny bubbles appear under the surface; add reserved flour as needed. Cover dough and let rest for 1 hour.

3. Divide dough into 4 parts and use 1 part at a time; it will keep in the refrigerator for several days and may be used as needed. Roll very thin on a floured surface. Cut into strips 3 inches wide, then into pieces 4 inches long. With a knife, make 3 or 4 gashes 1 inch long in each piece. To make interesting shapes, fold 1 or 2 corners through the gashes.

4. Drop dough into deep hot fat; it should float when frying. Fry until light brown on both sides. Sprinkle with powdered sugar before serving.

Slovenian Women's Union, Rockville, Maryland. South Slavic American Program, 1981

Taralles (Iced Cookies)

"This all-occasion cookie is a cousin to the Neapolitan taralli and is a necessity at special events — weddings, christenings, showers, and even when visiting sick friends. They are often made for holidays. Taralles can be served without icing — cut in half, buttered, and dunked in coffee.

My youngest daughter now makes the family's taralles; hers are better than mine because her hands are better. But when I prepared this cookie at the Smithsonian Folklife Festival in the summer of 1985, the children lined up to get them as quickly as I made them. They were very disappointed when the health inspector wouldn't let me give them away. He liked them too."

6 eggs
½ pound butter, melted
1 cup sugar
½ cup milk
1 teaspoon vanilla extract
6 teaspoons baking powder
5 cups flour

1 pound powdered sugar

Icing:
2 cups powdered sugar
4 to 6 tablespoons water
1 teaspoon vanilla extract

colored sprinkles or sugar crystals (optional)

1. Grease cookie sheets and preheat oven to 375°F.

2. Mix all ingredients with hands to a sticky, but not runny, consistency.

3. Working with floured hands, roll out a small amount of dough into a sausage shape, joining the ends firmly. Bake on greased cookie sheets for 15 minutes. Cool completely, then ice.

4. To make icing, combine sugar, water, and vanilla in a mixing bowl. Dip the top of each cooled cookie in the icing or spread on the icing by hand. Top with sprinkles or sugar crystals. Allow to dry.

Rose Notoris, Ambler, Pennsylvania. Cultural Conservation, 1985

Shoo Fly Wet Bottom

Crumb topping:
4 cups flour
1 cup brown sugar
½ teaspoon salt
1 cup shortening

Bottom:
2 cups molasses
2 cups cold water
2 teaspoons baking soda
1 egg, beaten

3 pie crusts

1. Mix flour, sugar, and salt for the crumb. Cut shortening into dry mixture.

2. Combine ingredients for the wet bottom. Add half of crumb mixture to molasses mixture. Pour into pie crusts and sprinkle remaining crumb on top.

3. Bake at 400°F for 10 minutes, then reduce heat to 375°F to finish baking for about 30 minutes. Yields 3 pies.

Sadie Kriebel, Hereford, Pennsylvania. Regional America: The Northeast, 1976

Schwenkfelder Saffron Cake

1. Thoroughly mix potatoes and sugar.

2. Dissolve yeast in potato water and add to potato mixture. Cover and set aside in a warm place for about 3 hours.

3. Bring milk to a boil; add shortening, eggs, sugar, and salt. Pour boiling water on saffron to draw out color and flavoring. Carefully drain saffron water into milk mixture; save saffron for crumb topping.

4. Cool to lukewarm, and add yeast mixture and 4 cups flour. Beat well. Cover and let rise until bubbly, approximately 1 to 1½ hours. Add remaining flour, or enough to make a dough that can be kneaded until smooth. Place in a greased bowl, cover, and let rise about 4 hours, or until doubled in size and light.

5. Make crumb topping by mixing flour, sugar, cinnamon, and crumbled saffron; cut shortening into dry ingredients.

6. Roll dough about ⅓ inch thick and place on a greased cookie sheet or baking pan. Cut into 4 cakes. Brush tops with melted butter, cream, or beaten egg. Cover with crumb topping. Let rise for about 1 hour. Bake in preheated 325°F oven for 20 to 25 minutes. Yields 4 9-inch cakes.

Sadie Kriebel

1 cup mashed
   potatoes
½ cup sugar
1 package dry yeast
1 cup potato water,
   lukewarm
1 cup milk
½ cup shortening
2 eggs, well beaten
1 cup sugar
½ teaspoon salt
¼ teaspoon saffron
   threads
¼ cup boiling water
about 8 cups bread
   flour

Crumb topping:
2½ cups flour
2 cups light brown
   sugar
1 teaspoon cinnamon
crumbled saffron
1 cup shortening
melted butter
   (or cream or
   beaten egg)

Hardtack Candy

"The candy must be stretched and cut with scissors as rapidly as possible as soon as it is cool enough to handle. Cool the cooked candy on a slab of marble pre-chilled in the refrigerator and spread with butter or margarine. Flavoring oils can be found in some drugstores or ordered directly from specialty manufacturers."

3¾ cups sugar
1½ cups light corn syrup
1 cup water
several drops food coloring
1 teaspoon flavoring oil (not extract)
powdered sugar

1. Mix sugar, syrup, and water in a large, heavy saucepan. Stir on medium heat until sugar dissolves. Boil without stirring until syrup reaches 310°F (hardtack). Remove from heat. Stir in food coloring and flavoring oil.

2. Pour onto a cold marble slab, 16 × 24 inches, that has been spread with butter or margarine. Cool candy by slipping a spatula underneath and gently flipping part of the mixture on top of the rest. Work in this manner until just cool enough to handle.

3. Pull or stretch small amounts into strips and cut with scissors into bite-size pieces. Dip in powdered sugar and let cool completely. Store in an airtight container. Yields 2¼ pounds.

Orville and Phyllis Bower, Rocky Mount, Virginia. Virginia Folk Culture, 1977

Fresco de Ensalada (Fruit Drink)

1 pineapple
1 red apple
1 green apple
1 yellow apple
1 maranon (cashew fruit)
1 package frozen nance
2 oranges
2 lemons
2 green mangoes
1 head lettuce
1 bunch watercress
sugar
water to cover

1. Chop fruit and vegetables and combine in a large glass jar or glazed crock.

2. Add sugar to taste and water to cover. Serve chilled.

Rita Torres Gonzalez, Washington, D.C. Cultural Conservation, 1985

Sow (Milk Drink)

3 quarts buttermilk
6 cups vanilla yogurt
2 cups sour cream
2 cups sugar
1 tablespoon white
    vanilla

1. Combine all ingredients in a large bowl or gallon jug. Mix well.

2. Add lots of ice and serve.

Anta Diop, New York, New York. Senegal Program, 1990

"Sow (pronounced so) is a drink of the Toucouleurs in Senegal. It is made by letting fresh cow milk sit outside to sour, then mixing it with lots of sugar and ice. This recipe was used at the Smithsonian Folklife Festival and is a close equivalent, at least in terms of taste. The quantity may be halved."

Apple Cider

1 bushel ripe apples
    (Yellow Delicious,
    York, and Stay-
    man)

1. To make good sweet cider, we mix Yellow Delicious, York, and Stayman apples. Make sure the apples are completely ripe.

2. Use an old hand cider press if you have one. Grind and press apples, then strain.

3. Put cider into jugs, if you have any left. Loosen caps and store in a cool place. You can drink it right away, or wait until it gets cool. Yields 2 gallons.

Note: If you want to make the cider turn to vinegar, put it in a warm place.

Merrill Snyder, Burnt Cabins, Pennsylvania. America's Appetite (for Energy), 1977

South

❖ · ❖ · ❖ · ❖

Linda R. Crawford

ealtime or not, in the South people sit "to visit" in the dining area or the kitchen, often disregarding the hostess's repeated efforts to relocate them elsewhere. Anyone relegated to another room automatically feels like company. But seated at the table, everyone feels right at home. And because the table is such a focal point of southern culture, food reinforces the South's rich sense of tradition. Certain dishes are associated with certain groups of people or the celebration of particular events. Served at the wrong time, a dish becomes a source of embarrassment. Served at the proper occasion, a meal defines the stature of an event and assures its social success. Even the name of a southern meal reflects its social importance. For example, custom dictates that the noon meal be called dinner and that supper be eaten at night. However, on the more ceremonious occasions, dinner becomes lunch, supper becomes dinner, and the average southerner's digestion becomes confused.

The Best for Guests

Brunch, that unnatural combination of breakfast and lunch, is suitable only for those rare occasions when it is considered socially acceptable to sleep late. Tea, by contrast, usually involves more food than beverage and is served in the afternoon. The more informal repasts are simply called snacks. This term conveniently covers anything from a handful of peanuts to an elaborate feast, provided it is served to guests at any time other than mealtime.

Feeding guests, after all, is a longstanding southern tradition. In the frontier and antebellum South, when travel was arduous and inns were few, travelers dropped in unexpectedly and stayed for extended periods of time. Pre–Civil War diaries chronicle an almost constant flow of visitors and the strain this habit placed on the household. Regardless of how severe this strain may have been, southern hospitality demanded that guests be fed the best available foods.

Previous pages: Sarah Mae Albritton surveys her Louisiana garden. (Susan Roach-Lankford)

And they were. As their letters and diaries show, antebellum visitors to southern plantations often sat down to meals that featured a choice of meats — turkey, ham, venison, and chicken — a variety of fruits, assorted vegetables, and several desserts. Even the more humble homes would present their finest foods to visitors, although in a less elaborate fashion.

Home gardens provided much of the variety for these meals. A typical nineteenth-century gardener might grow sweet potatoes, tomatoes, corn, beans, squash, field peas, butter beans, turnips, carrots, cabbage, and okra, to name a few plants. The region's long growing season produced a surplus of foods that were carefully preserved by canning, drying, or pickling so that they could be enjoyed throughout the year. Then, as now, the amounts and variety of foods generated by a home garden could be staggering.

So could the way food was prepared. Take the modern southern breakfast, for example. The grits and biscuits of the eastern and middle South are often replaced by hashbrown potatoes and toast farther to the north and west. And, while these variations may begin with breakfast, they continue through every meal, every occasion, and every type of food. Much of this variety can be attributed to shifting boundaries and circumstances within the region.

Theme and Variations

In this book, the South includes Louisiana, Arkansas, Kentucky, Tennessee, Mississippi, Alabama, North Carolina, South Carolina, Georgia, and Florida. Virginia and Texas are discussed in other regions, not because they are less southern, but because the food customs in these states tend to mingle more freely with those of the neighboring states and cultural regions. Along the northern edge of Texas, for example, traditional southern foods and food customs mingle with those of the Midwest. The western border blends with the Southwest. As a result, east Texans may consider themselves southerners, but west Texans are more likely to identify with the Hispanic southwestern states.

However one defines its geographic boundaries, the South is the least urbanized area within the United States. Some sixty-seven percent of its residents now live in communities of at least 2,500, but true metropolitan areas are relatively rare. Mississippi, North Carolina, and Arkansas are the most rural, Florida the least so. In terms of population, the South is largely composed of people of African and European extraction. However, because the South has had relatively little foreign immigration, especially of Caucasians, since the nineteenth century, most southerners base their sense of ethnicity on ancestral roots. Indeed, a disproportionate number of people in the South can trace their ancestry to settlers who arrived in the early 1800s, and many southerners identify with the national origins of their ancestors. This sense of identity is maintained by participating in the customs and traditions of a particular community, including the growing, preparation, and eating of its foods.

High on Hog

Food patterns tend to change gradually in any region, but perhaps particularly so in the South. When the European settlers first arrived, they ate what the Native Americans ate — corn, beans, squash, deer, turkey, fish, and the like. As soon as possible, however, they established herds of swine, thus adding pork to the southern diet. Pork was soon eaten at every meal. When hogs were killed, the chitterlings (intestines), knuckles, and livers were eaten immediately. Fat was rendered into lard. Meat was cured in a smokehouse, and sausages were made in a frenzy of activity. For early southerners, the butchering of hogs and the preservation of its parts were important survival skills.

Pork also affected the way foods were cooked. Many foods were either cooked in lard or flavored with it. Corn bread became crackling bread when cracklings were added for flavor. Pork grease added zest to vegetables, which many southerners considered inedible if they did not contain enough grease to "wink back" at the dinner guest. Pork lard also was used for frying a wide variety of foods. In an 1860 issue of *Godey's Lady's Book,* Dr. John S. Wilson of Columbus, Georgia, reported that southerners "indeed fried everything that is friable [*sic*], or that will stick together long enough to undergo the delightful process — hogs' lard is the very oil that moves the machinery of life, and they would as soon think of dispensing with tea, coffee or tobacco — as with the essence of hog."

Corn Culture

Corn also was a principal food crop. Once picked, it was boiled, roasted, ground, fried, and served as a vegetable in its own right — or turned into liquor and bourbon. Ground corn provided southerners with the flour they needed to bake bread. Hulled corn, when treated with lye, provided them with hominy. And when the hominy was dried and coarsely ground, corn provided southerners with grits. Even today, corn bread and grits are among the most universal of southern foods, although the methods of preparation vary regionally. For example, grits are sometimes served with fish in parts of the Carolinas down to Florida. However, in most parts of the South, they are cooked into a thick hot cereal, served for breakfast. Grits may be baked with cheese or sliced cold and fried in bacon grease.

Spoon bread, another southern corn specialty, is served in central Kentucky in the form of a soft custardlike bread. Just to the south, in Kentucky and in parts of Tennessee, a cornmeal batter is fried on a griddle and called hoecakes or corn cakes. Hush puppies, prepared with onion and other seasonings, are often served with fish, but not before first frying them, often in the same oil as the fish.

Originally, corn was a Native American plant. But just as African and European southerners adapted corn to their palate, the gardens that people continue to grow clearly illustrate the exchange of cultures within the region.

Opposite: A southern woman shows festival visitors how to weave a basket. (Kim Nielson)

Cultural Exchange

Native Americans introduced European settlers to corn bread, grits, sweet potatoes, squash, and beans.

Opposite: Aline Garrett of Louisiana prepares her mother's recipe for chicken pies at the 1984 folklife festival. (Kim Nielson)

In addition to corn, Native Americans grew beans and squash. African slaves contributed okra, yams, peanuts, watermelon, and collards. Europeans brought carrots, turnips, beets, cabbage, lettuce, and various herbs. Today, southern gardens are likely to contain plants from all three cultural sources. However, the true richness of southern foods does not emerge in the garden but around the table. There, one sees variety not only in the types of foods prepared, but also in the ways in which they are combined and the occasions on which they are served.

The first southerners, the Native Americans, may have contributed the most to traditional southern dishes. Native Americans introduced European settlers to corn bread, grits, sweet potatoes, squash, and beans. Settlers were also quick to learn what they could from the natives about wild plant foods — pecans, hickory nuts, blackberries, and muscadines. Today, nothing is more "southern" than pecan pie and pralines even though many Native Americans, the first people to cultivate the pecan tree, were decimated by disease and warfare or forcibly removed from the South in the 1830s.

Similarly, the "soul food" many people associate with traditional southern cooking came from Africa rather than Europe. Hot peppers and pepper sauce are typical of African American cuisine. Even gumbo, a dish universally associated with the Creole and Cajun cooking traditions of Louisiana, gets its name from the Bantu word for okra. And just as African food traditions took root in the South as slaves cooked for the owners of antebellum plantations, today many of these same culinary traditions survive because African Americans continue to cook food for special occasions and for many affluent southern households.

The European influence on southern cooking is evident from the time the first English settlers arrived in the seventeenth century. However, it was not until this ethnic group stabilized in the nineteenth century that its full influence emerged, particularly as English culinary traditions defined the way southern foods were combined and served. For example, Eliza Smith's *The Compleat Housewife: or, Accomplish'd Gentlewoman's Companion*, published by William Parks of Williamsburg, Virginia, in 1742, is actually a copy of a London cookbook. It carefully described how food should be combined and served in the proper social context. Mary Randolph's *The Virginia Housewife*, written in 1824, was the first truly southern cookbook. However, while it did reflect a thorough knowledge and use of regional produce, it nevertheless exhibited the strong influence of the English on southern cooking. For example, English traditions prevailed in Randolph's account of the proper table setting and proper foods for that special southern occasion.

Southerners of Scottish and Scotch-Irish descent used foods to perpetuate their heritage, too, and they do so today. Highland festivals that feature music, dance, crafts, and traditional dishes are held annually in Key Biscayne,

Orlando, and Miami, Florida; in Alexandria and Williamsburg, Virginia; in Carrollton and Glasgow, Kentucky; in Biloxi, Mississippi; and in Gatlinburg, Tennessee. German Oktoberfests accomplish the same thing in Morgan and Lawrence counties in Tennessee and in Cullman and Lauderdale counties in Alabama. People from the Salzburg region celebrate their heritage in Georgia, while those of Moravian descent can be found in both Georgia and North Carolina.

French Huguenots settled in the port city of Charleston, South Carolina, but it was in Louisiana that their culinary traditions truly flourished. [See the following essay on Cajun and Creole cooking.] Today, Cajun and Creole traditions are so strongly identified with south Louisiana that one tends to forget that the state is home to other ethnic groups as well. Eastern European Jews, for example, came to the region as early as 1733. Italians settled not only in Louisiana but also in eastern Florida, Alabama, and Arkansas. Many of their food traditions are tied to religious observances. The St. Joseph altars found throughout Louisiana, for example, are loaded with spaghettis, breads, cookies, and fish — but not meat. These foods are blessed as the ceremony begins. The public is served after the saints, and any food not eaten is given to the needy. Similarly, such dishes as kibbee, tabouli, humous, and baklava are now familiar to many southerners simply because Lebanese and Syrian people proudly shared their traditional foods with their new neighbors.

Asian Americans are seldom associated with southern cooking, but history suggests that to overlook their contribution would be a mistake. In the nineteenth century, as plantation agriculture declined, the owners stopped furnishing foodstuffs to their tenants. The Chinese living in the Louisiana and Mississippi Delta filled an important economic void by opening small grocery and supply stores that largely served the rural population. The Chinese have retained their distinct identity by relying on their nuclear and extended families and by preserving their many cultural traditions.

Cuban populations arrived in the South in the early 1800s, not, as some might assume, with the much-publicized sealift of the 1980s. In fact, since 1959, when the bulk of Cuban citizens settled in Florida, Cubans have formed distinct ethnic communities that have had their impact on southern food customs. Grocery stores and restaurants cater to dietary habits of Cuban descendants, as do countless homecooked meals. Latin cooking is also having a perceptible, if slow, effect on the broader southern palate. The same is true of Southeast Asian cooking. Immigrants from Vietnam, Cambodia, and Laos first began arriving in the 1950s, but their numbers have increased dramatically since the 1960s and 1970s. Each nationality has maintained its distinct cultural and ethnic characteristics, but Southeast Asian foods are slowly becoming better known — and appreciated — by their fellow southerners.

Everything from interstate highways to television to movies to "super" stores that aggressively market a wide variety of foodstuffs is having an effect on the way southerners regard their culinary traditions.

Clearly, the blending of traditions continues in the South, motivated by economic change, shifts in population, and emerging social patterns. For one thing, the indigenous population of the South is becoming more mobile. People move out of the region and then come back home again, joined by those of other regions searching for economic opportunities in the Sunbelt. These days, everything from interstate highways to television to movies to "super" stores that aggressively market a wide variety of foodstuffs is having an effect on the way southerners regard their culinary traditions. A number of southerners seem eager to try new dishes and new methods of food preparation. Brunswick stew, for example, no longer must contain squirrel and butter — margarine and another meat may be substituted. And microwave ovens are replacing the gas and electric stove in many households — just as these appliances replaced coal and wood stoves two generations ago.

But the essence of southern food traditions remains unchanged. Fried chicken is still plentiful at church suppers and "dinners on the grounds." Iced tea served in small diners still arrives at your table heavily sugared. Black-eyed peas are served on New Year's Day. And at Christmas, Thanksgiving, and other holidays, you can usually spot some culinary clue to the celebrants' ethnic heritage.

Nevertheless, this is the South. So while tradition is observed at most meals and on formal occasions, almost anything can happen when dinner is served at night.

Tradition Well Blended

Cajun and Creole

❀ · ❀ · ❀ · ❀

Maida Owens

Returning home from south Louisiana's Grand Bayou, Cajun fishermen grin and greet their friends, wives, and children as they unload three hundred pounds of redfish and speckled trout from their boat. One man shows his wife and daughter-in-law a few flounder that he caught. The women suggest stuffing several for their guests as the other fishermen and their families fill the back yard to clean the day's catch in preparation for a party. Suddenly, everyone is busy, even the children, the older ones practicing the delicate art of filleting the trout. Because twenty-five people will eat this afternoon, the cooks fry fish on large outdoor burners, make fish stew, and pull from the freezer stuffed crabs to bake with the few flounder taken in today's catch. Extra fish will be divided among the families and frozen for later use.

Similar gatherings of family, friends, and neighbors occur every weekend in homes throughout south Louisiana. The groups may be a couple and their children living on a bayou who pick crab meat from the shell to sell to a seafood market, neighbors gathering for a boucherie in a farming community on the prairies, or friends having a back-yard crawfish boil in a suburban neighborhood. Other days, people may gather to shell and can peas, preserve figs, butcher a pig, or stuff boudin — all good, solid south Louisiana cooking and eating activities.

A Longtime Borrowing

To fully appreciate south Louisiana foods, one must remember that Cajun and Creole cooking are the products of three hundred years of continuous sharing and borrowing among the region's many ethnic groups. For example, the French contributed sauces (sauce piquante, étouffée, stew, bisque), sweets (pralines, a modified French confection with pecans instead of the original walnuts), and breads (French bread, beignets or square doughnuts with powdered sugar, and corasse, fried bread dough eaten with cane syrup).

The Spanish added jambalaya (a spicy rice dish probably from the Spanish paella). Africans contributed okra, barbecue, and deep-fat frying and reinforced the tendency toward hot spices. Germans, who arrived in Louisiana before the Acadians, contributed sausages (andouille and boudin) and "Creole" or brown mustard. Caribbean influence is seen in the bean and rice dishes of red beans and rice and congri (crowder peas and rice). Native Americans contributed filé and a fondness for corn bread.

However, by no means is this a complete history of Creole and Cajun foods of south Louisiana. Most families of the region also enjoy Italian pasta and stuffed artichokes. In New Orleans, every ethnic group claims the muffuletta, a large sandwich with several meats and cheeses. South of New Orleans in Plaquemines Parish, Yugoslavs have contributed their knowledge of oystering and growing oranges. And most recently, the Chinese and Vietnamese have added their food traditions to the region's culinary history — so much so that Asian restaurants enjoy enthusiastic support and Asian chefs have begun to use such Louisiana fare as crawfish.

This cultural complexity makes it difficult to define clearly or separate Cajun and Creole food. The task is made more difficult by considerable seasonal and regional diversity. For example, the coasts and bayous yield an abundance of seafood dishes, while the prairies of southwest Louisiana, where ranching is important, provide such beef dishes as tasso, a smoked meat used as seasoning, and grillades, beef smothered in a seasoned gravy. Other variations cannot be explained by regional or seasonal factors, however. Local cultural preferences are the more obvious reason why one is more likely to find a dark brown roux on the prairies and a lighter, more delicate one in New Orleans.

Gumbo and Good Gumbo

The pride that individual cooks take in developing their own distinctive styles also accounts for many differences within the region. The incredible variations of gumbo illustrate the individuality of south Louisiana cooks. And while everyone makes gumbo, few cooks agree on what makes good gumbo. Frequently cooks disagree on ingredients or on how dark and thick the roux should be. Gumbo is a souplike dish — descended from the French bouillabaisse and renamed from the West African word for okra, guingombo — that usually features two or more meats or seafood and is served with rice. The most common types of gumbo are okra gumbo and filé gumbo. Okra gumbo depends on the smothered, or sautéed, okra for thickening. Filé gumbo starts with a roux made with hot oil in which flour has been slowly browned. Before serving, filé (ground sassafras leaves) is sprinkled on top to thicken it. A third, less common gumbo, gumbo z'herbes, is meatless. Originally served during Lent, this gumbo uses a combination of seven greens. The most common gumbos are chicken-sausage and seafood gumbo (shrimp, crab, and oysters), but turkey, duck, ham, squirrel, and other meats are also used.

What Is Creole? What Is Cajun?

At one time, it may have been possible to say that Creole cooking was the fancier cooking of New Orleans with more European influences and Cajun cooking was the simpler foods of the country folk, but this is no longer true. Today, it is difficult to distinguish between Cajun and Creole cooking as they are practiced in the home. In fact, the terms *Cajun* and *Creole* are frequently used interchangeably or together. When applied to food, Creole most often refers to the haute cuisine of New Orleans restaurants that developed from the intensive blending of the city's various food traditions, many of which originated with European-trained chefs. For example, Jules Alciatore of Antoine's Restaurant introduced baked fish en papillote (in paper) and oysters Rockefeller. The experimentation continues with such dishes as seafood pasta introduced by Ralph and Kacoo's, a more recent successful Cajun restaurant.

Opposite: Nola Guidry of St. Martinville, Louisiana, peels crawfish at the 1976 festival. (Smithsonian Institution)

The word *Creole* itself is difficult to define. People within Louisiana apply it to different groups and their language and food. Some argue that the descendants of the French and Spanish colonists in New Orleans are the only true Creoles. But Creole also refers to those of Afro-French-Caribbean heritage, many of whom do not live exclusively in New Orleans. Still others use Creole to refer to French-speaking blacks in rural southwest Louisiana and to similar descendants who live along the Cane River in Natchitoches Parish.

Cajuns, by contrast, are descendants of Acadians who were expelled from Nova Scotia and found their way to Louisiana. Between 1765 and 1795 many settled on Bayou Lafourche, Bayou Teche, and the prairies of southwest Louisiana. There, they lived in relative isolation, although each community absorbed a unique combination of Germans, Spanish, and Anglo-Americans who learned French. Today, the Cajun culture blends all of these cultures.

The Isleños of St. Bernard Parish are neither Creole nor Cajun. These Spanish-speaking settlers arrived in Louisiana from the Canary Islands about the same time as the Cajuns. Until recently, they lived in relative isolation just to the southeast of New Orleans. They continue to speak Spanish and live off the land by trapping and fishing. Caldo, one of their favorite dishes, is a soup made with white beans, vegetables, and meat.

Every Gathering a Food Event

Whatever their origin, the people of south Louisiana enjoy talking about food, exchanging recipes, and collecting cookbooks. They argue about the best way to cook rice, how dark a roux should be, and whether tomatoes belong in a gumbo. And everyone enjoys experimenting with, preparing, and, of course, eating food. Therefore, it is not surprising that the average cook possesses highly skilled culinary standards. And because both men and

women take pride in their cooking — and enjoy any opportunity to show off their skills — every gathering becomes a food event. Family food events in particular become social functions. Through food, families maintain a sense of generation and extension. Older family members pass family lore to the younger ones, and individuals learn about their cultural identity as well as about their nieces, cousins, and aunts.

A final glimpse of our Cajun fishermen a few weeks after their fishing trip shows clearly the social functions of food preparation.

The young woman walks next door to her mother-in-law's house while her children run ahead to hug their Maw Maw. After a cup of dark roast coffee, they begin preparing crawfish heads for bisque, a time-consuming task. The day before, they parboiled two hundred pounds of crawfish, scraped and cleaned the body portion of the crawfish — called the head — and peeled the tails. Today, they chop and cook onions, garlic, and celery to make a stuffing that is thickened with French-bread crumbs. They then add the crawfish tails and cook the stuffing, remove the cooked stuffing from the heat, add raw eggs to hold together the mixture, fill each head with stuffing, roll it in flour, and put it aside to be frozen for later use.

While they cook, the children run in and out, stopping occasionally to help stuff the crawfish heads. The women catch up on family gossip, and the mother-in-law tells stories of her own childhood in the swamp, her marriage, and her family's move into the city when her son was young. As family lore is passed to the next generation, mother-in-law and daughter-in-law grow closer and the younger woman learns what it is to be a Cajun.

That night, crawfish heads are used to make crawfish bisque. After making a very dark roux, the women add onions, celery, and garlic. Once these are sautéed, they add crawfish tails and the heads. Later, they will serve the bisque with rice to their families.

Another day, when family or friends drop by unexpectedly, the women will pull a package of crawfish heads from the freezer to make bisque for dinner. Everyone will be amazed that so excellent a dish could be prepared so quickly. The women will just smile.

Through food, families maintain a sense of generation and extension. Older family members pass family lore to the younger ones, and individuals learn about their cultural identity as well as about their nieces, cousins, and aunts.

Recipes

Baked Raccoon with Sweet Potatoes

Country Pan Sausage

Barbecued Bologna Sandwiches

Chicken Pies

Louisiana Catfish

Canned Carp Fish Cakes

Mirlitons and Shrimp

Crawfish Etouffée

Crawfish Boil

Chicken and Sausage Gumbo
with Oysters

Rice Dressing (Jambalaya)

Jambalaya

Caldo (Spanish Soup)

Poke Salad

Maquechoux (Smothered Corn)

Stuffed Artichokes

Hot Chowchow Relish

Corn Relish

Tomato Preserves

Pepper Jelly

Saw Mill Gravy

Plum Jelly

Homemade Cracklings

Crackling Bread

Mississippi Hush Puppies

Southern Corn Bread

Buttermilk Biscuits

Homemade Bread

Corasse (Fried Bread Dough)

St. Joseph's Day Bread

Blackberry Dumplings

Cracker Pudding

Hrstule (Bow Ties)

Chess Pie

Yugoslavian Pusharatas

Strawberry Shortcake

Old-time Syrup Cake

Sweet Potato Pie

Fig Cake

Aunt Mary's Apple Stack Cake

Fig Cookies

Old-fashioned Molasses Cookies

Syrup Pull Candy

Mississippi Pralines

New Orleans Creamy Pralines

Hot Mulled Wine

Baked Raccoon with Sweet Potatoes

"This recipe for raccoon is baked in a sauce and with sweet potatoes. I've done a few."

1 medium raccoon
salt
pepper
1 quart tomatoes, chopped
1 large onion, chopped
½ cup apple cider vinegar
½ cup brown sugar
6 to 8 sweet potatoes

1. Boil raccoon until tender, about 2 hours. Remove from liquid and drain. Put in a rectangular baking dish and season well with salt and pepper.

2. While raccoon is boiling, make a sauce with tomatoes, onion, vinegar, and sugar. Cook mixture on low heat until thick. Pour over meat.

3. Boil sweet potatoes until tender; remove skins and place around raccoon in baking dish. Bake for 1 hour at 325°F.

Mildred Johnson, Union City, Tennessee. Tennessee Program, 1986

Country Pan Sausage

5 pounds fresh pork
shoulder (or boned
ham), 80% lean
and 20% fat
1 tablespoon salt
1 ounce pepper
1 ounce ground sage
1 ounce red pepper
flakes
shortening, for frying

1. Cut meat into small pieces that will go through a meat grinder with a medium-grind plate.

2. Mix seasonings by hand and put on meat before grinding. If meat is too coarse, regrind, then mix thoroughly by hand to blend seasonings into meat. If meat is too thick and hard to mix, add a cup of water.

3. Pat meat into serving-size patties on wax-paper squares. Cook well in a frying pan with a small amount of shortening.

Fred and Bessie Kate Bentley, Pelham, Georgia. Community Activities and Food Preservation, 1980

"For good country Deep South eating, serve this sausage with syrup and biscuits and butter and hot coffee. Split open a biscuit and place the butter and sausage on it. Then close the biscuit back up and sop it with syrup."

Barbecued Bologna Sandwiches

Sauce:
¼ cup chopped onion
1 tablespoon butter
½ cup water
3 to 4 tablespoons
white vinegar

1 tablespoon Worces-
tershire sauce
¼ cup lemon juice
2 tablespoons brown
sugar
2 tablespoons honey
1 cup chili sauce

½ teaspoon salt
¼ teaspoon pepper

deli-style bologna
slices, ½ inch thick
white bread

1. Sauté onions in butter until almost brown. Add water, vinegar, Worcestershire sauce, lemon juice, sugar, honey, chili sauce, salt, and pepper. Simmer for 20 minutes on moderate heat until slightly thickened.

2. Grill both sides of bologna on a preheated charcoal grill and remove.

3. Marinate bologna in warm barbecue sauce for about 20 minutes. Serve on white bread with coleslaw or baked beans. Yields 2 cups.

Chuck Hauer, Memphis, Tennessee. Tennessee Program, 1986

"I was trained as an architect, but I've been a dedicated enthusiast of southern cooking since the days when I grew up in Natchez, Mississippi. Cooking holds a family together. I should know — I brought my father, sisters, brothers, nephews, and friends to help me cook at the folklife festival."

Chicken Pies

"In our household, we six children could always tell if the day was special — that's because momma made chicken pies. We children were taught to make the pastry and do other jobs involved in making chicken pies. Everyone quickly learned that with chicken pies, your middle name is 'flour' — flour on your nose, flour up to your elbows, and flour on your pants or skirt."

Filling:
4 tablespoons oil (or shortening)
6 tablespoons flour
1 large onion, diced
3 2½-pound chickens, cut up
salt
freshly ground pepper

3 stalks celery, chopped
1 green pepper, chopped
2 4-ounce cans mushrooms, drained
1 handful chopped green onions
1 handful chopped parsley

Dough:
8 to 9 cups flour
1 tablespoon salt
1¾ cups shortening
2½ cups cold water
3 egg yolks, beaten with a little water

1. For filling, make a roux of oil or shortening and flour, stirring constantly until brown. Add onion, cooking until golden.

2. Stir in chicken, seasoned with salt and pepper. Add celery and green pepper. Pour in enough water to almost cover chicken. Simmer, covered, for about 40 minutes or until tender. Add mushrooms, green onions, and parsley to stock. Simmer, uncovered, for about 20 minutes more to reduce sauce. Skin and bone chicken and return to sauce. Cool in refrigerator.

3. To make dough, combine 8 cups flour, salt, and ½ cup shortening in a bowl. Add water and stir until ingredients come together in a ball. If needed, add more water. Roll out dough into a square about ½ inch thick.

4. Spread another ½ cup shortening over dough, as for puff pastry. Sprinkle flour over shortening and fold, making two horizontal folds. Spread 1 tablespoon shortening at each end and sprinkle flour over shortening. Fold one end over the other like an envelope. Refrigerate for 30 minutes.

5. Roll out dough into a square again and repeat steps above; this time, however, do not set aside. Cut dough into 12 equal squares, then cut each in half. Roll each half, one at a time, into a flat circle. Fill each circle with 1 heaping tablespoon of chicken mixture. Fold over edges, crimping with fork tines.

6. Paint the pies with egg mixture. Bake at 400°F degrees for 20 to 30 minutes or until golden brown. Yields 3 dozen.

Aline M. Garrett, St. Martinville, Louisiana. The Grand Generation: Folklore and Aging, 1984

Louisiana Catfish

4½ cups water
1 8-ounce can tomato
    sauce
2 tablespoons oil
1 cup chopped onions
¾ cup chopped green
    onion tops
½ cup chopped
    parsley
1 tablespoon salt
1 teaspoon cayenne
    pepper
¼ teaspoon pepper
8 pieces catfish,
    1 inch thick
¾ cup flour

1. Combine water, tomato sauce, oil, onions, and parsley in a medium pot and bring to a boil. Cook on high heat for 15 minutes.

2. Season fish with peppers and salt, and roll in flour. Drop fish into boiling sauce, turn down heat, and cook on low heat for 35 minutes or until very tender. Serve over cooked rice. Serves 8.

Clementine Ardoin, Eunice, Louisiana. French American Program, 1983

"Folks here have been hunting and fishing in Louisiana lakes and bayous for their livelihood since they came to America. Preparing foods — especially catfish — brought home from those trips has always been a part of life for a Louisiana housewife."

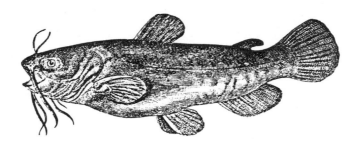

Canned Carp Fish Cakes

carp
½ teaspoon salt
1 egg
flour
cornmeal

1. Clean and cut carp into pieces; pack in pint jars with salt in each.

2. Seal jars and put in a pressure cooker or water bath. Cook for 10 to 15 minutes in pressure cooker or 20 minutes in water bath. Store in pantry.

3. To cook, open two pint jars of carp and put in a bowl with egg and enough flour and cornmeal to make fish stick together. Pat into small cakes and fry until brown on both sides.

Mildred Johnson, Union City, Tennessee. Tennessee Program, 1986

"These fish recipes were mostly used during depression days and when we were raising our six children. Because we never had money to run to town and get more modern food, we lived on what we could get off the farm and off Reelfoot Lake."

"Growing up in the French Quarter and the Tremé district of New Orleans — the two most Creole sections of the city — put me in contact with people from many different racial and ethnic backgrounds. The things I experienced there heavily influenced my cooking.

As a young girl I was taught to cook by the aunt who raised me and also the woman who cooked at the school I attended. Later I married a man who also loved to cook. The dishes that he learned to prepare in the country where his family, and my mother's family, came from also influenced me. It was he who taught me, for example, to prepare hogshead cheese, or fromage de tête. He also taught me to prepare congri, the Afro-Caribbean dish that is similar to the congris (the 's' is pronounced) found in Latin America."

Mirlitons and Shrimp

6 medium mirlitons (chayote or vegetable pears)
1 medium onion, finely chopped
½ green pepper, finely chopped

½ cup whole green onions tops, finely chopped
¼ cup finely chopped parsley
¼ cup oil

1 pound shrimp, peeled and deveined
salt
pepper
½ teaspoon sugar
¼ cup seasoned bread crumbs (optional)

1. In a large pot of water, boil whole mirlitons until tender, about 20 minutes. Cool.

2. Sauté onions, pepper, and parsley until onions are translucent.

3. Peel mirlitons, remove seeds, and mash. Add to sauteed vegetables. Cook until water evaporates (mirlitons create a lot of liquid).

4. Add shrimp and cook another 15 minutes. Stir in salt, pepper, and sugar. Bread crumbs may be added to absorb excess moisture and firm the mixture. Serve with steamed rice. Serves 4.

Note: Mirlitons also may be stuffed. Do not peel them, but scoop out pulp, leaving shells intact. Follow directions as above, stuff, and bake for about 15 minutes at 325°F to brown bread crumbs sprinkled on top.

Carmen Ricard, New Orleans, Louisiana. Louisiana Program, 1985

Crawfish Etouffée

¼ pound butter
1 medium onion, finely chopped
1 green pepper, finely chopped
1 stalk celery, finely chopped

¼ cup cream
½ teaspoon cornstarch
1 pound crawfish tails with fat
salt
pepper

⅛ teaspoon cayenne pepper
2 green onion tops, chopped
¼ cup chopped parsley

1. Using a large, heavy pot, sauté onion, pepper, and celery in butter (not margarine) for 30 minutes over low heat, until onions become clear, not brown.

2. Blend cornstarch with cream to remove any lumps. Add mixture and crawfish fat to vegetables. Cook for 5 to 10 minutes more.

3. Add crawfish tails and cover pot. Cook on low heat for 10 minutes. Add salt and pepper, plus cayenne to taste, starting with ⅛ teaspoon.

4. Add chopped onion tops and parsley just before serving. Serve over steamed rice.

Note: For shrimp étouffée, substitute 1 pound jumbo shrimp, cleaned and deveined, for the crawfish. Serves 3 to 4.

Maude Ancelet, Lafayette, Louisiana. French American Program, 1983

"Etouffée is best when made simply. The key to success is to let the crawfish and butter have their say (margarine will not do).

Most of the recipes we made at the festival were dishes from our garden and the fruit trees in our yard. Our garden is huge and we love harvesting it. My son-in-law, Willert, catches shrimp so we don't have much to buy. "

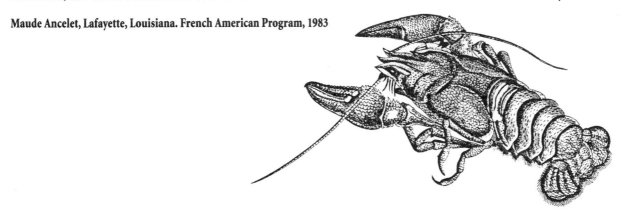

Crawfish Boil

15 pounds live
   crawfish
1 cup salt
¼ to ½ cup cayenne
   pepper
3 onions, chopped
2 green peppers,
   chopped
3 to 5 potatoes
3 to 5 ears corn

1. Boil a large kettle of water with enough water to cover crawfish. Add salt, cayenne pepper, onions, and green pepper.

2. Put in crawfish (3 to 5 pounds per person) and potatoes (1 or 2 per person). Boil for about 10 minutes. Add corn and boil until tender. Serves 3 to 5.

Nola and Sidney Guidry, St. Martinville, Louisiana. Louisiana Regional Program, 1976

"I was born and raised in St. Martinville, Louisiana, where my parents caught crawfish. Our three sons are carrying on our crawfish business now. The corn and potatoes in this recipe will absorb the hot spices and go perfectly with the crawfish."

Nola Guidry

"To make a good roux, constant stirring is a must. Don't answer the door if there's a knock, and don't answer the phone if it rings — a roux needs constant attention, so keep your eyes riveted to the inside of the pot the whole time. Start with slightly more flour than oil (the amount will depend on quality and recipe), making a cream-colored paste. About halfway through the process, the roux will become more liquid, but it will thicken to paste consistency again as it is nearing completion. Remember, stick with your stirring spoon.

As you become experienced, you will find that you can cook with a fairly high heat, but at first it is safer to reduce the heat until you get a feel for what is called stopping the roux. This involves recognizing the desired color — a rich brown (like a Hershey bar) for gumbos and a golden brown (like caramel) for piquante sauces, adding the chopped onions, celery, and pepper and removing the pot from the heat, still stirring all the while."

Chicken and Sausage Gumbo with Oysters

1½ cups oil
2 cups flour
3 medium onions, chopped
1 green pepper, chopped
2 stalks celery, chopped
1 gallon water
1 frying chicken (or hen or Guinea hen), cut up
2 cloves garlic
cayenne pepper
1½ pounds fresh seasoned pork (or beef) sausage
salt
pepper
1 pint oysters, with juice
green onion tops
parsley
flour (not self-rising)
oil (not olive)

1. To make a roux, use a heavy pot and heat oil until hot before adding flour. Cook to a rich brown.

2. Add onions, pepper, and celery. Lower heat and stir 1 minute longer so that roux will not continue cooking.

3. Slowly add water, stirring constantly. Bring to a rapid boil. Lower heat, then add chicken, garlic, and cayenne. (Old hens make better gumbo, but Guinea hens sometimes are considered the best.)

4. In a separate pot, cook sausage on low heat until brown. Remove grease and add sausage to gumbo. Salt and pepper to taste. Simmer about 1 hour if using a frying chicken, 1½ to 2 hours if using a Guinea hen, or 2 to 3 hours for an old hen.

5. Add oysters with juice, onion tops, and parsley and turn off heat. Serves 6.

Maude Ancelet, Lafayette, Louisiana. French American Program, 1983

Rice Dressing (Jambalaya)

4 to 5 tablespoons oil
2 pounds ground beef
1 pound fresh pork sausage, skins removed
½ pound dressing mix (ground liver, heart, and kidneys)

2 eggplants, chopped in ¼-inch cubes
1 large onion, chopped
1 medium green pepper, chopped
3 stalks celery, chopped

3 cloves garlic, minced
2 cups water
salt
pepper
cayenne pepper
4 cups uncooked white rice

1 small box mixed wild and white rice

½ cup green onion tops

½ cup chopped parsley

mushrooms, sliced (optional)

1. In a heavy pot, begin browning meats in oil. Add eggplant, onion, pepper, celery, and garlic. Stir well, cover, and sauté until meat is brown. Uncover and add water, salt, pepper, and cayenne pepper to taste. Simmer until meats and seasonings are cooked, about 1 hour.

2. Add onion tops and parsley. Sliced fresh mushrooms also may be added.

3. Cook rice according to directions. Thoroughly blend meat sauce and rice. Serves 16.

Maude Ancelet

> **"When visitors to the folklife festival were allowed to taste the results of our demonstrations, the samples disappeared in no time. Once I was so distressed at running out of food that I went behind the tent to cry. 'But Mama,' my son Barry said, trying to console me, 'we didn't come here to feed all of Washington!'"**

Jambalaya

½ pound sausage (smoked or pork), sliced

2 onions, finely chopped

1 bunch shallots, finely chopped

½ head garlic, minced

2 green peppers, finely chopped

4 stalks celery, finely chopped

oil, for cooking

1 4-ounce can tomato sauce

1 8-ounce can stewed tomatoes

2 bay leaves

2 pounds shrimp

½ pound crab meat (optional)

1 cup water

salt

pepper

2 to 3 cups cooked white rice

soy sauce

chopped parsley, for garnish

> **"I have my grown family and their children over every Sunday for dinner — sometimes we have as many as forty people. I love cooking and seeing them enjoying my food. In Louisiana, this jambalaya recipe is often varied by adding oysters or meat."**

1. Sauté sausage and chopped vegetables in a small amount of cooking oil.

2. Stir in tomato sauce, stewed tomatoes, and bay leaves; simmer for 15 minutes.

3. Add shrimp, crab meat, and water. Cook until shrimp is tender, about 15 minutes. Salt and pepper to taste.

4. Remove from heat. Add cooked rice. Mix well and sprinkle with soy sauce. Add fresh parsley. Let stand for 15 minutes or more before serving. Serves 6.

Louise Perez, St. Bernard, Louisiana. Louisiana Program, 1985

Caldo (Spanish Soup)

"The family of my husband, Irvan, is Isleno, originally from the Canary Islands. Although I have an Italian background and his is Spanish, we both grew up farming and fishing in Louisiana. We still grow a lot of vegetables and have fig, pear, and peach trees that produce enough for us to can and give away to family and friends. This soup is adapted from a recipe more than 200 years old. I learned it from my husband's grandmother, and I'm often asked to make it at our local festivals."

½ pound dried white beans
3 or 4 thick slices pickled pork (or slightly salted pork)
1 pound fresh snap beans (or 1 large can French-cut string beans)
2 turnips, quartered
2 to 3 carrots, cut into 2 to 3 pieces

2 yellow onions, finely chopped
1 package frozen mixed vegetables
1 package frozen lima beans
4 to 5 pieces corn-on-the-cob
6 red potatoes, quartered
1 can peas
1 8-ounce can stewed tomatoes

1 can whole corn
1 4-ounce can tomato sauce
1 small head cabbage, cut into small pieces
3 yellow squash, sliced (optional)
4 sweet potatoes, quartered

1. Wash beans and place in a large soup pot. Fill pot half- to three-quarters full with water. Add more water later, if needed for desired consistency.

2. When beans are half-cooked, add meat. When meat is almost tender, add all vegetables except cabbage, squash, and sweet potatoes. When red potatoes are half-tender, add cabbage, then squash, if desired.

3. In a small amount of broth from soup, cook sweet potatoes until tender. Serve with caldo.

Louise Perez, St. Bernard, Louisiana. Louisiana Program, 1985

Poke Salad

4 quarts young tender
poke shoots (or 2
cans poke salad
greens)
¼ cup bacon
drippings
1 teaspoon salt
3 eggs

1. Wash poke shoots well. Place in a large kettle with water to cover and bring to a boil. Drain. Cover again with water, bring to a boil, and cook for another 20 minutes. Drain well.

2. Place in a cast-iron frying pan with bacon drippings and salt. Cook at medium heat for 30 minutes.

3. Add eggs and stir until eggs are done. Serve with corn bread and green onions.

Janice Miracle, Middlesboro, Kentucky. Kentucky Program, 1973

"Pokeweed is a wild plant that grows almost anywhere there is a lot of sun. The roots are extremely poisonous but have been used for various medicinal purposes. The tender young shoots are edible and are considered a delicacy. With the coming of spring in the southern Appalachian Mountains arrives the craving for poke salad. Each June a Poke Salad Festival is held in Harlan, Kentucky. They serve many different poke dishes including the famous poke berry wine."

Maquechoux (Smothered Corn)

12 ears tender yellow
corn
2 fresh tomatoes,
chopped
1 green pepper,
chopped
1 onion, chopped
2 cloves garlic,
minced
½ cup oil
¼ cup water
¼ cup milk
salt
pepper
cayenne pepper
pinch of sugar

1. Cut corn from cob with a sharp knife. With the back of the knife, scrape the cob to remove all juice.

2. Put all ingredients in a heavy pot and cook on low heat, stirring occasionally for a few minutes. Cover and cook for about 1 hour, stirring occasionally.

Maude Ancelet, Lafayette, Louisiana. French American Program, 1983

Stuffed Artichokes

"A large number of Sicilian and Italian families settled in Louisiana to farm. I come from Italian roots — our family moved to St. Bernard Parish, about forty-five minutes from New Orleans. Although we may have adopted some Cajun and Creole dishes, we maintain our strong Italian ties. For example, this artichoke dish is usually served on Good Friday or other holidays."

Stuffing:

12 ounces Italian bread crumbs
8 ounces Romano or Parmesan cheese, grated
1 bunch shallots, finely chopped
4 stalks celery, finely chopped
½ cup finely chopped parsley
2 onions
1 head garlic
2 eggs, slightly beaten
juice of 1 lemon
pepper
olive oil

5 artichokes

1. In a large bowl, mix all stuffing ingredients. (No salt is needed, as cheese is salty.)

2. Wash artichokes with hot water to help open the leaves. Trim tops and bottoms. Open and stuff each leaf with stuffing, one at a time, starting with the outer leaves and going around until the center is reached. Put extra stuffing on the top.

3. Place artichokes in a large pot, side by side. Add 2 cups salted water and a small amount of olive oil. Pour additional olive oil over each artichoke.

4. Cover and simmer until tender. Artichokes are ready when the leaves are tender enough to be picked off easily.

5. Remove cover and allow to dry out on low heat for about 10 minutes. Serves 5.

Louise Perez, St. Bernard, Louisiana. Louisiana Program, 1985

Hot Chowchow Relish

1 quart chopped cabbage
1½ cups diced onion
1½ cups diced green pepper
1 red bell pepper, chopped

1½ cups chopped green tomatoes
3 to 4 cucumbers, diced
½ to 1 cup salt
1 quart vinegar
1 cup water

2½ cups sugar
5 large hot peppers
1 tablespoon dry mustard
1 tablespoon tumeric
1 tablespoon pickling spice

1. Combine all chopped vegetables; sprinkle with salt. Let stand for 5 hours or overnight. Drain well.

2. Combine vinegar, water, sugar, and spices. Simmer for 10 minutes, add vegetables, then bring to a boil. Pack mixture in hot, sterilized jars and seal. Process in hot water for 15 minutes. Yields 8 pints.

Sarah Mae Albritton, Ruston, Louisiana. Louisiana Program, 1985

Corn Relish

18 ears corn kernels
6 large onions, chopped
6 green peppers, chopped
3 red bell peppers, chopped
½ gallon vinegar
2 tablespoons salt
1 cup mustard

2 tablespoons dry mustard
3 cups sugar
6 green tomatoes, chopped

1. Mix all ingredients.

2. Cook on medium heat for 45 minutes. Pack in sterilized jars and process in hot water for 15 minutes. Yields 7 to 9 pints.

Minnie Pearl Brown, Tifton, Georgia. Community Activities and Food Preservation, 1980

Tomato Preserves

2 gallons ripe tomatoes
10 cups sugar
½ teaspoon nutmeg

1. Scald tomatoes in boiling water for several minutes. Remove and run under cold water to slip off skins. Chop.

2. Mix with sugar and nutmeg and cook for 1½ hours until thick. Pour into sterilized jars and seal. Yields 7 pints.

Minnie Pearl Brown

Pepper Jelly

1 cup chopped green
  peppers
3 banana peppers,
  seeded and
  chopped
½ cup chopped hot
  peppers
1½ cups apple cider
  vinegar
6½ cups sugar
½ teaspoon salt
1 6-ounce bottle
  gelling agent

1. Combine peppers, vinegar, sugar, and salt. Boil for 20 minutes.

2. Add gelling agent and cook for 10 minutes. A few drops of green or yellow food coloring may be added. Pour into hot pint jars. Yields 6 to 8 pints.

Peggy Miller, Sylvester, Georgia. Community Activities and Food Preservation, 1980

Saw Mill Gravy

1 tablespoon bacon
  drippings
3 heaping tablespoons
  white cornmeal
½ teaspoon salt
2 cups milk
dash of pepper

1. Place bacon drippings in a pan. Add cornmeal and salt. Cook on medium heat, stirring until brown.

2. Add milk and let boil until it thickens, stirring vigorously to keep it from lumping. Season with pepper to taste.

Janice Miracle, Middlesboro, Kentucky. Kentucky Program, 1973

"During the early years of our country, many logging camps sprung up in the mountains where virgin timber was prevalent. In these lumber camps cooks would prepare breakfast for a hundred or so hungry lumberjacks. One of the common foods was gravy made from coarsely ground cornmeal. When made from whole-grain cornmeal, this gravy was very nutritious and would give the lumberjacks strength to carry out their jobs.

The gravy's name comes from the fact that these men worked at a saw mill, and sometimes when the gravy would be coarse and thick, the lumberjacks would accuse the cooks of substituting sawdust for cornmeal."

Plum Jelly

5 pounds tart plums
   with skin
3 cups water
7½ cups sugar
1 box fruit pectin

1. Crush plums, add water, cover, and boil for 15 minutes.

2. To extract juice, pour plums into a colander, press out juice, and cool. This should produce 5½ cups.

3. Pour juice into a damp jelly bag over a stand or colander and drain. To get a clear jelly, do not squeeze the bag.

4. Pour juice into a kettle and stir in sugar. Cook on high heat until it comes to a rolling boil that cannot be stirred down.

5. Add pectin and boil until jelly sheets form on a spoon. Remove from heat and quickly skim off foam. Pour immediately into hot containers and seal. Yields 4 pints.

Sarah Mae Albritton, Ruston, Louisiana. Louisiana Program, 1985

"When I was seven years old — Lord, that was a long time ago, in 1943 — mother sent my sisters and me to pick wild plums and blackberries. It was a three-mile walk down the railroad track to the berry patch. We picked for a long time because motherdear told us to pick three gallons of berries and one gallon of plums. Picking berries was hard, and the red bugs almost ate us up.

When we got home, motherdear put coal oil (kerosene) on our legs and arms.

That night we bragged on who would eat the most jelly. Motherdear called us into the kitchen and let us lick the large black pot. Boy, was it good.

The following morning, motherdear fixed our breakfast: rice, salt pork, biscuits, and one spoonful of jelly. I ate my jelly fast and asked for more. Motherdear said no, and went into all the reasons why I could not have any more. She only earned $3 per week, there was a depression, sugar was rationed, and so on. Her reasons were good enough, but I just kept begging and she kept saying 'no more jelly today.' 'Please mother.' 'No!'

I could see motherdear getting upset. I was really mad. I ran from the kitchen and went under the house, crying. 'When I grow up and get me a job,' I said, 'I'm going to make all the damn jelly I please and my children can eat all they want.' I kept this promise."

Homemade Cracklings

5 cups fresh pork
fatback with skin
shortening

**"Cracklings are
especially good with
baked sweet potatoes. You
also may cut the meat off
the rind and use the meat
to season dried peas and
beans or greens."**

1. Cut fatback into 1½-inch pieces. Put in a slow cooker or fish cooker with enough shortening to cover meat.

2. Cook on high heat until meat floats to the top of the grease. Serve.

3. Use remaining skins to make pork rinds by parching them in the oven at 350°F until fluffy, about 30 minutes.

Fred and Bessie Kate Bentley, Pelham, Georgia. Community Activities and Food Preservation, 1980

Crackling Bread

2 cups cracklings
(see preceding
recipe)
½ teaspoon salt
5 cups cornmeal
water, hot

1. Preheat oven to 350°F.

2. Soak cracklings in hot water to cover.

3. Combine cornmeal with salt. Add enough hot water to make a soft dough. Mix in cracklings. Shape dough into pones (small oblong loaves) or hoe cakes and bake until golden brown, about 45 minutes.

Fred and Bessie Kate Bentley

Mississippi Hush Puppies

1½ cups white
cornmeal
½ cup sifted flour
2½ teaspoons baking
powder
1 teaspoon salt
¼ teaspoon pepper
½ cup milk

1 egg, beaten
⅓ cup finely chopped
onion
3 tablespoons fat
(or oil), melted

1. Sift together dry ingredients. Add remaining ingredients and stir just until blended.

2. Drop by tablespoons into deep fat that has been heated to 350°F. Fry for 2 to 3 minutes, or until golden brown. Drain. Yields 18.

Catfish Farmers of Mississippi, Jackson, Mississippi. Mississippi Program, 1974

Southern Corn Bread

2 cups cornmeal
¼ cup flour
3 teaspoons baking
　powder
1 teaspoon salt
¼ teaspoon baking
　soda
2 egg yolks
1½ cups milk
2 tablespoons short-
　ening, melted

1. Preheat oven to 450°F.

2. Combine all ingredients and mix well.

3. Pour batter into a hot, greased cast-iron frying pan and bake for 25 to 30 minutes.

Ora Watson, Deep Gap, North Carolina. Corn Culture, 1969

"My grandmother taught all of us children how to cook. I raised seven children on a wood stove. I canned all our vegetables and baked all our bread and cakes and cookies. I am eighty-two years old and I still quilt and cook for me and my husband."

Buttermilk Biscuits

2 cups flour
2¼ teaspoons baking
　powder
¼ teaspoon baking
　soda
1 teaspoon salt
⅓ cup shortening
¾ cup buttermilk
2 teaspoons shorten-
　ing, melted

1. Preheat oven to 450°F.

2. Sift flour and then measure. Combine with remaining dry ingredients and resift 3 times.

3. Cut in shortening with a pastry blender or rub with fingertips. Stir in buttermilk until thoroughly mixed.

4. Turn dough onto a lightly floured surface and knead about a dozen times. Roll out to ½ to ¾ inch thick, then cut with a floured biscuit cutter. Place biscuits on a greased baking sheet. Brush tops with melted shortening. Bake for 12 to 15 minutes. Yields 14 to 16.

Ora Watson

Homemade Bread

"**My mother was of German descent and married into a French family. She baked bread every day and always took a part of the dough out to make a morning corasse.**"

1 package dry yeast
2 cups water at room temperature
½ teaspoon salt
2 tablespoons sugar
2 tablespoons oil
5½ cups flour

1. Soak yeast in water. Add salt, sugar, and oil.

2. Gradually add flour and knead dough until smooth. Let dough rise. Roll, then let rise again.

3. Divide into two loaves. Let rise until double in size. Bake at 375°F for 30 to 35 minutes, or make corasse (following recipe). Yields 2 loaves.

Lucy Sedotal, Pierre Part, Louisiana. Louisiana Program, 1985

Corasse (Fried Bread Dough)

1 homemade bread dough (see preceding recipe)
1 quart oil
1 pint maple (or cane) syrup

1. Let the bread dough rise overnight.

2. Heat oil until very hot. Pull off 1-inch square pieces of dough, and stretch into a long and thin circle. Fry until light brown. Repeat with remaining dough. Serve with syrup for breakfast.

Lucy Sedotal

St. Joseph's Day Bread

12 tablespoons sugar
5 teaspoons salt
4 cups warm water
6 packages dry yeast
5 pounds flour

5 double-yolk or
    extra-large eggs
14 tablespoons
    shortening

1 teaspoon anise
    flavoring
oil
beaten egg
sesame seeds

1. Stir sugar and salt into warm water, then add yeast.

2. Add about half of the flour and mix well with a wooden spoon. Stir in 1 egg and a little shortening; alternate eggs and shortening while mixing well. Add anise at the end and mix.

3. Add remaining flour and mix gently to avoid toughening the bread. Knead well. Pour in a little oil and knead well.

4. Put dough in a well-oiled large bowl, cover, and let rise in a warm place for about 1 hour.

5. After the first rising, punch down the dough and knead again. Let rise 1 more hour. Knead again, then cut into small pieces and make desired shapes, such as fish, braided wreaths, and loaves; larger pieces such as crosses may be made. Put in pans to rise again. Brush with beaten egg and sprinkle with sesame seeds.

6. Bake at 375°F until brown on top. Be sure that smaller loaves do not overcook; large pieces should be baked at a lower temperature such as 300°F for several hours.

Lucy Mike King, Hammond, Louisiana. Louisiana Program, 1985

"It is a Sicilian tradition to prepare elaborate food-filled altars to honor St. Joseph's Day (March 19) every year in my Italian community in Hammond, Louisiana. I've been baking this symbolic bread in shapes such as lambs, crosses, ladders, and other religious figures for more than sixty years."

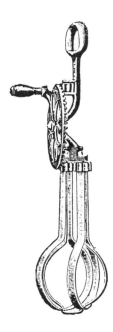

Blackberry Dumplings

Dough:
3 to 4 cups self-rising
   flour
½ cup milk
½ cup buttermilk
1 cup shortening

1 quart blackberries
1 cup sugar
2 cups water

1. To make dumplings, fill a large mixing bowl almost full with sifted flour and make a hole in the middle. Mix in buttermilk, milk, and shortening. Knead dough, then tear off pieces.

2. Bring blackberries, sugar, and water to a boil. Drop in dumpling dough. Cover and simmer until dough is done.

Bessie Mae Eldreth, Boone, North Carolina. Cultural Conservation and Language: America's Many Voices — Appalachian Americans, 1987

Cracker Pudding

6 eggs, separated
1 can sweetened
   condensed milk
2 cans evaporated
   milk
1 evaporated-milk
   can water

2 teaspoons vanilla
   extract
¼ pound butter,
   melted
¾ pound crackers
6 tablespoons sugar

1 teaspoon vanilla
   extract
1 teaspoon baking
   powder

1. Preheat oven to 400°F.

2. Stir egg yolks, add condensed milk, evaporated milk, water, vanilla, and butter. Crumble crackers into mixture. Put in a buttered 9 × 13-inch glass baking dish. Let set for 10 to 15 minutes.

3. Beat egg whites to soft peaks. Add sugar and vanilla and beat. Add baking powder and beat until stiff. Pour over pudding mixture. Bake for 8 to 10 minutes or until light brown. Serve warm or cool.

Lucy Sedotal, Pierre Part, Louisiana. Louisiana Program, 1985

Hrstule (Bow Ties)

6 egg yolks
2 tablespoons white vinegar
2 tablespoons whiskey
2 tablespoons lemon juice
1 teaspoon vanilla extract
4 tablespoons sugar
1 teaspoon salt
3 cups cake flour
oil, for frying
powdered sugar

1. Combine egg yolks, vinegar, whiskey, lemon juice, and vanilla.

2. Mix sugar, salt, and flour and add to wet ingredients. Make a soft dough similar to a pie crust.

3. Divide dough into 6 pieces and form each into a ball. Roll out each ball as thin as possible. Cut dough into 10 to 12 strips about 1-inch wide. Fold over each strip and fry in deep oil. Drain on paper towels, then sprinkle with powdered sugar.

Alena Cerinich and Jackie Gilich, Biloxi, Mississippi. Mississippi Program, 1974

Chess Pie

½ pound butter
3 cups sugar
2 tablespoons flour
6 eggs
1 can evaporated milk
2 teaspoons vanilla extract
3 8-inch pie crusts

1. Preheat oven to 300°F.

2. Cream butter, sugar, and flour. Slowly stir in eggs. Then add milk and vanilla and mix well.

3. Pour into unbaked pie crusts and bake for about 45 minutes. Pie is done when the center is set.

Helen Howard, Henderson, Tennessee. Tennessee Program, 1986

"I learned to make these Yugoslavian pastries from my father, Steve Martin Sekul, and my mother, Elena Trebotich Sekul. They were both born on the island of Brac on the Dalmatian Coast of Yugoslavia on the beautiful Adriatic Sea and emigrated to the United States in 1903.

My first recollection of my father making the pastries was around holidays, especially Christmas. He would always start making them before Midnight Mass. Our whole family — my one brother and my four sisters and myself — would gather to enjoy this tradition. As our family grew, our spouses, children, and other relatives would join in the festive occasion where we would sing Yugoslav songs and dance to the delightful folk music of the country. I am now continuing this rich heritage with my own children and grandchildren."

Jackie Gilich

Yugoslavian Pusharatas

"There is a great settlement of Yugoslavian people on the Mississippi Gulf Coast, especially in my hometown of Biloxi. Some of our leading citizens are of Yugoslav descent. The first doctors, lawyers, dentists, pharmacists, judges, priests, seafood packers, and restaurant and grocery store owners in Biloxi were Yugoslavian. The first ones to settle here, however, made their living as fishermen. They came to the Gulf Coast because it reminded them of the coast of Yugoslavia where they were born."

Jackie Gilich

2 pounds self-rising flour
2 tablespoons cinnamon
1 cup sugar
1½ cups chopped pecans
2 cups raisins
juice and grated rind from 2 oranges, separated

2 red apples, grated with peels
1 tablespoon lemon juice
¼ cup bourbon
¼ cup port wine
3 tablespoons vanilla extract
2 cups milk
oil, for frying

Icing:
3 pounds powdered sugar
1 large can evaporated milk
1 tablespoon vanilla extract

1. Sift flour and cinnamon; add sugar, pecans, raisins, orange rind, and apples. Mix well, adding orange juice, lemon juice, bourbon, port, and vanilla. Slowly add milk while mixing all ingredients. Batter should not be runny.

2. In a deep fryer, heat cooking oil to 350°F. With a teaspoon, drop mixture into hot oil. Cook until golden brown, then drain on paper towels.

3. Make icing by mixing powdered sugar, evaporated milk, and vanilla. Dip each pusharata in icing and let dry on wax paper.

Alena Cerinich and Jackie Gilich, Biloxi, Mississippi. Mississippi Program, 1974

Strawberry Shortcake

¼ pound butter
1 cup milk
1 cup self-rising flour
1 egg
1 cup sugar
1 quart strawberries
1 cup sugar

1. Preheat oven to 350°F.

2. Melt butter in a saucepan. Stir in milk; then add flour, egg, and sugar. Mix well and pour into a greased rectangular cake pan.

3. Bake for 35 to 40 minutes, or until a toothpick stuck in the center comes out clean.

4. Cut off caps of strawberries, wash until clean, slice, and combine well with sugar.

5. Spread strawberries over top of cooked short-cake. Serve with whipped topping.

Mildred Johnson, Union City, Tennessee. Tennessee Program, 1986

Old-time Syrup Cake

1 cup sugar
1 cup shortening (or margarine)
3 eggs
1 cup molasses
1 teaspoon baking soda
2 cups self-rising flour
1 teaspoon cinnamon
1 teaspoon cloves
1 teaspoon ginger
1 teaspoon allspice
⅔ cup boiling water

1. Preheat oven to 300°F.

2. Cream sugar and shortening. Add eggs and molasses, mixing after each addition.

3. Combine baking soda and flour. Add to egg mixture, then mix well with cinnamon, cloves, ginger, and allspice. Add water. Pour into a greased 9 × 13-inch pan.

4. Bake for 1 hour without opening the oven door.

Irene Bedell Blackwell, Covington, Louisiana. Louisiana Program, 1985

"We learned to cook a lot of things with the syrup we made from the cane we grew. We knew how the syrup was cooked off and canned and sealed. We helped our dad and mom do this. We never did have much real sugar in the house, so we had to use our molasses to sweeten our cookies and cakes and save the rock sugar for coffee and tea."

"I plowed the mule for fifty-seven years, and I could pick five hundred pounds of cotton in a day from when I was nine years old until I was fifty-three. At fifty-three years, I picked 612 pounds in one day. I was married to Florril Brown in the year of 1931. To this union fifteen children were born: twelve boys and three girls, with three sets of twins.

My husband drowned on January 15, 1968, and left me with seven children to raise, one boy in college, six in junior high school. I was the only one working. For $1.75 an hour, I worked seventeen to eighteen hours a day to try to make ends meet. Now God blessed me to raise eleven children, and he blessed me to work and pay for three homes. My house burned on March 14, 1968, and I lost everything I had, but God has been good to me. Now I have seventy-seven grandchildren, thirty-four great-grandchildren, thirty-three great-great-grandchildren, and I was at the Smithsonian Folklife Festival."

Minnie Pearl Brown

Sweet Potato Pie

6 medium sweet
  potatoes
½ pound butter
3½ cups sugar
dash of nutmeg
½ teaspoon allspice
  (or 1 teaspoon
  vanilla extract)
1 cup milk (or 1 can
  evaporated milk)
4 9-inch pie crusts

1. Peel sweet potatoes and cut into ¼-inch squares. Cover with water, boil until tender, then drain.

2. Preheat oven 400°F.

3. Mash potatoes in a bowl with a fork until smooth. Beat in butter, sugar, nutmeg, and allspice or vanilla. Add milk in small quantities until the filling reaches the proper consistency, similar to pumpkin pie filling (firm but not too thick). If filling seems too soft, do not use all of the milk. Pour into crusts.

4. Bake for 20 minutes, until crust is brown, then reduce heat to 350°F and bake for 15 minutes more (less for a gas oven).

Minnie Pearl Brown, Tifton, Georgia. Community Activities and Food Preservation, 1980

Fig Cake

3 eggs
1 cup sugar
2 cups flour
1 cup milk
¼ pound margarine
½ teaspoon baking
  soda
2 teaspoons
  cinnamon
1½ to 2 cups chopped
  pecans
1½ cups cooked fig
  preserves

1. Preheat oven to 350°F.

2. Beat together eggs and sugar. Add flour, milk, margarine, baking soda, and cinnamon. Blend and beat for 2 minutes. Add pecans and figs. Beat another minute.

3. Pour into a greased and floured bundt pan and bake for about 1 hour.

Maude Ancelet, Lafayette, Louisiana. French American Program, 1983

Aunt Mary's Apple Stack Cake

1 cup lard (or butter)
1 cup sugar
¾ cup molasses
1 egg
6½ to 7 cups flour
3 teaspoons baking powder

1½ teaspoons baking soda
½ teaspoon salt
1 teaspoon cinnamon (or ground cloves)
1 teaspoon ginger
1 cup buttermilk

Fruit topping:
2 16-ounce packages dried apples
sugar
1 teaspoon ginger
1 teaspoon cinnamon

"Aunt Mary was a paraplegic from age eight, but she lived to be eighty-six. Her mother, who lived to the age of 105, taught her how to make this masterpiece. Aunt Mary always made these cakes as gifts at Christmas."

1. Mix lard or butter, sugar, molasses, and egg. Beat until fluffy.

2. Sift 3 cups flour with baking powder, baking soda, salt, cinnamon or cloves, and ginger. Add to molasses mixture, small amounts at a time, alternating with buttermilk. Stir well after each addition. Add small amounts of remaining flour to dough, stirring until stiff enough to roll.

3. Preheat oven to 375°F. Divide dough into 8 pieces, each about the size of a medium orange. In a well-greased 9-inch cast-iron frying pan, pat out each round of dough to a thin circle. Dough will rise in baking to about ¼ inch thick.

4. Bake for about 20 minutes, or until all layers are cooked and golden brown. Take from oven and remove from pan. Cool.

5. To make topping, soak apples in water to cover overnight. Drain and cook on very low heat with sugar to taste until thick; add spices. Spread thinly between layers and on top of cake. Set in a cool place (but not the refrigerator), for 2 to 3 days until moist.

Janice Miracle, Middlesboro, Kentucky. Kentucky Program, 1973

Fig Cookies

"We grow our own figs in the back yard, and I put up a lot of fig preserves. Fig cookies and fig cake are the family's favorite way to use these preserves."

3 cups flour
2 cups sugar
3 eggs, slightly beaten
1 stick margarine, melted

1½ cups chopped pecans
½ teaspoon baking soda

1 teaspoon cinnamon
1½ cups cooked fig preserves, drained

1. Preheat oven to 350°F.

2. Combine all ingredients, using hands; batter will be very thick.

3. Spoon onto greased cookie sheets and bake for 15 to 18 minutes. Yields 4 dozen.

Maude Ancelet, Lafayette, Louisiana. French American Program, 1983

Old-fashioned Molasses Cookies

½ cup shortening
½ cup sugar
1 egg
1 cup molasses
1 tablespoon lemon juice
3½ cups flour, sifted
1 teaspoon cinnamon
¾ teaspoon ground cloves
½ teaspoon ginger
2 teaspoons baking soda
½ teaspoon salt
⅓ cup boiling water

1. Preheat oven to 350°F.

2. Cream shortening and sugar, and beat in egg. Add molasses and lemon juice. Blend well.

3. Sift dry ingredients. Add to creamed mixture, then add boiling water and mix. Chill thoroughly.

4. Drop by a teaspoon onto a greased and floured cookie sheet. Bake for 15 to 18 minutes.

Irene Bedell Blackwell, Covington, Louisiana. Louisiana Program, 1985

Syrup Pull Candy

1 quart Georgia cane
   syrup
1 tablespoon vinegar
1 cup nuts
2 tablespoons butter

1. Put all ingredients in a heavy saucepan. Bring to a boil on high heat. Cook to the hard-crack stage (300°F) on medium heat, about 30 minutes.

2. Pour into a buttered platter to cool. When cool enough to handle, pull until bright in color, about 15 minutes. With buttered hands, break candy into pieces.

Jewell and Grady Bryan, Sr., Lenox, Georgia. Community Activities and Food Preservation, 1980

"I grow green government cane. Some of it is planted in the fall, and some of it is grown from stubble (roots left in the ground). I fertilize it with 4-9-3 guano. I cut the cane down after the first frost and have it ground in a power mill. I have an old-timey mule-drawn mill for a standby in case the power mill breaks down.

I have a double furnace with two kettles. Fifty gallons of juice is poured into the kettle. This is cooked slow until all the skimmings or dregs are removed. Then the heat is increased. It takes about 2½ hours to cook a boiling of syrup. When it is ready to be taken up, the level of syrup will be back down to the level that the juice was when it was put in the kettle. The syrup is then strained and put in bottles or jars.

I have been making syrup for forty-nine years. I have five boys and five girls, seven of whom are married. There are sixteen grandchildren and two great-grandsons. They all love syrup and homemade biscuits. I remember my grandpa and daddy making syrup. Now my boys help me make syrup and plan to carry on the syrup-making tradition.**"**

Grady Bryan, Sr.

"We made pralines back in my childhood days. There was no TV, so family and friends would gather on my grandmother's porch, where we sang songs and told stories. My grandmother, mother, and I would go in the kitchen and make batches of pralines.

In 1938 we began making pralines in a shop on a very busy highway. We could barely keep up with demands, but we did and soon began shipping them all over the United States and Europe. As the girls got older, they worked in the shop making pralines like these."

Elouise S. Taillac

Mississippi Pralines

2½ pounds sugar
12 ounces water
4 tablespoons butter
½ cup corn syrup
2 heaping table-
    spoons marsh-
    mallow cream
vanilla extract (or
    maple flavoring)
4 cups pecan pieces

1. Combine sugar, water, and butter. Cook on low heat to 238°F on a candy thermometer. Once it begins to boil, do not stir. Remove from heat.

2. Add marshmallow cream and beat with a mixer until mixture begins to harden around the edges of the pot. Then reheat slowly, adding flavoring and pecans.

3. Pour mixture on wax paper in 2-inch round patties. Yields 4 dozen.

Elouise S. Taillac and Jackie T. Noto, Bay St. Louis, Mississippi. Regional America: The South, 1976

New Orleans Creamy Pralines

3 cups evaporated
    milk
3 cups granulated
    sugar

½ stick butter
1 teaspoon vanilla
    (or rum) extract
1½ cups pecan pieces

"One of twelve children, I'm the third generation of candymakers in my family. We made pralines at Christmastime to give away as gifts to friends and family. Originally from St. Bernard Parish, I now live in New Orleans and have a praline shop in the French Market."

1. In a heavy pan on medium heat, cook milk and sugar for about 20 minutes, until it reaches the soft-ball stage or 235°F on a candy thermometer.

2. Remove from stove and add pecan pieces. Put back on stove for 5 minutes, then add butter and vanilla or rum extract.

3. Cook another 5 minutes, stirring the whole time. Remove from stove and drop by a tablespoon onto greased wax paper. Yields 20.

Note: If you want chocolate pralines, add ¾ cup chocolate chip morsels when adding butter. Add several tablespoons milk if mixture becomes too thick.

Loretta Harrison, New Orleans, Louisiana. Louisiana Program, 1985

Hot Mulled Wine

1 pint light red wine
4 cloves
1 cinnamon stick
2 slices lemon
sugar (optional)

1. Put ingredients in a stainless-steel saucepan and heat until it gets foamy.

2. Remove from heat before wine boils and serve in cups. When using a glass or crystal cup, pour wine over a silver teaspoon to keep cup from cracking.

Maria Agner, Fitzgerald, Georgia. Community Activities and Food Preservation, 1980

"I'm originally from Würzburg, Germany, a beautiful town in northern Bavaria. It has a relatively mild climate and is surrounded by hills with vineyards. The quality of the wine produced there is excellent — far too valuable for cooking!

This mulled wine is heartily recommended for cold weather and the holiday season."

Upper Great Lakes

☾ · ☾ · ☾ · ☾

Yvonne R.
Lockwood
and
Anne R. Kaplan

Young Irving A. Dunsmoor moved with his parents to the Midwest in 1853. "My mother," he later recalled, "was very fond of dandelion greens, and missed them very much, as she could find none growing about our place. So she sent back to Maine for seed and planted them." This Yankee woman's experience was a typical one for the many people who eventually settled in what is now known as the Upper Great Lakes region: northern Ohio, Illinois, and Indiana as well as Michigan, Wisconsin, and Minnesota. Like the Native Americans before her and the dozens of groups from all over Europe, Asia, the Middle East, Africa, and Latin America who came later, Mrs. Dunsmoor settled in a land filled with both strange and familiar food resources. And like them, she imported what she could and made do with what was on hand.

Since the days of the region's first settlers — Ojibway, Dakota, Winnebago, Potowatomi, Menominee, Ottawa, Oneida — the natural bounty of the Upper Great Lakes states has given the area a distinct regional identity that distinguishes it from the midwestern heartland with which it is so often grouped. These Native Americans discovered an abundant supply of fish in the Great Lakes and in the many rivers, streams, and inland lakes that dot the countryside. Berries were plentiful, especially in the northern reaches, and mushrooms grew in the moist, shady forests and meadows. Sugar could be tapped from maple trees. Deer, moose, elk, bear, duck, geese, pigeon, and other small game birds also were plentiful. The first settlers supplemented the area's natural bounty with summer gardens of corn, beans, and squash. They boiled foods in bark containers suspended over an open fire. They smoked fish and meat in strips on racks. They parched wild rice on scaffolds or in pits and dried berries in the sun, often compressing them into cakes.

Not surprisingly, the natural resources of the land also lured settlers from the seventeenth through the early twentieth centuries. They first came to

Previous pages: Musicians on a break at the Smithsonian Folklife Festival use their bass fiddle as a table. (David Sutherland)

trade for furs, then to farm, fish, mine, and log. Later settlers found a more industrialized region, but they also adapted their cuisines to regional food customs that could be traced back to the original inhabitants.

Settlement by Euro-Americans destroyed much of the area's natural environment and, with it, the subsistence way of life of their predecessors. Today, Native Americans live in all the major cities around the Great Lakes and on reservations scattered throughout the region. Native foods are still cherished, because they taste better and because they are believed to be healthier than the processed "white man's food." But more important, traditional foods are a crucial part of the Native American's heritage. It is not unusual for urban residents to join their relatives on the reservation for a particular harvest. Such activities naturally reinforce family and social ties, as they perpetuate food traditions.

The wild rice harvest in early fall is a time of shared labor and great sociability among extended families and friends. This aquatic grass once flourished throughout the Great Lakes region and today remains a major staple of the Ojibway of Wisconsin, Minnesota, and Canada. Handpicked, hand-parched wild rice has a taste and texture unrivaled by the domesticated and mechanically processed version sold in grocery stores. Soaked in water and then boiled, it is a delicious staple, traditionally seasoned with maple sugar, berries, or animal fat. It makes excellent gruel and is a thickener in soups, stews, and dressings. Popped wild rice is a traditional favorite of the children. Dishes bearing names such as Chippewa wild rice casserole, made with canned cream of mushroom soup, are another matter. These modern Euro-American creations have little to do with traditional native foods.

Today, many Native Americans continue to fish and hunt to supplement their larders, although the catch is as likely to be frozen as smoked. Berry gathering and the making of maple sugar also continue, although usually more as a means of teaching children about their heritage than for subsistence. On the other hand, the powwow circuit is a good place to find modern Native American food in all of its variety. At these dance competitions, a kind of pan-Indian food holds sway: frybread, wild rice and venison stew, buffalo burgers, and wild rice or corn soup.

Among the Europeans, the French were the first to settle in the Upper Great Lakes region. In 1620 they arrived in what is now Michigan to establish fur-trading routes that led south and west. These trappers and traders learned about Native American foods and, in time, disseminated their knowledge to later settlers. Much later, in the late nineteenth and early twentieth centuries, the mass migration of Europeans turned the Great Lakes region into an industrial, multicultural microcosm of the entire nation. Today, the largest number of Poles not living in Poland reside in Chicago, as

Native Foods Meet Euro-American

do large numbers of Mexicans and Lithuanians. Cleveland's Slovenian population is surpassed only by that of Slovenia itself.

States in the region have distinct ethnic characteristics. For example, Wisconsin and Ohio are home to many third- and fourth-generation German Americans and numerous Swiss. Michigan contains one of the largest Arab and Arab American populations in the United States, the largest Maltese community outside Malta, and large numbers of Belgians, Mexicans, Poles, Canadians, Finns, Dutch, San Marinese, Greeks, Macedonians, and other Slavs. Minnesota includes many Scandinavians, Finns, and Germans, but it also contains the nation's third-largest concentration of Hmong, an ethnic minority from Southeast Asia. Smaller groups of southern, eastern, and central Europeans also live in Minnesota. Such multicultural settlers have contributed to the regional diet.

Fish for Every Taste

Fishing is an important sporting and subsistence activity. Perch, pike, smelt, suckers, trout, chubs, and whitefish (the predominant commercial catch) are consumed in a variety of traditional ways: whole, filleted, sliced, in chunks, ground, boiled, stewed, baked, smoked, fried, grilled, planked, steamed, pickled, and canned. In addition, such delicacies as roe and livers are relished.

Boiled fish has been the fare of commercial fishers since the late 1800s, but in the last several decades community fish boils have become popular social events. Men, especially fishing men, usually are in charge. Public fish boils are a good excuse for a back-yard gathering or a local fund raiser. Women frequently take charge when the boil is prepared for the immediate family. The menu seldom varies. The fish can be served plain, with potatoes and onions, or with onions, carrots, and tomato juice.

Canning, pickling, smoking, and drying are old methods of preservation. Although canning and pickling are home-based methods, smoking fish remains both a commercial and a private enterprise in this region, particularly in the north. Smoking technique is individualized by selecting a certain type of fish and wood, by varying the amount of salt or time the fish is soaked, and by creating different balances between the temperature and the smoking. Smokers themselves range from gutted refrigerators to handcrafted buildings; at the sign of billowing smoke, neighbors gather around the smoker with six-packs of beer, eager to test the fish.

Stalking the Wild

Hunting and trapping remain important to the region, both as subsistence and as recreation. The region's unique combination of heavy forests, rich farmlands, and wetlands is an ideal environment for its abundant wildlife. This wildlife attracts people from across the Midwest. In deer season alone, millions are spent so that venison can be consumed in roasts, stews, and burgers. Other popular uses include pasty, sausage, and jerky.

Trapping, too, has its faithful legions. The eighteenth-century French valued muskrat for its fur and as an important winter food. Muskrat is trapped and eaten throughout the Great Lakes region, but perhaps nowhere with such significance and pride as in Monroe, Michigan. There, descendants of the area's early French community are known as "mushrat French," a term that distinguishes them from Quebequois and French nationals. In Monroe muskrat dinners not only are community fund raisers, they also serve as important family events. In fact, the "rat" is so integrated into this community that legends, anecdotes, and jokes about it are common. The animal is trapped from November to February and immediately skinned and gutted. Before cooking, the musk glands and every bit of fat must be removed or the meat will become foul tasting and almost inedible. Typically, muskrat is fried, roasted, or boiled. For public dinners and in some homes, people roast muskrat in cream-style corn, whereas in many French homes, it is often fried and smothered in onions and roasted. Old-timers consider the brains and tongue a delicacy, and some even make bouillabaisse from the heads.

Other riches of the Great Lakes include morels, wild berries, and maple syrup. Morels are delicious wild mushrooms, simple to identify and generally safe to eat, if you can find them. Folk wisdom has it that morels grow in the farmlands toward the south and in the aspen groves and mixed stand of trees in the north. However, morel hunting remains shrouded in secrecy and rich with legend. Otherwise rational people behave strangely, and even spouses and siblings may not share with each other their knowledge about a special hunting area. During morel season, usually in late April and May, cars line country roads near good hunting grounds. Morels are cooked in various ways and dried. Only recently have they been domesticated and made available in gourmet shops.

Decades ago berry picking was essential to the subsistence of many Native Americans and newly arrived immigrants. More recently, forest fires and deforestation by the lumber industry have created an environment in which berries thrive. Despite mosquitoes, heat, bears, and uneven terrain, berry picking remains a popular family activity. Depending on the growing zone, pickers will find strawberries, blueberries, raspberries, blackberries, cranberries, chokecherries, and thimbleberries — the latter in limited areas in the vicinity of Lake Superior. Berries are turned into jams and jellies, sauces, soups, pies, tortes, juices, and syrups. In the past twenty years thimbleberry jam has become a tourist item, perhaps because this berry is rare and slightly exotic.

Maple syrup is often associated with Vermont, but Michigan, Wisconsin, and Minnesota are important syrup-producing areas as well. State-of-the-art commercial enterprises and one-person operations make syrup for retail outlets and home consumption. Early settlers learned how to tap a maple tree by

Riches for the Picking

observing Native Americans, who drank the sap or boiled it down and made cakes of the crystals for later use as flavoring. Today, as in the past, candy is made by dribbling syrup in the snow. Public pancake breakfasts held near the sugarbush and sugarhouses are quickly becoming a Great Lakes tradition.

Ohio is Johnny Appleseed country, but according to legend he also strewed apple seeds throughout the region of the Great Lakes. In Minnesota, the ability to produce apples became part of eighteenth-century boosters' claims that the state had an ideal climate. Apples are especially abundant in Ohio and Michigan. Just as sugarhouses are the destination of group outings in the spring, apple orchards and cider mills with offers of apples, cider, and doughnuts are the target of family activities on chilly autumn days. Many orchards offer "pick-your-own" apples.

Michigan also grows peaches and pears, but cherries are one of its major crops. The first cherry trees were planted in the mid-1800s around Grand Traverse Bay, which is known as cherry pie country. Today, sweet and sour cherries are turned into jams, juices, syrups, breads, desserts, and dried fruit.

The abundance and diversity of the region's natural resources affected the food traditions that new settlers brought to the region.

A small number of African Americans have lived in the Upper Great Lakes region since the early settlement days. In 1802 Pierre Bonga, a free fur trader, plied his trade in what is now Minnesota. In the 1820s vacationing southerners and officers at Fort Snelling (present-day Minnesota) brought their slaves to the territory. In the Civil War era, some African Americans fled via the underground railroad to southern Michigan; others went on to Canada. The Quakers helped some slaves purchase land in rural Michigan. Today, in southwestern and central Michigan, African Americans own large farms and form a special community.

Elsewhere, African Americans tended to settle in urban centers. The first migration began at the end of the Civil War, with the largest increases occurring in the 1920s, 1940s, and 1950s. Most of the area's African American food customs can be traced to a particular region of the South that a family calls home, and home cooking, church suppers, fund-raising dinners, and street or ethnic food festivals all offer variations on what is commonly known as southern or "soul food." African and Caribbean specialty foods, such as roasted goat, also have been revived recently. In large urban centers such as Detroit and Chicago, butchers sell possum, rabbit, and other specialty meats. Where populations are smaller, informal networks ensure that city dwellers can obtain traditional foods not sold commercially. For example, in Minneapolis and St. Paul, families go on outings to secure Mississippi River snapping turtles or rabbits, then share the bounty with friends or advertise it on modest placards propped up in home and store windows.

An Ethnic Cornucopia: Africans...

Opposite: A German woman wears a traditional bridal headdress during the 1975 festival. (Jim Pickerell)

Germans...

The Germans were one of the first European immigrants to leave established areas on the East Coast and homestead large tracts of land in Ohio, Michigan, Illinois, Indiana, Wisconsin, and Minnesota. Many then moved farther west, and newer immigrants went directly to the region's cities and farms during the mid-nineteenth century. Cities such as Milwaukee, for example, are famous for their German flavor. In such small towns as New Ulm, Minnesota, and Frankenmuth, Michigan, the German heritage has become a tourist attraction. Even rural areas have a distinct German presence. The German American population includes Prussians, Bavarians, Swabians, Berliners, Ruhr and Rhine valley dwellers, and Volga Germans. Among them are Roman Catholics, Jews, Protestants, including the Amish and Mennonites — each group with its own traditional foods.

Opposite: Norwegian rosette cookies are deep fried using a rosette iron for 1984 festival visitors. (Richard Hofmeister)

At holidays and festivals, German cooks excel at complicated dishes. Sauerbrauten (beef marinated for as much as three days before it is roasted and covered with gravy) is often served with spätzle (a soft egg noodle), potato dumplings, or potato pancakes and red cabbage. Or the cook may prepare roulade (pounded beef steaks wrapped in bacon and filled with chopped vegetables). Pork roasts with cabbage are another common holiday centerpiece, often followed by a profusion of cookies such as anise-flavored pfeffernüse or lebkuchen, literally "love cookies," and stollen, a fruit-studded yeast bread.

A great many people enjoy sausage and beer, but the Great Lakes Germans certainly consume their share. Bratwurst, made from pork, veal, and eggs, is a signature dish, especially when served with sauerkraut. Blood sausage, egg liverwurst (eier leber-wurst), sausage with oats (grütz-wurst), braunschweiger, Thüringer (a smoked sausage popular in east-central Germany), and various summer sausages are frequently used for lunches, picnics, sports events, and casual suppers.

Like other central Europeans, Germans eat their share of potatoes: as warm potato salad, dumplings, pancakes, and boiled, mashed, fried, or baked. Noodles, too, are a popular part of the German cuisine, especially spätzle. Soups are also popular and vary from delicate clear marrow broth to hearty potato soup, even cold cherry or poppy-seed soup. A salad of wilted greens with a vinegar-sugar-and-oil dressing frequently accompanies meals. Desserts range from poppy-seed pastries and rich blitz torte to cookies and kuchen, a tart that traditionally featured fruit in season.

Scandinavians...

The Scandinavians also came relatively early and in great numbers, many of them settling in western Wisconsin and Minnesota — the latter now referred to as a Scandinavian haven. Scandinavians are known for their baked goods: rye breads, hardtack, and desserts rich with cream and butter. Holidays see an abundance of delicate white cookies, from Danish pretzel-shaped kringler flavored with cardamom to Swedish rosettes, Norwegian

krumkake, and the shared versions of sandbakkels, fattigmann, and spritz. Rice pudding is another pan-Scandinavian Christmas dessert. In it, one almond is hidden, promising good luck to the person who finds it. The rich Norwegian kransekake (kransekage in Danish, kranskaka in Swedish) is another perennial favorite, a pyramid of baked rings made of almond paste, sugar, and egg whites. This dense, festive pastry is drizzled with white sugar icing and decorated with miniature national flags or other items appropriate to the celebration — weddings, anniversaries, landmark birthdays, and national holidays.

Each Scandinavian nationality is also known for certain specialty foods: Swedish meatballs, in their distinctive gravy; lussekatter, the Swedish saffron-flavored bun traditionally served on St. Lucia's Day in December; smørrebrød, Danish open-faced sandwiches; and communal torsk suppers, in which Norwegian Americans serve fish with drawn butter and lefse, a tortilla-thin potato bread, all washed down with healthy shots of akevitt, an anise-flavored liquor.

Cornish...

If it is a good cup of tea you crave, you should visit a Cornish home. Cornish heavy cake, saffron rolls, and currant (Cousin Jack) cookies just seem to go with tea, which the Cornish have been enjoying in America since the 1840s. With their knowledge of deep mining, they first came to work the copper mines of Michigan and, later, the Wisconsin lead mines and Michigan and Minnesota iron deposits.

No traditional Cornish food is better known than the pasty, a turnover with a pielike crust that is filled with meat and vegetables. Although the pasty is the national dish of Cornwall, it became part of the home cooking of other immigrant groups who worked in the mines.

Finns...

To the chagrin of the Cornish, the pasty has also become identified with both the Finns of the Upper Peninsula (U.P.) of Michigan and the region itself. The sizeable Finnish population in Michigan no doubt accounts for some of this association; the Finns also have a similar food and have played an important role in disseminating the pasty in the past. In any event, the Finns encourage this association by serving pasty at their ethnic suppers. The truth of the matter is that almost everyone eats pasty. This once monoethnic Cornish food has become a multiethnic regional specialty and traditionally is filled with beef (and sometimes pork) or venison and potatoes, onions, and rutabagas or carrots. The Cornish have maintained a few ethnic variants, such as the date pasty and the eggy pasty, in which a whole egg is placed on top of the ingredients.

Finnish Americans constitute one of the largest ethnic groups in the culture area that stretches from Michigan's Upper Peninsula to Minnesota's Iron

Range. Despite this fact, Finnish bakeries are limited and restaurants are rare. It is in the home that one sees the widest variety of festive and everyday Finnish food. Visitors are offered coffee, served with homemade cardamom bread, called nisu, pulla, kahvileipää, or biscuit. Eaten with butter and jam, or plain, cardamom bread is perhaps the most evident culinary link with Finland. Also, korppua (a dry, rusklike toast) is distributed by bakeries in Michigan and Minnesota to Finnish American communities or made at home and served with jam and butter for breakfast, with midday coffee, or as a snack.

Other Finnish American foods are the provenance of the older generation and are sought by relatives visiting the region. Kalakukko, for example, is filleted fish or small whole fish wrapped in rye dough and baked slowly for a long time. This version and another made with beef are cousins of the Russian pierogi. Squeaky cheese also is a traditional food. Because this delicacy requires a large quantity of unpasteurized milk, or first milk when available, Finnish farmers with cows are the most likely source. The cheese gained its English name from its consistency: served in chunks or wedges, it squeaks against the teeth when chewed. Old-timers dunk it in their coffee or even put chunks directly in the cup. Viili, a soured milk erroneously likened to yogurt, also is a traditional Finnish American food, eaten for breakfast, as a snack, as dessert, with cinnamon and sugar, with salt, or plain. Not everyone appreciates its stretchy, almost slimy consistency, however. But those who like it seek it out, and visitors carry starter cultures home to make their own.

Often heavy on butter yet delicate and subtle to the palate, Finnish American foods and desserts are not for those seeking a zesty wallop. Much that distinguishes this food is the cooking style itself, not the ingredients. Typical dishes include mojakka, either an unthickened beef stew prepared with allspice or fish stew made with water or milk; scalloped potatoes and fish, usually salted salmon; whole-grain homemade bread; rice pudding and fruit soup, made with prunes and raisins or fresh berries; cereals cooked in milk; and oven-baked pancakes, called pannukakku or kropsua.

☾ · ☾ · ☾ · ☾

The truth of the matter is that almost everyone eats pasty. This once mono-ethnic Cornish food has become a multiethnic regional specialty.

☾ · ☾ · ☾ · ☾

Arabs...

Arab Americans from many different nations brought with them both discrete customs and customs shared by many Arab speakers, including food and food customs. The Detroit metropolitan area has the largest Arab population in North America. Before World War II the majority of immigrants were Christian laborers and peddlers. Since 1948, however, most have been middle- and upper-class Moslems. The populations include Lebanese, Palestinians, Yemeni, Iraqi, Syrians, Jordanians, Egyptians, and Chaldeans.

Many have settled in enclaves by national origin and religion. The south end of Dearborn, Michigan, is one of the area's best-defined and highly concentrated Arab communities. In addition to a wide range of social, cultural, and political organizations, grocery stores provide cooking equipment and every packaged or bulk-food item that can be imported. Restaurants serve Arab meals and provide women a respectable place to go for coffee and soft drinks. Bakeries sell Arab bread, meat and spinach pies, lahamageen, and an assortment of sweet pastries, as well as such locally prepared specialties as pickled turnips and labanee balls in olive oil. Imagine Arab cuisine without lamb, rice, yogurt, olive oil, tahini, mint, lemon, pine nuts, onions, fresh vegetables, and dried legumes (lentils, garbanzos, and fava beans)! Fortunately, Arab Americans do not have to. Varieties of lamb and vegetable stew, babaganoon, hummus, an array of lamb kebabs, falafil, mojjadara, mint tea, and "Turkish" coffee also typify Arab foods of this region.

Eastern Europeans...

Eastern European migration to the Great Lakes following World War II augmented the existing communities, and many groups located in specific urban centers. Cleveland, for example, is the center for Slovenes. Southern Michigan is noted for its Romanians, Macedonians, Greeks, and Albanians. Northern Ohio and southern Michigan are populated by a good sprinkling of Hungarians, while the Chicago area includes among its population a large number of Serbs, Croats, and Bosnians. Poles and other eastern European ethnic groups also are well represented in the area. Hamtramck, Michigan, for example, is regarded as an "urban village" of Poles and Ukrainians. Kielbasa is as much a part of Hamtramck and Chicago as it is of Poland. Detroit has more than two hundred Macedonian bakers, who service the needs of other ethnic groups as well as their own. For Serbian slavas, for example, they roast whole lambs and piglets. For Polish Fat Tuesday, they make paczki — raised dough, deep fried and filled with custard or prune or berry jam, or left plain.

The foods of eastern Europe, and especially southeastern Europe and the Balkans, are complex. For centuries that area has served as the route between East and West for invading armies, the Crusades, merchants, and migrating peoples. The numerous population shifts during the time of the great empires (Ottoman Turkish and Austro-Hungarian) resulted in mixed populations. In the process, foods crossed cultural boundaries and diffused with little or no change. Today, food is strongly maintained as an aspect of cultural identity, and many variants of the same foods are claimed by people of different cultures. The most identifiable cultural influences on the foods of this region are Turkish, Austrian, Hungarian, and Italian.

As immigrants to the United States, Serbs, Croats, Slovenes, Macedonians, Bosnians, Bulgarians, Romanians, Greeks, and Albanians were again subject to a variety of influences (region being only one) that are exhibited in their food customs. Nonetheless, certain foods have held tenaciously despite, or

Opposite: A festival participant uses a steady hand to demonstrate traditional Ukrainian and Polish egg decorating. (Jim Pickerell)

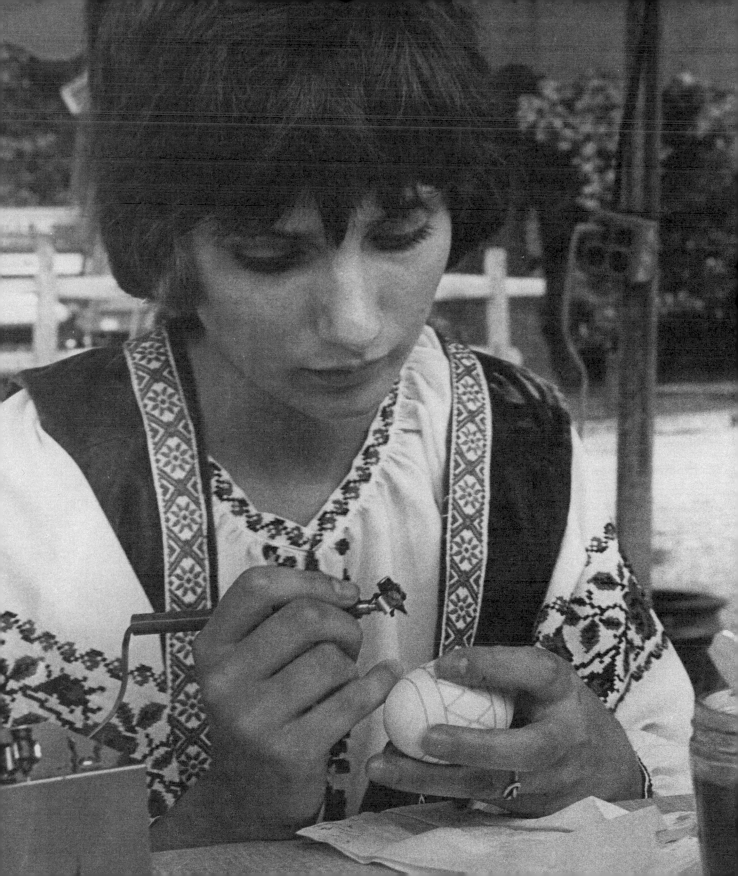

perhaps because of, the pressures of assimilation.

Stuffed cabbage is one of the most symbolically important items in the diet and traditions of eastern European descendants. According to tradition, stuffed cabbage is made with ground meat and rice and rolled in leaves of cabbage or whole-head sauerkraut. This dish is a must at holidays and for such celebratory meals as weddings. Spit-roasted lamb is another specialty for people from Yugoslavia. Men usually prepare, cook, and serve roast lamb, which appears regularly at ethnic picnics, saints' days, homecomings, anniversaries, and name days.

Strudel, pita, burek, and banitza are some of the names used to describe the same southeastern European paper-thin pastry, variously filled with fruit, cheese, meat, spinachlike greens, squash, potatoes, and walnuts. The dough is rolled up, like a jellyroll, and baked either in straight rolls or coiled in a round pan. This thin, unleavened dough is also prepared in layers with various fillings. Potica, or povitica, is another ethnic specialty of this region. It contains raisins, ground walnuts, or poppy seeds and is rolled into a thin yeast dough. Among Slovenes and Croats, it is an essential food during holidays and other celebratory events. Wine and distilled alcohol from fruits are other ritual and everyday necessities. Sljivovica, made from prune plums, is considered a cure-all and, according to the code of hospitality, is offered to guests. Some first-generation immigrants built stills so that they would have a supply. Today, a number of European countries mass-produce sljivovica, but one-liter bottles of sljivovica, made in villages and brought to America, are treasured most highly.

Traditional foods prepared in U.S. homes and restaurants range from what would be everyday fare in the Old Country to holiday foods. Everything from dried beans, cornmeal mush, corn bread, fowl, grilled meats, stuffed vegetables, dumplings and noodles, salads, and one-pot meat and vegetable dishes to desserts, liqueurs, and fruit brandies receives the local or ethnic touch. Smoked meats and sausages are part of many household diets. Old-timers recall the hard work and good times of butchering pigs to fill the family larder. Although smoked meats and sausages are still essential to the diet, they are more often obtained today at a local Croatian, Hungarian, or Polish butcher than prepared at home.

☾ · ☾ · ☾ · ☾

Stuffed cabbage is one of the most symbolically important items in the diet and traditions of eastern European descendants.

☾ · ☾ · ☾ · ☾

Mexicans...

Unlike nineteenth-century European settlers, most Mexican Americans arrived in the region as twentieth-century migrants, working in the fields or canning factories. Gradually, however, some of these immigrants supplemented their summer agricultural labors with winter jobs in St. Paul and Chicago's packing houses and stockyards, on railroads, road crews, and in factories. What had been a transient rural population settled eventually in the area's large cities: Chicago, Detroit, and Minneapolis–St. Paul.

Most Americans are familiar with such popular Mexican foods as tacos, enchiladas, salsa, deep-fried tortillas, and refried beans. Just as day-old tortillas are transformed into chips, refried beans, reheated in lard, are one way for thrifty Mexican American cooks to use leftovers. Much more desirable are frijoles de la olla (beans fresh from the pot), which add a minimum of fat to flavor pinto beans. Other traditional home dishes include guisado (stew), various sopas (soupy dishes with noodles), and seasoned meats (for example, pork with green chile sauce). Reserved for special occasions because of the time needed to prepare them are such foods as tamales and chicken or pork mole. Mole is a sauce that features chiles, peanut butter, crushed sesame or pumpkin seeds, Mexican chocolate, and garlic.

While some women regularly make flour tortillas, the more time-consuming corn tortillas are rarely made at home, except for holiday meals. Instead, they are purchased at the tortillarias and Mexican grocery stores that serve as informal social centers as well. Mexican American markets often include a wide variety of fresh, dried, and powdered chile peppers, tomatillos and nopales (cactus) when in season, cilantro, chorizo (a spicy pork sausage), cornhusks, cheese, baked goods, and canned or packaged Mexican items. If a store sells menudo (a soup made with tripe and hominy), you can be fairly certain that it caters mainly to Mexican American patrons. Menudo is particularly popular for Sunday breakfast, in part because of its reputation as a hangover cure.

Southeast Asians...

The Indochinese who fled Southeast Asia after the fall of Saigon in 1975 are the most recent immigrants to the Great Lakes region. Vietnamese, Hmong, Lao, Thai, and Cambodian people met and mingled in the larger cities of their native lands, as they did again in the Asian refugee camps. Their cuisine in the United States reflects this fact. The Vietnamese came earliest and in greatest numbers to the region, scattering throughout the Great Lakes region. Vietnamese restaurants have introduced Americans to spicy stir-fried dishes flavored with lemon grass and star anise, served over transparent, skinny rice noodles or mung-bean threads. Spring rolls, similar in concept to Chinese egg rolls, enclose chopped meat, vegetables, spices, and sometimes bean threads in a deep-fried rice-paper wrapper. Fish sauce and hot peppers, cilantro, ginger, and onions lend a distinctive taste to sauces and garnishes.

The Hmong are an ethnic minority who never had a homeland of their own. For centuries they lived and farmed in the Laotian highlands. Between 1976 and 1980 about 60,000 Hmong arrived in the United States, and more than 10,000 settled in Minnesota, placing it behind only California and Texas in the number of Hmong living outside Southeast Asia. Like the Vietnamese, the Hmong eat vegetables and stir-fried, seasoned pieces of chicken, pork, and beef. These foods are served with — never over — fluffy white rice, sticky rice, or noodles. Hot-pepper sauce, a combination of minced peppers, green onions and fish sauce, is a fiery companion to most meals. Cool water is a preferred drink. The traditional Hmong diet consists of few sweets.

The region's Indochinese often have to make substitutions in their cuisine — water buffalo, after all, are hard to find in the United States, as are many native greens and tubers. Avid gardeners among the Hmong, however, have managed not only to supply themselves and their neighbors with native foods, they also have educated the general public. For example, many stands in St. Paul's farmers market now display bitter melon, unusual varieties of eggplant, cabbages, greens, yard-long beans, and other exotica. At first, other Southeast Asians and the area's Chinese, Korean, and Filipinos were the only buyers. Gradually, others began asking questions and experimenting with these foods.

Clearly, the food history of the Upper Great Lakes is a story of interethnic mingling that nonetheless encourages the maintenance of regional, national, religious, and ethnic specialties. In the seventeenth and eighteenth centuries, the Native Americans taught French, French-Canadian, and British trappers and traders about muskrat and wild rice. Centuries later, that same process continues, but the foods now flow both ways.

☾ · ☾ · ☾ · ☾

Recipes

Muskrat with Corn

Roasted Muskrat

Cornish Pasty

Bistek Ranchero

Lebanese Lamb and Green Beans

Fish in a Crust

Pan-fried Fish

Spätzle

Karjalanpiirakat
(Karelian Rice or Potato Pasties)

Squeaky Cheese

Huevos al Rabo de Mestiza

Ensalada de Nopalitos (Cactus Salad)

Dandelion Greens

Skillet Corn Bread Fritters

Finnish Flat Bread

Finnish Sour Rye Bread

Pulla
(Finnish Cardamom Coffee Braid)

Zopf Brot
(German Braided Bread)

Moravian Love Feast Buns

Saffron Buns or Bread

Finnish Oven Pancake

Qtayif
(Stuffed Pancakes)

Nammura (Farina Cakes)

Cornish Saffron Cake

Moravian Sugar Cake

Blitz Torte

Thimble Tarts

Belgian Pie

Cousin Jack Cookies

Belgian Lukken Cookies

Norwegian Spritz Cookies

Krumkake Cookies

Rosettes

Cherry Dumpling Soup

Maple Sugar Candy

Maple Cream Candy

Muskrat with Corn

3 muskrats
cabbage leaves
1 tablespoon cider
    vinegar
1 teaspoon dill weed
1 teaspoon dried basil
1 bay leaf
1 whole clove
4 onions, sliced
½ stalk celery

Roasting sauce:
2 cans whole-kernel
    corn
2 cans cream-style
    corn
salt
pepper
2 tablespoons
    margarine

1. Clean muskrats by removing heads, feet, and all fat. Split hind legs and remove musk balls in each leg as well as musk balls and fat between the shoulders. Soak in salted water for 2 hours, then wash until clean.

2. Parboil by lining the bottom of a large kettle with cabbage leaves. Lay muskrat on top of cabbage. Add vinegar and seasonings. Cover with water and bring to a boil. Cook until a fork can be inserted in the meat. Remove from kettle and wash until clean.

3. Preheat oven to 350°F.

4. Combine corn, adding salt and pepper to taste. Place half of muskrat in a roasting pan and dot with margarine. Cover with half of corn mixture, then layer on remaining meat and corn; top with margarine. Bake for 1½ hours.

Hudson and Elda Peltier, Monroe, Michigan. Michigan Program, 1987

❝If muskrat is not available, try beaver. Just cut the beaver into stew-size chunks, remove fat, and follow the recipe. ❞

Judy Lunning

Roasted Muskrat

1 muskrat
flour
shortening, for frying
salt
pepper
½ to 1 cup diced
    onion
½ to 1 cup diced
    celery

1. Clean and remove as much fat as possible from muskrat, then cut into 6 pieces. Soak in salted water overnight. Drain and pat dry.

2. Roll pieces in flour and brown in shortening.

3. Preheat oven to 325°F.

4. Place meat in a roasting pan and add salt, pepper, onion, celery, and water to fill pan ⅛ to ¼ inch deep. Cover and bake for 1½ hours.

Judy Lunning, Mio, Michigan. Michigan Program, 1987

Cornish Pasty

Crust:
1 cup flour
½ teaspoon salt
⅓ cup shortening
milk (or ice water)

Filling:
1 cup sliced potatoes
½ rutabaga, sliced
½ cup sliced onion
¼ cup diced flank
  steak
¼ cup diced pork
  steak
salt
pepper
1 tablespoon
  margarine

1. To make crust, mix flour and salt. Cut shortening into dry ingredients. Add enough milk or ice water for dough to hold together. Roll out to a 9-inch circle.

2. Preheat oven to 400°F.

3. Layer uncooked filling ingredients on half of dough circle. Top with margarine. Fold over crust, then seal and crimp edges. Bake on a baking sheet for 1 hour. Serves 1 to 2.

Lucille Brown, Wakefield, Michigan. Michigan Program, 1987

❝Both sides of the family had miners who emigrated to America from Cornwall, England, so the pasty is part of our family tradition. It furnished miners with a nourishing meal underground. I make them on a regular weekly basis, and when our family is all together, they are a must meal.❞

Lucille Brown

❝Aunt Melva, on my husband's side, told me when I make Cornish pasties not to use any meat of lesser quality than sirloin, as 'the pasty is as good as the steak that you put in.' ❞

Eunice Jewell

Bistek Ranchero

1 8-ounce T-bone
  steak

Sauce:
½ medium onion,
  sliced

2 tablespoons butter
  (or lard)
1 tomato, sliced
1 jalapeño chili,
  seeded and finely
  diced

1 clove garlic, crushed
pinch of cumin
salt
pepper

1. To prepare sauce, sauté onion in butter. Stir in tomato, chili, and garlic. Add cumin, salt, and pepper. Cook on low heat for 5 to 10 minutes.

2. Cook steak in a frying pan. Pour sauce over steak and heat for a few seconds. Serve with tortillas or bread. Serves 2.

Maggie Garcia, Grand Rapids, Michigan. Michigan Program, 1987

Lebanese Lamb and Green Beans

1 pound lamb (or beef), cut into 1-inch cubes
1 onion, chopped

1 pound fresh green beans, cut into 1½-inch lengths
1 20-ounce can tomatoes, with juice
1 teaspoon salt

¼ teaspoon pepper
dash of allspice
pinch of peppermint
½ teaspoon dried parsley

1. In a large nonstick pan, sauté meat until pinkness is gone. Stir in onion and cook until onion is soft.

2. Add beans, tomatoes, and seasonings. Cover and simmer for 1 hour. Serve hot over rice or rice pilaf. Serves 4.

Helen Mohammed Atwell, Dearborn, Michigan. Michigan Program, 1987

Fish in a Crust

1 package dry yeast
1 cup warm water
1 teaspoon salt
¼ cup shortening
1½ cups rye flour
1½ cups white flour
2 pounds fresh fish (trout or whitefish), cleaned and boned
salt
pepper
1 small onion, thinly sliced
4 tablespoons butter

1. In a bowl, dissolve yeast in warm water. Add salt, shortening, and flours. Mix well and knead in additional flour as necessary to make a soft dough. Cover and let rise until double in size.

2. Preheat oven to 350°F.

3. Roll out dough on a floured surface to a rectangle 12 × 10 inches and ½ inch thick. Place fish on dough and top with salt, pepper, onion, and 2 tablespoons butter. Fold dough over fish. Moisten edges to seal in juices. Shape like a loaf of bread.

4. Bake until crust is brown. Lower heat to 325°F and continue baking for a total of 1½ hours. Remove from oven and brush top with remaining butter, melted. Cover to soften crust. Slice like a jellyroll to serve.

Anna Lassila, Mohawk, Michigan. Michigan Program, 1987

Pan-fried Fish

½ cup cornmeal
1 cup flour
pinch of salt
dash of pepper
pinch of sugar
1 whole trout (or
    similar fish),
    cleaned
oil, for frying

1. Combine dry ingredients.

2. Fill a frying pan with ¼ inch oil and heat.

3. Rinse fish and pat dry with towels, then roll in flour mixture. Drop in hot oil and cook for at least 12 minutes or until golden brown.

Marguerite L. Berry-Jackson and Marie L. Cross, Lansing and Mecosta, Michigan. Michigan Program, 1987

"Because we lived on the shores of School Section Lake, fish was our main dish. When a fish was caught, it was cleaned immediately and put in salt water to soak overnight. Fish was served most often at breakfast, although at our noon dinners, spoonbread, potatoes, and canned fruit also became part of the menu. We add sugar when frying fish to help it brown."

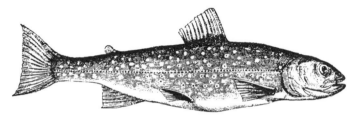

Spätzle

2 cups flour
5 eggs
¾ tablespoon salt
½ cup milk
¼ pound butter,
    melted
1 pound Swiss cheese,
    grated
1 medium-large
    onion, sliced

1. Beat flour, eggs, salt, and milk. When dough is the right consistency (soft enough to be piped through a pastry bag), press it through a noodle maker.

2. Drop noodles into salted boiling water. Noodles should swell up; they will shrink somewhat when cool. Use a slotted spoon or sieve to remove noodles from water; drain.

3. Pour some of melted butter over noodles while still warm. Layer noodles with cheese and let stand for 10 minutes. Brown onion in remaining butter and pour over noodles.

Wives of the Alte Kamaradan Band, Mequon, Wisconsin. Old Ways in the New World: German American, 1975

Karjalanpiirakat (Karelian Rice or Potato Pasties)

"A most colorful and rich heritage of Finland comes from Karelia, the land of song. The easternmost province of Finland, most of Karelia was dissolved into the Soviet Union after the Winter War of 1944, so the Finns in melancholy memory epitomize the Karelians as being the most fun-loving, the most lively people.

Karelian rice pasties are popular throughout Finland today and can be purchased in bakeries and supermarkets, made fresh daily. Although the most popular version has a rice filling, a potato filling also is used."

Rice filling:
1 cup water
3 cups milk
¾ cup rice
salt
butter

Potato filling:
4 large potatoes
   (about 1 pound)

1 cup hot milk
salt
pepper
butter

Pastry:
1 cup water
1½ teaspoons salt
1½ cups rye flour
1 cup flour

Glaze:
1 cup boiling milk
¼ cup butter

Egg butter:
1 hard-boiled egg
1 cup butter, firm

1. To prepare rice filling, combine water, milk, and rice in a heavy saucepan. Simmer for 1 hour or until rice has absorbed all of the liquid, stirring frequently. Add salt and butter to taste.

2. To make potato filling, peel and cut up potatoes. Place in a pot with water to cover and cook until tender. Drain and mash, then add hot milk, salt, pepper, and butter to taste. Beat until light.

3. To prepare pastry, mix water, salt, and flours to make a smooth dough. If necessary, add more water.

4. Shape dough into a rope as thick as your wrist. Cut into 20 equal portions. Shape pieces into flat round cakes and roll each out to make a very thin circle about 6 to 8 inches in diameter. Set aside.

5. Preheat oven to 450°F and lightly grease 2 baking sheets.

6. Fill the center of each dough circle with about 3 tablespoons rice or potato filling. Fold over 2 sides of dough to form an oval shape, but leave exposed about a 1-inch wide strip of filling. Crimp the edges. Place pies on baking sheets.

7. To make glaze, mix boiling milk and butter. Brush on pies and bake for 10 to 15 minutes or until light brown. Glaze again once during baking and after the pies are removed from the oven. Cool. (Pasties will soften as they cool; you may want to cover them in aluminum foil while warm to soften throughout.)

8. To prepare egg butter, chop hard-boiled eggs with butter until blended. Put in a bowl and serve as a topping or spread for the pasties. Yields 20.

Beatrice Ojakangas, Duluth, Minnesota. Old Ways in the New World: Finnish American, 1974

Squeaky Cheese

3 gallons milk
¼ rennet tablet
1 tablespoon water
2 tablespoons salt

1. Heat milk until warm but not hot (about 100°F). Dissolve rennet in water and add with salt to milk, stirring well. Cover with a towel and let sit for at least 1 hour, until mixture starts to form curds. Do not stir or touch during this time.

2. Test curd after about 1 hour by placing a spoon in the center to see whether a hole is left when spoon is removed. Pour curd onto the center of a large towel that has been draped over a pail or large dish pan. Bring together the corners of the towel to make a bag. Let it drain, and keep squeezing and shaping the mass until it is fairly dry. Touch only the outside of the towel, not the cheese.

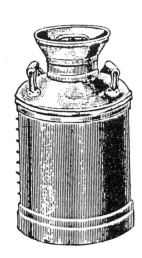

3. Place a hand underneath, open the towel, and invert cheese onto an ungreased pizza pan. Let cheese sit; drain off the whey that separates from the cheese. Sprinkle on some salt and place cheese under the broiler. Have another pizza pan ready; when cheese is brown and starts snapping, in about 15 minutes, flip it over onto the other pan.

4. Sprinkle a little extra salt on top and return cheese to broiler for another 15 minutes. Watch closely to avoid burning. Have pail or dish pan close by and keep draining and discarding the whey that separates from the cheese. Remember not to touch the cheese with your hands. When light brown, remove cheese from oven and drain whey again. Cool.

Lilja White, Aurora, Minnesota. Finnish Americans, 1980

Huevos al Rabo de Mestiza

Salsa:
½ poblano chili
1 jalapeño chili
1 tomato
2 tablespoons oil
  (or margarine)
¼ large onion
  (or 1 bunch green
  onions)
salt
4 sprigs coriander,
  chopped
½ pound white Oax-
  aca cheese, grated

2 tortillas
4 eggs

1. Prepare salsa by roasting chiles and tomato over an open flame until they turn black and blister. Transfer to a bag, close, and let sit for 10 minutes. Peel away charred skin, seed peppers, and dice.

2. Heat oil in a frying pan and sauté onion. When onion softens, add chiles and tomato, and salt to taste. Cook until vegetables are done, then add coriander, cheese, and a little water. Remove from heat.

3. Warm tortillas on low heat and put on a plate. Fry eggs sunny side up and place 2 on each tortilla. Cover with sauce. May be served with refried beans or fried potatoes. Serves 2.

Maggie Garcia, Grand Rapids, Michigan. Michigan Program, 1987

Ensalada de Nopalitos (Cactus Salad)

2 ancho chiles, dried
4 guajillo chiles, dried
1 26-ounce can San
  Marco cactus
1½ green onions
1 tablespoon
  chopped cilantro
1 tomato, diced
¼ pound enchilada
  cheese, diced
lettuce leaves, for
  garnish
1 lime, sliced, for
  garnish

1. Sauté chiles until brown. Add water to cover and simmer for 10 minutes on low heat. Purée chiles in a blender, return them to pan, and simmer until slightly thickened.

2. Combine remaining ingredients. Add chiles and marinate in the refrigerator.

3. Place lettuce in a salad bowl, add salad, and garnish with lime slices.

Maggie Garcia

Dandelion Greens

dandelion greens
bacon (or salt pork)
salt
pepper

1. Wash greens several times and parboil for 15 minutes.

2. While parboiling, fry bacon or salt pork until crisp. Remove meat from frying pan, crumble, and set aside. Drain half of grease from pan.

3. Drain greens and add to pan. Simmer until tender. Season with salt and pepper and put in a serving bowl with crumbled bacon on top.

Marguerite L. Berry-Jackson and Marie L. Cross, Lansing and Mecosta, Michigan. Michigan Program, 1987

Skillet Corn Bread Fritters

1 cup yellow
   cornmeal
1 cup flour
1 teaspoon sugar (or
   honey)
1 teaspoon salt
3 teaspoons baking
   powder
1 egg
⅓ cup oil
⅔ cup milk
1 cup shortening

1. Sift dry ingredients. Make a well in the center and add egg, oil, and milk. Beat vigorously for several minutes.

2. In an iron frying pan, heat shortening until smoking and drop in batter by tablespoons. As batter browns, turn fritters. Cook for about 3 minutes.

Marguerite L. Berry-Jackson

"By the time spring finally arrived, we were so eager for a change in our menu, we could hardly wait for the dandelions to get big enough to gather. One thing was sure, they were not the nuisance people say they are today. They never had a chance to go to seed. From the time they got as big as a saucer, they were gathered by cutting them off, leaving the root in the ground. If the hens were laying well, an egg was boiled and it too was sliced and put on top. Makes a pretty delicious dish.

We also used wild leeks, especially early in the spring, to add a different flavor to boiled potatoes, which we served with butter, browned or milk gravy, and usually pork drippings."

Finnish Flat Bread

"Breads are the mainstay of the Finnish diet. Rye and barley ripen during the short growing season, so these two grains are used almost exclusively. Sour rye bread is a special favorite of the Finns. Before yeast was commercially available for leavening, the dough was left to ferment, thus creating the gas that soured the dough and made it rise.

Wheat flour was not available in Finland until after 1900. Because it had to be imported, it was reserved for fancy baking and holiday breads. Wheat flour is added to the bread because it makes the dough easier to handle. Yeast is also added to shorten the process."

Geraldine Kangas

2 packages dry yeast
2 cups warm water
2 cups milk, scalded and cooled
1 tablespoon salt
1 egg

2 tablespoons honey (or brown sugar)
¾ cups graham flour
¾ cups cracked-wheat flour
½ cup farina wheat germ (optional)

9 to 11 cups white flour
½ cup margarine (or shortening), softened
butter, for glaze

1. Dissolve yeast in warm water. Add cooled milk, salt, egg, and honey. Gradually stir in graham flour, cracked-wheat flour, farina, and, if desired, wheat germ. Slowly add white flour, beating well after each addition.

2. When dough becomes stiff, turn it out onto a floured surface. Work in margarine or shortening, kneading until smooth. Shape into flat loaves and place on a lightly greased baking sheet. Prick all over with a fork. Let rise for only a short time.

3. Preheat oven to 375°F. Bake for 30 minutes or until light brown. Brush with butter while hot.

Karen Kiviluoma, Makinen, Minnesota.
Finnish Americans, 1980

Finnish Sour Rye Bread

Starter:
1½ cups buttermilk
1 cup medium rye flour (or pumpernickel rye graham)

1 package dry yeast
¼ cup warm water
2 tablespoons salt
1½ cups buttermilk
2½ cups rye flour

3½ to 4 cups flour
2 tablespoons cornmeal

1. Four days before making bread, combine buttermilk and flour. Put starter in a bowl, crock, or jar and leave in a warm place. Stir once a day. If it becomes dry, add small amounts of water.

2. Dissolve yeast in warm water and let stand for a few minutes. Mix in starter, salt, and buttermilk. Stir in flours.

3. Turn out dough onto a floured surface and knead for 5 minutes. Place in a greased bowl and let rise for 1 to 1½ hours.

4. Shape dough into 2 round loaves. Sprinkle baking sheet with cornmeal. Place bread on baking sheet and let rise for about 35 minutes. Preheat oven to 375°F.

5. Bake for 45 to 60 minutes. If bread becomes too brown, reduce heat to 350°F. Cool on a wire rack. Yields 2 loaves.

JoAnn Salo, Embarrass, Minnesota. Finnish Americans, 1980

"Coffee and pulla was the standard after sauna heat. The flavor of the pulla improves as it ages."

Patricia Salo Downs

Pulla (Finnish Cardamom Coffee Braid)

1. Dissolve yeast in warm water with 1 teaspoon sugar and let stand until spongy.

2. Scald milk, and add butter, salt, and remaining sugar. Cool to lukewarm. Add some of milk mixture to yeast.

3. Sift 2 cups flour with crushed cardamom and stir into yeast. Let stand for a few minutes.

4. Add remaining milk mixture. Gradually stir in 2 more cups flour. Mix in eggs and gradually add remaining flour. Keep the dough spongy, adding just enough flour so it is not sticky.

5. Knead dough for about 5 minutes and let rise for 1 hour. Preheat oven to 350°F. Divide dough into 6 portions, shape into braids, and use 3 braids to make each of 2 loaves. Let rise for about 1 hour.

6. Bake for 30 to 35 minutes. Brush braids with a syrup made of coffee and sugar. Serve with strawberry preserves, jelly, or jam. Yields 2 loaves.

JoAnn Salo

1 cake yeast
½ cup warm water
2 cups milk, scalded
½ cup butter
1½ teaspoons salt
½ cup sugar
7 to 8 cups
    unbleached flour
8 cardamom seeds,
    shelled and finely
    crushed
2 eggs

Syrup:
coffee
sugar

Zopf Brot (German Braided Bread)

1 ounce dry yeast
2 cups milk
1 cup sugar
¼ pound butter
1 tablespoon salt
1 egg, beaten
6 cups flour
1 cup raisins
1 tablespoon butter,
   melted

1. Warm 2 tablespoons milk. Dissolve yeast in milk with 2 tablespoons sugar.

2. Scald remaining milk and add butter, remaining sugar, salt, and egg. Combine with yeast.

3. Add a little flour and mix well. Add remaining flour, mixing to form a dough. Knead until smooth. Let rise until double in size, about 2 hours.

4. Preheat oven to 350°F. Punch down dough and knead in raisins. Divide dough into 3 parts and form into a braid (or make 2 braided loaves with 6 strands). Place on a baking sheet or in 2 loaf pans. Bake for 40 minutes. Brush with melted butter. Yields 1 or 2 loaves.

Wives of the Alte Kamaradan Band, Mequon, Wisconsin. Old Ways in the New World: German American, 1975

Moravian Love Feast Buns

"In the Moravian Church, a 'love feast' is a spiritual gathering consisting of worship, singing, talking, and enjoying a simple meal together. In 1971, when the members of the John Heckewelder Memorial Moravian Church gathered on the Mall to celebrate their 'love feast,' they were surprised to see a crowd of hippies gathering to join in what they thought was to be a love-in!"

Reverend Melvin Klokow

1 quart warm milk
3 cakes yeast
1½ cups sugar
¾ pound butter,
   softened
2 teaspoons salt
3 teaspoons
   cinnamon
flour

Glaze:
sugar
egg yolk
milk

1. Dissolve yeast in warm milk with 1 tablespoon sugar. Mix yeast with remaining ingredients, adding enough flour to make a soft dough.

2. Knead dough on a lightly floured surface and let rise until double, about 1 hour. Form into buns and place on greased baking sheets. Let rise again.

3. Preheat oven to 375°F. Brush buns with glaze of sugar, egg yolk, and milk. Bake until brown, about 30 minutes. Yields 25.

John Heckewelder Memorial Moravian Church, Gnadenhutten, Ohio. Ohio Program, 1971

Saffron Buns or Bread

10 to 15 grains
  saffron
1 teaspoon salt
1 cup boiling water
3 packages dry yeast
1 teaspoon sugar
1 cup flour
1 cup warm water
8 cups flour
2 cups sugar
¾ pound margarine
1 cup warm milk
1 cup currants
1 4-ounce package
  candied lemon peel
1 tablespoon salt

1. The night before making bread, steep saffron and salt in water.

2. The next day, make a sponge with yeast, 1 teaspoon sugar, 1 cup flour, and warm water. Let rise for about 15 minutes.

3. Combine remaining flour and sugar, then cut in margarine to make a dough.

4. Add warm milk to saffron mixture, then mix with yeast sponge. Stir in currants, lemon peel, and salt. Add to dough and mix well. Dough should come off hands easily. Let rise until double, about 1 to 2 hours.

5. Shape into buns or loaves, place in greased pans, and let rise again 30 to 40 minutes. Bake at 350°F for 30 minutes. Makes 3 dozen buns or 2 loaves.

Lucille Brown, Wakefield, Michigan. Michigan Program, 1987

"This is a traditional English 'background' food that can be made into buns or loaves. The rich, distinctive flavor of the saffron, along with the currants and lemon peel, makes this a family favorite, especially at Christmas and Easter."

Finnish Oven Pancake

1. Preheat oven to 375°F to 400°F.

2. In oven, melt butter in 2 8-inch round pans.

3. Beat eggs. Add milk, sugar, salt, and flour, beating constantly with a wire wisk.

4. Pour batter into the sizzling hot pans and bake for 30 to 40 minutes. Remove from pans as soon as possible to avoid sticking. Serve with jelly, syrup, or sugar.

Geraldine Kangas, Aurora, Minnesota. Finnish Americans, 1980

¼ cup butter
2 eggs
2 cups milk (or 1 cup
  each whole and
  evaporated milk)
2 tablespoons sugar
1 teaspoon salt
1 cup flour

Qtayif (Stuffed Pancakes)

"The oven pancake is a traditional Shrovetide food, originally using what we call 'new milk.' When the cow has a calf, the first and second milking cannot be used. By the third milking, the milk is not as strong and is used for the oven pancake, as well as to prepare cottage cheese, oven cheese, and squeaky cheese.

In demonstrating the preparation of the oven pancake at the Smithsonian Folklife Festival, we found out that most European countries make a similar pancake. The Swedish add salt pork, the Dutch and Jewish people add powdered sugar, and the Germans add apples. The English eliminate the sugar and use the fat from a beef roast to make their Yorkshire pudding. Oven pancakes are easy to prepare and excellent when served with strawberries."

Geraldine Kangas

Pancakes:
2 eggs
½ cup sugar
2 tablespoons oil
2 cups flour
1 teaspoon salt
3 teaspoons baking
    powder
1½ cups water

Cheese filling:
1½ pounds ricotta
    cheese (or farmer's
    cheese)
½ cup sugar
1 teaspoon orange-
    blossom water

Walnut filling:
1 cup ground walnuts
¼ water
1 tablespoon
    cinnamon
sugar (optional)

Syrup:
1 cup sugar
1 cup water

1. Mix ingredients for pancakes. Pour ¼ cup batter into a hot, greased pan or griddle. Cook pancakes, browning only 1 side. When bubbles appear on top, remove each pancake to a cookie sheet to add choice of filling.

2. To prepare cheese filling, mix cheese with sugar and flavoring; beat until smooth.

3. For walnut filling, grind walnuts in a blender with water; drain nuts and pat dry. Stir in cinnamon and, if desired, sugar.

4. Put a small amount of filling on half of each pancake, fold over the other side, and seal edges. Place on a greased cookie sheet and bake at 350°F for 10 minutes.

5. While baking, make syrup by dissolving sugar in water and boiling for 10 to 15 minutes. Pour syrup on pancakes when ready to serve.

Helen Mohammed Atwell, Dearborn, Michigan. Michigan Program, 1987

Nammura (Farina Cakes)

4⅔ cups farina
　　(or cream of wheat)
2½ cups sugar
2 teaspoons baking
　　powder
1 cup clarified butter
2⅓ cups milk
1 tablespoon oil
1 tablespoon rose water
pine nuts (or almonds)

Syrup:
2 cups sugar
1¼ cups water
1 tablespoon lemon
　　juice

1. In a mixer, blend farina, sugar, and baking powder. Combine wet ingredients and add to farina mixture, stirring until well mixed.

2. Pour batter into a greased 9 × 13-inch baking pan and place a pine nut in the center of each 1-inch square area. Bake at 350°F for 30 to 45 minutes.

3. While cake is cooking, combine syrup ingredients and cook for 5 to 10 minutes. When cake is done but still warm, cut into squares and cover with syrup.

Helen Mohammed Atwell

Cornish Saffron Cake

15 grains saffron
1 cup boiling water
½ cup butter
1½ cups sugar
¼ teaspoon lemon
　　extract
2 eggs
2¾ cups flour, sifted
2 teaspoons baking
　　powder
1 cup raisins
1 cup currants
1 cup candied fruit

1. Steep saffron in boiling water and let sit until cool, or overnight.

2. Preheat oven to 350°F. Grease and flour a 9 × 13-inch pan.

3. Cream butter and sugar; add lemon extract. Add eggs and mix well.

4. Combine dry ingredients with fruit. Add to butter mixture, alternating with saffron liquid.

5. Pour into prepared pan, sprinkle with sugar, and bake for 45 to 50 minutes.

Eunice Jewell, Dodgeville, Wisconsin. Old Ways in the New World: British American, 1976

❝When I was married in 1950, the cost of fifteen grains of saffron was twenty-five cents. When I went to Washington in 1976, it cost $1. Today, it costs $2.50 at our local corner drugstore. In many areas, saffron costs $7 to $9 for fifteen grains. And if you're Cornish, you need saffron to make the twelve loaves of saffron bread you give away at Christmas. This is so people will have twelve months of good luck. At Christmas, to ensure good luck every month, extra loaves are given and received with joy. ❞

Moravian Sugar Cake

1 cup hot mashed
   potatoes
1 cup sugar
1 package dry yeast
1 cup warm water

¾ teaspoon salt
1 cup margarine (or
   butter), melted
2 eggs, beaten
4 cups flour

Topping:
¼ pound cold butter,
   cut into chips
1 pound brown sugar
cinnamon

1. Combine potatoes and sugar, mashing sugar so it dissolves.

2. Dissolve yeast in warm water. Add to potato mixture with salt, margarine, and eggs, stirring well after each addition. Sift flour and add to batter, mixing until smooth.

3. Cover with a tea towel and let rise in a warm place for about 5 hours.

4. Spoon batter ½ inch deep into 8-inch cake or pie pans. Let rise for about 1 hour, until puffy.

5. Preheat oven to 350°F. Punch holes about 1 inch apart in batter. Put in chips of cold butter, pushing down with brown sugar; do not make holes too deep, or the sugar and butter will go to the bottom of the pan. Put more sugar on top of cake. If holes are covered up, punch more so sugar can run. Sprinkle lightly with cinnamon. Bake for about 25 minutes. Cool for 5 minutes in pan. Yields 6.

John Heckewelder Memorial Moravian Church, Gnadenhutten, Ohio. Ohio Program, 1971

Blitz Torte

"Blitz torte was one of the cakes that good German cooks served. Guests in the old days didn't concern themselves with diet and cholesterol problems, and one of the marks of a good cook was her rich, tasty desserts."

½ cup sugar
½ cup butter
6 eggs, separated
3 tablespoons milk
1 cup flour
1 teaspoon baking
   powder

¾ cup powdered
   sugar
1 cup slivered
   almonds

Custard:
1 egg

1 cup milk
½ cup sugar
1 tablespoon flour
pinch of salt
1 teaspoon vanilla
   extract

1. Preheat oven to 350°F.

2. Cream sugar and butter. Add egg yolks and milk. Mix dry ingredients and add to batter. Spread in 2 buttered 9-inch pans.

3. Adding powdered sugar gradually, beat egg whites until stiff. Spread on top of batter, sprinkle with almonds, and bake for 20 to 25 minutes. Cool.

4. Mix custard ingredients and boil until thick, stirring constantly. Spread on top of cooled torte.

Wives of the Alte Kamaradan Band, Mequon, Wisconsin. Old Ways in the New World: German American, 1975

Thimble Tarts

---

2 cups flour
1 teaspoon salt
¾ cup lard
   (or shortening)

1 egg
5 tablespoons water
butter, softened
jelly or jam

1. Preheat oven to 375°F.

2. Mix flour and salt, and cut in lard or shortening. Beat egg with water and add to dry ingredients.

3. Gently knead dough. Roll on a floured surface, then cut into 2- to 3-inch rounds with a cookie cutter. Using a thimble, make a small hole in the center of half of the rounds. Butter all rounds on one side. Sandwich 2 rounds, placing buttered sides together. The round with the thimble hole becomes the top.

4. Bake on greased cookie sheets or in muffin pans until golden brown, about 15 to 20 minutes. Cool slightly.

5. Pull apart tarts and spread your favorite jelly or jam on the center of the bottom piece. Top with the round that has the thimble hole. Tarts may be covered with whipped cream, but most people enjoy them with the bright jelly showing in the center.

Eunice Jewell, Dodgeville, Wisconsin. Old Ways in the New World: British American, 1976

"We took advantage of every opportunity to visit the historic sights of Washington; but we especially enjoyed our contact with the guests who came from different areas of the United States and those from foreign countries — the Pearly Queen from London, the Gaelic singers, the Morris dancers, Jean Ritchie, ballad singers, clog dancers, storytellers, musicians, fiddlers, dulcimer players, and many others. The folk music that was played long into the night remained with me for a long time; strains still awaken in me memories of that time."

Belgian Pie

Dough:
2 ounces dry yeast
½ cup warm water
1 tablespoon sugar
6 eggs
¼ cup sugar
1 cup cream, scalded
   and cooled slightly
½ pound butter,
   softened
5 cups flour

Prune filling:
3 pounds prunes,
   pitted
¾ cup sugar

Rice filling:
⅔ cup uncooked rice
¾ cup water
1 quart milk
4 eggs, beaten
¾ cup sugar
vanilla extract

Cheese topping:
3 pounds dry cottage
   (or baker's) cheese
1 cup sugar
2 tablespoons flour
4 eggs

1. Dissolve yeast in warm water with 1 tablespoon sugar and let stand until bubbly. Beat eggs with remaining sugar. Combine yeast mixture, cream, and butter. Stir in flour.

2. Divide dough into 12 balls. Let stand for 10 minutes, then roll out each to fit a greased pie pan. The dough will be soft and may require a little more flour.

3. To make prune filling, soak prunes with water to cover and cook until tender. Drain and save the juice. Mash prunes and add sugar and enough juice to make a spreading consistency.

4. For rice filling, cook rice with a small amount of water until tender. Add milk and simmer until rice is done. Add eggs and sugar and simmer on low heat until thick. Add vanilla to taste.

5. Make cheese topping by beating all ingredients. If it is too thick to spread, add a little cream.

6. Preheat oven to 350°F. Put filling on dough and spread with cheese topping. Bake for about 15 minutes. Yields 12 (6 of each filling).

Mary Jane Porath, Casco, Wisconsin. Old Ways in the New World: Belgian American, 1976

Cousin Jack Cookies

2 cups flour
½ cup sugar
2 teaspoons baking
   powder
pinch of salt
pinch of nutmeg
½ cup shortening
1 egg
½ cup milk
1 cup currants
   (or ¼ cup chopped
   candied lemon
   peel)

1. Preheat oven to 350°F.

2. Sift dry ingredients. Cut in shortening as for a pie crust.

3. Beat together egg and milk. Add to flour mixture, with currants or lemon peel.

4. Pat dough out on a floured surface. Cut in circles with a cookie cutter and place on a greased baking sheet. Bake at 350°F for 15 minutes.

Lucille Brown, Wakefield, Michigan. Michigan Program, 1987

"When the miners came to America, they would send back to England saying that they had a 'cousin' who could work in the mine here. A lot of them were called Jack, thus 'Cousin Jack' cookies."

Belgian Lukken Cookies

1 pound butter,
   softened
2 cups sugar
1 egg
2½ ounces whiskey
   (or brandy)
1 teaspoon vanilla
   extract
4 cups flour
1 teaspoon salt

1. Cream butter and sugar. Stir in egg, whiskey, and vanilla, mixing well. Add flour and salt, mixing thoroughly.

2. Refrigerate in a covered plastic container until the dough is stiff enough to handle, about 2 to 3 hours.

3. Roll chilled dough into finger lengths and put in the center of a hot wafelizer iron that has been buttered or sprayed with a nonstick cooking or baking spray. Count to 12 or 15 before turning cookie. Cook until light brown, then lift cookies from iron with a spatula; place on paper towels to cool. Store in a covered container in a cool place.

Evelyn A. VanPuyvelde, Moline, Illinois. Old Ways in the New World: Belgian American, 1976

"Lukken are a waffle cookie, wafer thin, made one by one using a special wafelizer placed on top of a gas burner. They are very fragile and break easily. Lukken are served primarily during the holidays."

Norwegian Spritz Cookies

1 cup butter
1 cup sugar
1 egg
2½ to 3 cups flour
2 teaspoons baking
  powder
¼ teaspoon salt

1. Cream butter and sugar, then add egg. Mix flour (start with 2½ cups), baking powder, and salt. Add to butter mixture. Dough should be soft enough to go through a spritz iron easily. (The iron makes the distinctive S shape.)

2. Preheat oven to 375°F.

3. Make 4 cookies as a test to determine whether dough has enough flour. If cookies spread out too much, add remaining ½ cup flour.

4. Bake 2 pans of cookies for 4 minutes, then reverse pans on oven racks, changing pan directions also, front and back, and bake for 4 or more minutes. Edges should be barely brown. Yields 5 dozen.

Gudrun Vaatveit Berg and Barbara B. Swenson, Bemidji and Tonka Bay, Minnesota. The Grand Generation: Folklore and Aging, 1984

"Every Christmas my mother, Gudrun Vaatveit Berg, would bake cookies just as her mother had done. Of course, baking these special delicacies started after Thanksgiving, for we had to have seven different cookies, one for every day of the Christmas week. A good Scandinavian cook can stake her reputation on the fragility of her cookies.

Mother would bake one cookie batch each day, made mostly of butter and sugar because they are so very delicate. In fact, when we took cookies to someone else's house for a holiday gathering, we would carefully place them in a box on top of a pillow on the car seat. At home, Mother would then hide the cookies in a big dress box on the top shelf of the linen closet, but I knew where they were and could stuff several in my mouth before Mom discovered what I had done.

At the Smithsonian Folklife Festival, we worked in an archaic kitchen tent with a gas stove that was difficult to regulate, and the weather was hot and muggy. Our conditions were not much better than our pioneer ancestors in the prairies of the Midwest! When we had a failure during our demonstration, we reminded our audience that these were winter cookies baked at Christmastime. They have to be stored in a dry, slightly warm place — freezing would destroy rosettes and krumkake."

Barbara B. Swenson

Krumkake Cookies

½ cup whipping
   cream
3 eggs
1 cup sugar
1¼ cups flour, sifted
¼ pound butter,
   melted
1 teaspoon vanilla
   extract

1. Whip cream. Beat eggs lightly and add to cream. Stir in remaining ingredients.

2. Bake on a krumkake iron on top of the stove. Turn iron once while baking. Remove cookies from iron with a spatula and roll at once around a wooden krumkake roller. Set aside to cool.

Gudrun Vaatveit Berg and Barbara B. Swenson

Rosettes

2 eggs
1 teaspoon sugar
¼ teaspoon salt
1 cup milk
¼ cup cornstarch
¾ cup flour
lard, for frying

Topping:
whipped cream
peanut brittle
   (optional)
sugar

1. Beat eggs lightly, then stir in sugar, salt, and milk. Sift cornstarch with flour and add to eggs.

2. With a rosette iron in a deep frying pan, heat lard to 375°F to 400°F. Spread a thick cloth or cloths next to pan, and tap iron on cloth to remove some lard. Dip iron in batter, then in hot fat to fry rosettes. Remove cookies from iron by tapping iron lightly with a fork.

3. Top rosettes with whipped cream and, if desired, sprinkle with crushed homemade peanut brittle. Just before serving, dip each rosette in a bowl of sugar to cover completely.

Gudrun Vaatveit Berg and Barbara B. Swenson

Cherry Dumpling Soup

Dumplings:
1 tablespoon butter
3 tablespoons sugar
3 eggs
½ cup milk
½ teaspoon nutmeg
½ teaspoon salt
½ teaspoon baking
    powder
1 to 1½ cups flour

2 quarts canned
    sweetened cherries
    (or 2 quarts fresh
    cherries plus 2 cups
    sugar)
1 lemon slice
½ cup cherry wine
    (optional)

1. In a mixer, beat dumpling ingredients, adding enough flour to make a soft dough.

2. Boil 3 to 4 cups water and drop in batter by teaspoonfuls; dumplings will float to the top when done.

3. Add cherries and lemon slice, and simmer until cherries are cooked. Stir in wine, if desired, just before serving. Serve hot or cold.

Wives of the Alte Kamaradan Band, Mequon, Wisconsin. Old Ways in the New World: German American, 1975

"Our area was settled by German families who farmed. The farmers raised dairy cattle for income and had a variety of other crops to provide for most of the family food needs, including fruit orchards. Cherries ripened around July 4, and the women made cherry dumpling soup as a refreshing, cool lunch or supper treat to be eaten during some of the hottest days of the year.**"

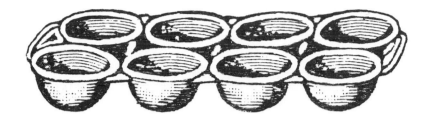

Maple Sugar Candy

1. Boil 1 quart maple syrup to 236°F. Stir while hot until milky in appearance and almost set.

2. Pour into muffin tins or molds. Cool until sugar cakes will drop from tins or molds. Yields 2 pounds.

Paul Richards, Chardon, Ohio. Ohio Program, 1971

Maple Cream Candy

1. Boil 1 quart maple sugar briskly to 234°F, or soft-ball stage. Keep sides of the pan free of crystals.

2. Pour syrup about ¾ inch deep into a shallow dish. Do not scrape pan when pouring syrup. Cool until lukewarm.

3. Stir with a spoon until light and creamy. Pour into a greased dish. Cut into squares. Yields 2 pounds.

Paul Richards

"Maple sugaring has been a large part of our family livelihood since my parents started in the maple business in 1910. Today, two of our children and one son-in-law work in our business, and now the grandchildren are eager to learn. This year, the seven-year-old boy tapped trees and made four gallons of maple syrup."

Great Plains

➤ · ➤ · ➤ · ➤

Lynne Ireland

T he "great American desert," some call it. Flat, treeless expanses stretch for miles in some places; where it is not flat, hills roll like endless ocean waves. There is hardly a respectable feature to divert the eye. Pretty dull territory, compared to purple mountains' majesty. For many the Great Plains were, and continue to be, a place to get through, an endurance trial to survive on the way to somewhere else. But others have come to know that the region's plain appearance is deceiving. A treasure trove of flora and fauna and unique land and water masses exist, largely unnoticed, on the Great Plains. The largest sand-dune area in the Western Hemisphere is here, covered with grass in what is now Nebraska. Underneath the sandy surface lies the Ogallala Aquifer, an underground water system that extends from Texas to North Dakota and gives truth to the old saying that on the plains the rivers run upside down — sand on the top, water down below.

Like the Great Plains environment, plains people have been characterized as predictably boring. Everyone knows these folks — farmers wearing bib overalls and seed caps, sporting white foreheads and red noses, flanked by plump women who are accustomed to being called "the missus."

Anything but Plain

Plains food is as easy to dismiss. Everyone knows that this is the land of white bread, meat and potatoes, and hot dishes made with cream of fill-in-the-blank soup. Salads and desserts both are spelled J-e-l-l-O. Like most stereotypes, these monotonous visions have some basis in fact. Yet, plains food is anything but plain.

Take, for example, the food at a German Russian wedding dance. Simple food, maybe — roast beef, potatoes, kraut, pickles, chicken noodle soup with butterballs, rye bread with caraway seeds, and custardy, fruit-filled kuchen. Then there is the "lunch" served late in the evening, after hours of dancing polkas and waltzes have rendered the earlier, substantial meal a memory. Out

Previous pages: Canning the harvest is a tradition developed to survive on the plains. (Janet Gilmore)

from the kitchen come the cooks with trays of garlic sausage and heaps of rye bread and crisp sour pickles. Beer washes it all down, the perfect complement.

Some of the best food I have ever eaten I found on the plains, some of it served in the most unpretentious settings: that German-Russian wedding feast at the Legion hall on the Scottsbluff-Gering highway in Nebraska's panhandle. Roast lamb, spinach, and feta cheese under the shelter of the cottonwood grove on Connie (Constantine) Laposotes's farm near Bayard. Tortillas warm off the cast-iron stove lid that Joe Moreno's mom used instead of a griddle on top of her electric range. Sourdough pancakes spread with chokecherry jelly, the wild fruit gathered on a Sandhills ranch. The Swedish cheese pudding, ostkaka, its creamy whiteness splashed with the magenta of tart lingonberry sauce. On the Great Plains, as elsewhere, traditional foods feed the body and the soul.

These days especially, traditional foods face an uphill battle. In many small towns, the young measure culture in terms of proximity to McDonald's. And yet, traditions survive. Long after Nebraska families of Swedish descent moved off the farm — and lost their ready access to raw milk — they still search out a quasi-legal source of this vital ingredient for ostkaka. "Sure, I'll sell you raw milk," the dairy farmer says, "but you have to bring your own container." In the days before Christmas a wonderful black market operates just outside Nebraska's capital. City folks pull up in the farmyard and appear at the back door, jars and picnic jugs in hand. As one family loads its contraband into the car, headlights in the driveway signal the arrival of another raw-milk smuggler. Those departing greet the new customers with a nod and a question that is more like a password, "You here for ostkaka?"

Such traditions may seem like a lot of trouble, but food has only lately become a take-it-for-granted proposition on the plains. The Native American tribes that moved into this region centuries ago had much to learn about their new home's resources. The Omaha, Ponca, Oto, Pawnee, and Sioux became masters at using what the plains offered. Corn and buffalo were the kingpins of a food system that incorporated a surprising variety of meat, fish, fowl, and flora — chokecherries, ground cherries, milkweed pods, arrowroot, and cattail, to name a few. Most European and American settlers on the plains chose not to benefit from the native people's experience. The newcomers were unsure about the safe use of unfamiliar plants and even less certain about consuming "native" food. Accordingly, monotony was the standard bill of fare as homesteaders established claims and planted crops.

Corn was the great staple; easily grown, it produced the added bonus of cobs for fuel. An 1861 edition of the *Nebraska Farmer* suggested thirty-one

On the Great Plains, as elsewhere, traditional foods feed the body and the soul.

Corn and Still Corn

dishes to make from cornmeal, including mush, johnnycakes, muffins, griddle cakes, Indian pudding, corn dodgers, whitpot, and samp. Mush and corn bread, the most commonly eaten cornmeal dishes, appeared at every meal in some pioneer households. Toppings and side dishes — milk, sorghum, fried salt pork (sowbelly), or meat drippings — provided variety, but as the saying went, "No matter how you disguised it, it was still corn."

Families experienced monotony during feast times as well as famine. Drying was the only preservation method available to women who lived far from the railroad or were too poor to afford canning jars. So people ate garden produce when it was ripe — and ate it and ate it. More than one kid grew up hating watermelon. And more than one complaining youngster spouted, "Spit in my ears and tell me lies, but give me no more dried-apple pies."

Make-do Spirit

Scarcity was as much a fact of life as monotony. Nutrition was calculated on a monthly, or yearly, basis. Fresh meat, fresh fruits, and fresh vegetables were not available for "one-a-day" consumption. In the 1870s small game populations dwindled, and deer, antelope, and buffalo became rare in some parts of the plains. Pork became the staple meat. Hogs were butchered in the chill of autumn, and for a few meals the family knew the luxury of fresh meat. Most of the cuts were smoked, salted, or packed away in lard. All too soon the household was down to eating sowbelly and beans again.

Fresh vegetables also were a seasonal delight. Lamb's-quarters, purslane, dock, and mustard were welcome additions to a spring meal. When it rained rain and not grasshoppers, gardens yielded beans, carrots, potatoes, and other vegetables for the summer months, with some to spare. Women nursed fruit trees through blistering summers and frigid winters and lived on wild plums, chokecherries, buffalo berries, and gooseberries until domestic fruit stock produced. Dried apples and canned fruits such as peaches and pears could be acquired by bartering at the nearest store. The farm wife's eggs and butter were the usual medium of exchange. And when there simply was no fruit, cooks improvised. Soda crackers and spice made a surprisingly adequate "apple" pie. Vinegar replaced scarce-as-hen's-teeth lemons for a tart, meringue-topped dessert.

The same make-do spirit applied to beverages. Coffee, an expensive commodity when available, was extended or replaced by roasted barley, wheat, carrots, and native chicory. Native and domestic herbs were brewed for teas to quench the thirst and cure the body's ills. Summer coolers such as switchel were mixed from such unlikely ingredients as brown sugar, vinegar, molasses, and water. Elderberries, dandelions, and plums were gathered for the wine barrel.

These patterns of monotony, scarcity, and making-do were part and parcel of the homesteading experience. Similar hard times were known by peo-

➤ • ➤ • ➤ • ➤

"Spit in my ears and tell me lies, but give me no more dried-apple pies."

➤ • ➤ • ➤ • ➤

ple who settled along the rivers in the 1860s, those who branched out from the railroad lines in the 1880s, and those who ventured out onto the high plains in the new century.

If scarcity and monotony challenged "American" homesteaders, immigrants faced these troubles and more. The Germans, Scandinavians, Bohemians, German Russians, Poles, and, later, Mexicans and southern blacks who came to this region were in for a rude surprise. Gone were the herbs, mushrooms, vegetables, fish, cheese, bake oven — the tastes of home. Shocked by a new climate of interminable subarctic winters, Saharan summers, and ceaseless wind, immigrants tried to find what solace they could in a semblance of traditional food.

Willa Cather described one Bohemian family's Old Country culinary prize in *My Antonia*. "As we rose to go, she opened her wooden chest and brought out a bag made of bed-ticking, about as long as a flour sack and half as wide, stuffed full of something.... When Mrs. Shimerda opened the bag and stirred the contents with her hand, it gave out a salty, earthy smell, very pungent, even among the other odors of that cave. She measured a teacup full, tied it up in a bit of sacking, and presented it ceremoniously to grandmother. 'For cook,' she announced. 'Little now; be very much when cook,' spreading out her hands as if to indicate that the pint would swell to a gallon. 'Very good. You no have in this country. All things for eat better in my country.'" The American grandmother in the story was not convinced and threw the package and its contents of little brown roots into the stove. But her grandson "bit off a corner of one of the chips.... I never forgot the strange taste; though it was many years before I knew that those little brown shavings, which the Shimerdas had brought so far and treasured so jealously, were dried mushrooms. They had been gathered, probably, in some deep Bohemian forest...."

Cooks coaxed something like the food of home out of cast-iron stoves fueled with cobs, if they were lucky, or with cow chips, if they were not. Chips were another challenge. More than one woman had to overcome the distaste she felt not only for gathering manure, but also for bringing it into the home and cooking over it. Chips burned hot but quickly, so maintaining even minimal standards of cleanliness was a chore. In *Western Story: The Recollections of Charley O'Kieffe, 1884–1898*, the task was described this way: "Here is the rundown of the operations that mother went through when making baking powder biscuits... stoke the stove, get out the flour sack, stoke the stove, wash your hands, mix the biscuit dough, stoke the stove, wash your hands, cut out the biscuits with the top of a baking powder can, stoke the stove, wash your hands, put the pan of biscuits in the oven, keep on stoking the stove until the biscuits are done (not forgetting to wash the hands before taking up the biscuits)."

Coaxing Flavors of Home

From Privation to Plenty

In time, the privations of homestead days gave way to plenty for Yankee settler and foreign farmer alike. Still, values of frugality prevailed. Hard times have a way of coming back on the plains. Maybe the watermelon the family grew to hate could not be canned, but once there were sugar and jars, the rind could be pickled. Willa Cather defined a type of plains woman — the inveterate canner — in her description of one Swedish immigrant in *O Pioneers!*: "Alexandra often said that if her mother were cast upon a desert island, she would thank God for her deliverance, make a garden, and find something to preserve." In the Sandhills and on the high plains where shifting sandy soil and slight rainfall made farming impossible, people established food traditions that continue to this day.

Beef — not corn — is, and was, the staple. City slickers are pointedly reminded that they will not find anything resembling a plow on a ranch. Cattlemen bristle at the suggestion that we would be healthier if we ate less beef. Beef is consumed two or three times a day, in cheerful defiance of the two or three times a week recommended by the American Heart Association.

On both ranch and farm, the meal patterns are dictated by work schedules. Breakfast comes a couple of hours after the day's labors have begun. Dinner is the noon meal, and depending on where the work is, the meal often comes to the field. Supper is eaten at night — sometimes well after dark. The term *lunch* designates the sweet rolls, coffee, sandwiches, pickles, and cake that are delivered to the fields mid-morning and mid-afternoon.

Some traditional plains food has had an impact beyond its original community. "Rocky Mountain oysters," once a spring dish that appeared on ranch tables at castrating time, have become a snack in taverns and steakhouses across the region. Kolaches (sweet rolls with apricot, prune, poppyseed, cherry, or cheese fillings) beckon from grocery bakery cases, although they resemble the traditional version of the Czech pastry about as much as the coffee-cart "Danish" takes after its progenitor. Cops, construction workers, and political cronies crowd Omaha's Sons of Italy hall for the weekly pasta feed. Far removed from its traditional context, the German Russian pridoch (a combination of ground beef, cabbage, and onions baked inside bread dough) has become the trademarked Runza, sold by the thousands at fast-food outlets in Kansas, Nebraska, Colorado, Illinois, Iowa, and Las Vegas. In an ironic twist of fate, the descendants of German Russian immigrants who left Russia to find a better life in the United States are returning to the Soviet Union to sell Runzas to the Russians.

Food enthusiasts have discovered traditional foods, but if they cannot experience the food in context, they can at least eat the Sunday "duck 'n' dumplings" dinner at Harold and Heidi's Café in Crete, Nebraska, and wait in line with Mexican customers at Jacobo's in Omaha for the once-a-week offering of tamales. But finding a market for traditional foods does not guar-

Opposite: Kolaches and other Czech pastries are common fare in some parts of the plains. (James P. Leary)

antee their survival. Food fads change quickly, and the food hobbyists will soon move on to something else.

The Food Remains

Ultimately, the fate of traditional plains foods will rest with the plains people who call those traditions their own. Even where the tongue of the Old Country is silent, the old songs forgotten, the food remains. It would probably be easier to let these traditions fade and to eat only what television tells us to. But traditions die hard. On the plains, at powwows and family reunions, at birthdays and funerals, at the breakfast table and the picnic table, old food customs are faithfully carried on. One family still follows grandmother's rule: regardless of the time of day, if the food on the table includes potatoes, then it is a meal, and you have to say grace. In another family, certain recipes are such a valued asset that they are bequeathed in wills.

The future of farm and ranch food is more precarious. Every census count since 1920 has shown that most parts of the Great Plains continue to lose people. The number of farms dwindle every day; family-owned farms do not have to become a thing of the past, but they well may. Still, the traditions of plains people are powerful. Maybe the number of people will continue to drop. Maybe the farms will be owned by multinational corporations. Maybe the farmers will become salaried employees. But I would be willing to wager that at noontime the plains worker will still stop for "dinner." And even if it is delivered in a pickup bearing a corporate logo, at ten in the morning and four in the afternoon, people will still stop for "lunch."

➤ · ➤ · ➤ · ➤

Recipes

Gollodetz
(Jellied Pork Hocks)

Baked Round Steak with Dressing

Bierocks
(Mennonite Baked Sandwich)

Schweitzer Käse (Swiss Hard Cheese)

Kaese Beroggi
(Cottage Cheese Pockets)

Riven Ost Kartofler
(Grated Cheese Potatoes)

Noodles with Prunes

Rødkaal (Danish Red Cabbage)

Halupsy (Cabbage Rolls)

White Bread

Cherry Dumplings

Kuchen (German Coffee Cake)

Grebble (Fried Pastries)

Czech Kolaches

Ableskage
(Danish Apple Cake)

Danish Puff Pastry

Danish Aebleskivers

Wine Soup

New Year's Cookies

Gollodetz (Jellied Pork Hocks)

2½ pounds fresh
   pork hocks
1 teaspoon salt
1 quart water
¼ teaspoon pepper
1 bay leaf
1 clove garlic, minced

1. Boil pork hocks with salt in water. Add seasonings and simmer until tender.

2. Let broth sit until cold, then remove the fat and bay leaf. Cut the meat off the bones and put it back into the liquid.

3. Thoroughly chill mixture to jell, then cut into slices.

Note: Chicken may be substituted for the pork hocks.

Anne Roesch Larson, Aberdeen, South Dakota. Regional America: Northern Plains, 1975

Baked Round Steak with Dressing

2 pounds round steak
salt
pepper
1 small onion,
   chopped
4 tablespoons mar-
   garine (or butter)
4 cups bread crumbs
½ cup chopped celery
¼ teaspoon sage
¼ teaspoon salt
1 egg, beaten
water

1. Season steak with salt and pepper to taste.

2. Make dressing by frying onion in margarine until brown. Mix with remaining ingredients, adding enough water to moisten well.

3. Spread dressing on steak, roll up, and tie securely. Place in a covered roasting pan. Bake at 325°F for 2 to 2½ hours. Slice and serve with baked potatoes. Serves 4.

Genevieve Trinka, Lidgerwood, North Dakota. Regional America: The Heartland, 1976

Bierocks (Mennonite Baked Sandwich)

1 pound lean ground
   beef
1 large onion, diced
salt
pepper
5 cups shredded
   cabbage
dough for 24 buns

1. Brown meat and onion with salt and pepper.

2. Add cabbage and cook until done, stirring occasionally.

3. Roll out dough for each bun to a 4-inch circle. Fill with ¼ cup filling. Bring together opposite corners in the center. Press edges to seal.

4. Turn bierocks smooth side up on a greased cookie sheet. Let them sit for 15 minutes, then bake at 350°F until brown. Serve hot. Yields 24.

Meta Goering Juhnke, Moundridge, Kansas. Regional America: The Heartland, 1976

Schweitzer Käse (Swiss Hard Cheese)

"Early in this century, in the spring, my grandmother would make hard cheese when there was a surplus of milk on the farm. She emigrated from Volhynia (then Polish Russia) to Kansas in 1874, but originally her people were Amish and came from Switzerland. The recipe is called Swiss cheese, but it is possible that she and her family learned about it in Volhynia.

My own family lived on a farm in the 1970s. We milked a cow and had more milk than we needed, so I made many rounds of cheese, which became a favorite food for my six children. At the 1976 Festival of American Folklife, an interpreter told a group of Polish sausage demonstrators what I was doing, and they were so excited because their families made cheese much as I did. You see, the recipe had survived the migration and was now a bridge across national boundaries."

2 gallons raw milk
½ rennet tablet

1 Hansen's cheese-colored tablet (optional)

½ cup cold water
1 teaspoon salt

1. Allow 1 gallon evening milk to ripen overnight in a cool place, about 50°F to 60°F. (If raw milk is not available, add 1 pint cultured sour milk or cream to commercial milk.) Pour in 1 gallon fresh morning milk. This combination gives a better cheese than if only fresh milk is used.

2. Warm milk to 86°F in an enamel or tin pail. If yellow cheese is desired, dissolve cheese-colored tablet in 1 teaspoon water and stir into milk.

3. Dissolve ½ rennet tablet in water and stir until completely dissolved. Add rennet solution to milk, stirring thoroughly for 1 minute. Let stand undisturbed for 35 to 40 minutes, until a firm curd forms.

4. Test firmness of curd with your finger; if it breaks cleanly over your finger, it is ready to cut. Cut curd into ⅜-inch squares, using a small butcher knife so that the blade will go to the bottom of the pail. Stir curd by hand for about 15 minutes, and carefully cut up the largest pieces that rise from the bottom.

5. Slowly warm curd on low heat to about 102°F, raising the temperature every 1½ to 5 minutes. Stir vigorously to keep curd from sticking together. Leave curd in the warm whey until it becomes firm enough so that the pieces will easily shake apart when pressed together, about 1 hour.

6. Pour curd into a cheesecloth 3 to 4 inches square. Hold the corners in each hand and let the curd roll back and forth without sticking together for 2 or 3 minutes, allowing the whey to run off. Then sprinkle with salt and mix well with hands. Tie cloth corners, forming curd into a ball. Hang up for ½ to ¾ hour to allow whey to drip off.

7. Take a long cloth the size of a dish towel and fold to about 3 inches wide. Wrap tightly around cheese ball, forming a round loaf about 6 inches in diameter. Firmly press down cheese. Place 3 or 4 thicknesses of cloth above and under cheese. Put in a cheese press or an improvised wooden frame, and place 2 bricks on top. Let stand overnight.

8. The next morning, remove cloths from cheese and place on a board for a half day, turning occasionally until the rind is completely dry.

9. Dip cheese in paraffin heated to 110°F to 120°F in a deep pan.

10. Store in a clean, cool, frost-free cellar. Turn over each day for a few days and then 2 or 3 times a week. The cheese is usually good to eat after 3 or 4 weeks. Yields 1½ to 2 pounds.

Meta Goering Juhnke, Moundridge, Kansas. Regional America: The Heartland, 1976

Kaese Beroggi (Cottage Cheese Pockets)

1 egg plus 1 egg white
¾ cup milk
 (or water)
2 cups sifted flour
½ teaspoon baking
 powder
½ teaspoon salt

Filling:
2 egg yolks
1 pint dry cottage
 cheese
½ teaspoon salt
dash of pepper

Sauce:
1 tablespoon
 shortening
1 tablespoon fine
 bread crumbs
½ cup half and half

1. Mix egg and egg white with milk or water.

2. Add dry ingredients and stir or knead to make a medium-soft dough. Add a little flour if the dough is sticky. Let stand for 1 hour. Roll out ⅛ inch thick and cut into 3-inch squares.

3. To make filling, mix all ingredients.

4. Put 1 tablespoon filling on each dough square, fold into a triangle, and pinch edges to seal.

5. In a large pan of boiling water, cook the beroggi, adding a few at a time, for 7 to 8 minutes. Lift out with a slotted spoon.

6. To prepare sauce, melt shortening in a large frying pan. Brown bread crumbs, stirring constantly. Add half and half and bring to a boil. Keep beroggi warm by adding them to the sauce. Cover and turn the heat to low until ready to serve.

Note: For kraut beroggi, substitute 2 tablespoons drained sauerkraut for the cheese mixture.

Meta Goering Juhnke

❝Beroggi are like the Polish pierogi. In our community, the Ukrainian term 'verenika' (varenyky) is used for these dumplings when the sauce is made with fried bacon and onion bits cooked with cream or half and half.❞

Anna K. Juhnke

Riven Ost Kartofler (Grated Cheese Potatoes)

6 potatoes
¼ cup flour
¼ cup grated
   Parmesan cheese
¾ teaspoon salt
⅛ teaspoon pepper
⅔ cup butter

1. Peel potatoes and cut into quarters.

2. In a bag, mix flour, cheese, salt, and pepper. Shake potatoes in mixture.

3. Melt butter in a flat baking dish and add potatoes. Bake at 350°F for 1 hour. Serves 6.

Esther A. Jorgensen, Viborg, South Dakota. Regional America: Northern Plains, 1975

Noodles with Prunes

3 eggs
3 tablespoons milk
1 teaspoon salt
flour
2 quarts milk
prunes (or raisins),
   cooked
bread cubes
butter

1. Beat eggs and add 3 tablespoons milk and salt. Stir in enough flour to make a firm dough.

2. Turn dough onto a floured surface and knead in flour until dough is stiff. Roll out very thin, in round sheets. Dry on towels until dry but flexible. Roll up like a jellyroll, then cut roll into thin slices. Fluff and separate the noodles.

3. Bring milk to a boil in a large pot. Add noodles and simmer until cooked, about 20 minutes.

4. Garnish with slices of cooked prunes or raisins and top with bread cubes browned in melted butter.

Anne Roesch Larson, Aberdeen, South Dakota. Regional America: Northern Plains, 1975

Rødkaal (Danish Red Cabbage)

1 medium head red
cabbage
1 tablespoon butter
½ cup vinegar
¼ cup sugar
1 teaspoon salt
¼ cup currant jelly
(optional)

1. Remove outer leaves and core of cabbage and finely shred.

2. Melt butter in a large pot or kettle. Add cabbage, vinegar, sugar, and salt, and simmer for about 2 hours, until tender.

3. Season to taste with additional vinegar, sugar, or salt and currant jelly, if desired. Serves 4 to 6.

Esther A. Jorgensen

Halupsy (Cabbage Rolls)

1 head cabbage
water
½ cup vinegar

Filling:
1 pound ground beef
½ pound ground
pork
1 cup uncooked rice
1 large onion,
chopped

Sauce:
1 16-ounce can
stewed tomatoes
1 pint sour cream (or
half and half)

1. Steam cabbage in a large pot with some water and vinegar. Break off the leaves and cut out the heavy rib. Reserve the liquid.

2. To make filling, combine uncooked meat, rice, and onion.

3. Place a heaping tablespoon of meat mixture on a leaf of cabbage. Fold in the sides and roll to make a neat package.

4. Place rolls in a roasting pan and add some of the water and vinegar mixture to cover the rolls halfway. Cover and bake at 325°F for 2 hours.

5. Uncover and add tomatoes and sour cream or half and half. Cover and bake for another 30 minutes. Uncover and let stand for 15 minutes before serving. Serves 6 to 8.

Anne Roesch Larson

"Mother made these cabbage rolls with heads of sauerkraut that she had preserved in a crock. The cabbage was salted and covered with a cloth and weighted down, usually with a heavy stone. After the cabbage had soured, she would take out the head, wash it, and use the leaves for the cabbage rolls."

White Bread

2 cakes yeast (or 2 packages dry yeast)
2 cups water, lukewarm
4 tablespoons sugar
5 tablespoons lard (or shortening)
2 cups milk (or 2 cups potato water), scalded and cooled
12 cups unbleached flour
4 teaspoons salt

1. Dissolve yeast in water, then dissolve sugar and lard or shortening in lukewarm milk. Combine both mixtures.

2. Mix flour with salt. Beat half of flour into milk mixture. Fold in 5 more cups and knead in the remaining flour, adding as much as necessary. Knead dough until it leaves the edges of the bowl. Form into a round ball, cover, and let rise until double in size.

3. Deflate dough, knead again, and cut ball of dough into 4 pieces. Form each piece into a round ball and let rise for 10 minutes.

4. Shape each ball into a loaf and place in a well-greased 9 × 4-inch bread pan. Let rise in pans until double. Preheat oven to 400°F.

5. Bake for 10 minutes, then reduce temperature to 375°F and bake for 45 minutes more, until tops are golden. Remove from pans and brush tops with butter. Yields 4 loaves.

Note: Dough may be refrigerated overnight; then remove from refrigerator, let rise, and form into loaves.

Anne Roesch Larson, Aberdeen, South Dakota. Regional America: Northern Plains, 1975

"When I baked bread during the festival on the Mall, I baked large loaves and always baked a little loaf to give to a child, as I always did at home. I told one of the children that the bread had to bake first, so if she came back a bit later, she could have it. She came back — and became one of the happiest children I had ever seen."

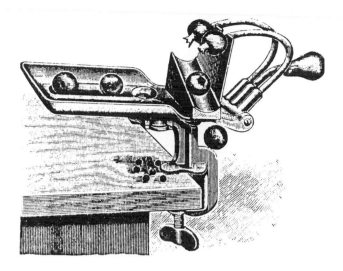

Cherry Dumplings

2 cups flour
3 eggs
½ teaspoon salt
few drops water
1 can cherry pie (or
    other fruit) filling
whipped cream
2 pieces bread
butter

1. Combine flour, eggs, salt, and a few drops water to make dough knead well.

2. Divide dough into 2 pieces, roll out ⅛ inch thick, and cut into 4- to 5-inch squares.

3. Add 1 to 2 tablespoons filling to the center of dough squares. Bring up all corners and pinch together to seal.

4. Drop into boiling salted water and stir a little to keep from sticking to the bottom of the pot. Dumplings are done when they float to the top, about 5 minutes.

5. Remove from water with a slotted spoon and put in a bowl. Cover with whipped cream. Toast bread, then fry in butter until brown; crumble over whipped cream.

Mary Fahlbusch, Scottsbluff, Nebraska. Old Ways in the New World: Germany, 1976

Kuchen (German Coffee Cake)

"When I was making the kuchen dough, I would recite 'Pat-a-cake, Pat-a-cake' in German. People appreciated that. 'Bache, bache, kuchen.... The baker must have seven ingredients: eggs and salt, milk and lard, sugar and flour, saffron to make it yellow.' My mother always said that as she was making the kuchen dough."

1 cup milk, scalded
   and slightly cooled
1 package dry yeast
   (or 1 cake yeast
   dissolved in ¼ cup
   warm water with
   1 teaspoon sugar)
1 teaspoon salt
½ cup sugar
2 eggs, slightly beaten
4¼ to 5 cups flour
½ cup butter,
   softened

Custard:
1 egg
½ cup cream (or sour
   cream or unsweet-
   ened evaporated
   milk)
1 tablespoon sugar

Fruit filling:
fruit (apples, cooked
   pitted dried
   prunes, raisins in
   cottage cheese,
   peaches, pears, or
   blueberries)
cinnamon

Bacon filling:
bacon, finely chopped
garlic salt
   (or onion salt)

Crumb filling:
butter
sugar
flour
cinnamon

1. When milk is lukewarm, add yeast, salt, and sugar in a large mixing bowl.

2. Stir in eggs and 2 cups flour. Beat well with a mixer or wooden spoon. Add butter, beat well, then stir in 2½ cups more flour. Work well with spoon until mixture leaves the edges of the bowl and forms a soft ball.

3. Sprinkle with ¼ to ½ cup flour, and knead until it is a smooth ball and easy to handle. Cover and let rise until double in size. Dough may be covered and refrigerated overnight.

4. Cut dough into 8 pieces; form each into a ball and roll into a flat round on a floured surface. Place in well-greased 8- or 9-inch pie pans. Pull dough up pan sides and let rise while preparing fillings. (Different fillings may be used for the 8 rounds.)

5. To make custard, mix egg, cream, and sugar.

6. For fruit filling, spread a layer of fruit on dough. Pour custard over fruit and sprinkle with additional sugar (amount depends on kind of fruit used; apples and pears require about 4 tablespoons). Sprinkle with cinnamon. Bake at 375°F for 15 to 20 minutes.

7. To make bacon kuchen, brush top of dough with a thin coating of custard and sprinkle with bacon and garlic or onion salt. (This kuchen may also be baked in a round cake pan, leaving the edges flat.) Bake at 375°F for 12 to 15 minutes.

8. For crumb kuchen, mix equal parts butter and sugar and 2 parts flour. Brush top of dough with a thin coating of custard and sprinkle with crumb mixture and cinnamon. Bake at 375°F for 10 to 15 minutes.

Anne Roesch Larson, Aberdeen, South Dakota. Regional America: Northern Plains, 1975

Grebble (Fried Pastries)

1 cup buttermilk
16 ounces sour cream
3 eggs, beaten
3 teaspoons baking powder
1 teaspoon baking soda
¼ cup sugar
1 teaspoon salt
4½ cups flour
½ teaspoon dry yeast
oil, for frying

1. Mix buttermilk, sour cream, and eggs.

2. Combine dry ingredients and mix gently into egg mixture. (The dough will be sticky.) Add just enough flour to handle, the less the better. Chill overnight.

3. Pinch off small amounts of dough. Roll out ⅛ inch thick, cut into 5-inch squares, and twist. Fry in deep fat until done.

Mary Fahlbusch, Scottsbluff, Nebraska. Old Ways in the New World: Germany, 1976

"Grebble is one of my family recipes, part of the German traditions still celebrated in Scottsbluff. It is usally served on Good Friday, together with a fruit soup."

Czech Kolaches

1 2-ounce cake yeast
  (or 3 tablespoons
  dry yeast)
½ cup lukewarm
  water
1 teaspoon sugar
2 cups milk, scalded
  and slightly cooled
¾ cup sugar
2 teaspoons salt
½ cup oil
½ teaspoon mace
½ teaspoon nutmeg
1 tablespoon grated
  lemon rind
2 tablespoons lemon
  juice
3 eggs, well beaten
7 cups unbleached
  flour

Fillings:
apricot
prune
poppy seed

Glaze:
1 egg, beaten with
  1 tablespoon water
1 cup sugar
⅓ cup flour
2 tablespoons butter,
  softened

1. Dissolve yeast in water with 1 teaspoon sugar.

2. In a large mixing bowl, combine all ingredients except 2 cups flour; beat well. Add remaining flour, stirring with a wooden spoon. (The dough will be quite soft.) Place in a large, greased container, cover, and refrigerate overnight.

3. Common kolache fillings are apricot, prune, and poppy seed. Canned fillings may be purchased, but homemade are preferable. To make apricot filling, finely cut dried apricots, simmer in water until thickened, and add lemon rind, lemon juice, and sugar to taste. For prune filling, simmer pitted prunes until tender, adding sugar and cinnamon to taste. For poppy-seed filling, lightly grind seeds and cook with dark corn syrup; finely grated raw carrots may be added to reduce the richness.

4. To shape kolaches, place a portion of dough on a floured surface; leave the remainder in the refrigerator to be shaped later. Pat dough into a rectangular shape about ¼ inch thick and cut with a sharp knife into 2-inch squares. Working with a few squares at a time, stretch slightly and drop 1 teaspoon filling in the center. Draw together the corners at the center, 2 diagonal corners at a time.

5. Brush the tops with beaten egg mixture. Mix sugar, flour, and butter and sprinkle on top. Place on greased cookie sheets. Let rise for about 30 minutes. Preheat oven to 350°F and bake until light brown.

Genevieve Trinka, Lidgerwood, North Dakota. Regional America: The Heartland, 1976

Ableskage (Danish Apple Cake)

2 cups crumbs
½ cup butter
1 tablespoon sugar
2½ cups applesauce
½ pint whipping
    cream
2 tablespoons white
    (or brown) sugar
red fruit jelly
    (optional)

1. Brown crumbs well in frying pan with butter and sugar. (The crumbs may be from dried bread, cake, zwieback, or a combination.)

2. Place crumbs in a serving dish or a mold. Layer alternately with applesauce. Refrigerate to harden.

3. Whip cream and use to top cake. Add sugar and decorate with dabs of red fruit jelly, if desired. Serve cold. Serves 6.

Esther A. Jorgensen, Viborg, South Dakota. Regional America: Northern Plains, 1975

"This is a very popular Danish dessert — a must for Christmas in my family, dating back to my grandmother in Denmark in the 1870s and then in America after 1910."

Danish Puff Pastry

1 cup flour
½ cup butter
1 tablespoon water
pinch of salt

Filling:
1 cup water
½ cup butter
1 cup flour
½ teaspoon salt
1 teaspoon almond
    extract
3 eggs

powdered sugar icing

1. Mix flour, butter, water, and salt as for a pie crust. Pat out onto an ungreased cookie sheet in two strips, 3 × 15 inches.

2. To make filling, heat water and butter and stir in flour until smooth like cream puff filling. Cool. Add salt, almond extract, and eggs, one at a time. Beat well.

3. Spread filling over dough. To make it puff, do not pat it down; pile it gently and push it to the edges with a spatula. Bake at 350°F for 50 to 60 minutes. Cool. Drizzle on a powdered sugar icing flavored with almond extract, swirling it to make a pattern.

Esther A. Jorgensen

Danish Aebleskivers

"To make aebleskivers, you must have an aebleskiver pan, which is cast iron with seven round wells. This pan may be hard to find, so look for one in old hardware stores, antiques shops, any place where Danish and Norwegian crafts are sold. The Danish way to eat aebleskivers is to dip them in sugar and eat them with your fingers. They are good with syrup and jelly.

3 eggs, separated
2 tablespoons sugar
1 teaspoon salt
2 cups buttermilk
2 cups flour
1 teaspoon baking soda
1 teaspoon baking powder
shortening (or oil)
powdered sugar

1. Beat egg yolks and add sugar, salt, and buttermilk. Sift flour, baking soda, and baking powder. Add dry ingredients to egg mixture.

2. Beat egg whites until they form stiff peaks, then fold into batter.

3. Place a small amount of shortening or oil in each well of an aebleskiver pan and heat. Pan should be hot before adding the dough. Fill each well about ⅔ full. When dough starts to bubble, begin turning aebleskivers with a steel knitting needle or an icepick. Keep turning and testing doneness by sticking needle in the center. If it comes out clean, they are done.

4. Dip aebleskivers in sugar; they may be served with syrup and jelly. Yields about 35.

Esther A. Jorgensen, Viborg, South Dakota. Regional America: Northern Plains, 1975

Wine Soup

1 egg
½ cup cream
1 cup water
1 cup sweet red wine
sugar (optional)
toast

1. Beat egg and add cream.

2. Mix with water and wine and simmer for a few minutes.

3. Serve over slices of toast.

Anne Roesch Larson, Aberdeen, South Dakota. Regional America: Northern Plains, 1975

"We were never allowed to have any wine as we were growing up, except when we were sick. Then, Mother made this wine soup for us, using wine my parents made from grapes. Here, they bought the grapes; in Glukesdahl, Russia, where they came from as German Russians, they raised their own grapes."

New Year's Cookies

2 cups potato water
1 cup evaporated milk
2 packages dry yeast
1 cup sugar
3 eggs, beaten
½ cup margarine, melted
3 teaspoons salt
¼ teaspoon nutmeg
1 tablespoon vanilla
8 to 8½ cups flour
2 cups raisins
oil, for frying
sugar

1. Combine potato water and milk and heat to lukewarm. Add yeast, sugar, eggs, margarine, salt, nutmeg, vanilla, and half of the flour. Beat until smooth, then gradually add remaining flour and raisins.

2. Knead on a floured surface to form a ball. Put dough in a bowl and let rise in a warm place until double in size.

3. With greased hands, pinch off balls 1½ inches in diameter. Place on slightly floured cookie sheets several inches apart and let rise until almost double.

4. Deep fry at 325°F to 350°F until golden. Turn only once. Drain on paper towels and roll in sugar. Yields 70 to 75.

Esther D. Schmitt, Newton, Kansas. Regional America: The Heartland, 1976

"This is a traditional Mennonite recipe. My mother and grandmother always made these cookies for New Year's Day. They are also served at our church's annual meeting around the first of the year. In fact, everyone in our community makes New Year's cookies. They freeze well and can be reheated in the microwave."

West and Southwest

▲ · ▼ · ▲ · ▼

**Lin T.
Humphrey
and
Theodore C.
Humphrey**

Smothered with gravy in Oklahoma, covered with chiles in New Mexico, barbecued in Texas, blanketed with sauerkraut in a German community in Utah, surrounded by wild onions and mushrooms in Oregon, nestled in baby oysters in Washington, or simmered with zucchini and prunes in California, pot roast is still pot roast — even when it metamorphoses into mutton in Colorado and venison in Nevada. In fact, not just meats but vegetables and fruits also display regional variations. That is why people avoid fancy Continental restaurants and go instead to the produce section of the local market. And if you are a culinary traveler, local produce vendors can tell you about the crops in the area; they can also suggest recipes for preparing them — when in doubt, sauté in butter. Specials at markets and restaurants are another dead giveaway to the culinary tourist. You can always eat flash-frozen berry pie and mussel pizza at home — fresh-picked corn and sun-dried pinto beans must be eaten here and now.

But that is not all that people in the West and Southwest eat. The old canard that all the loose nuts and screws end up in the Golden West still leaves a bad taste in the mouths of those of us who live on the western side of the mountains. And speaking of bad taste, that is another epithet tossed at foods here. Unfortunately, songs of the pioneer movement in America as well as records and journals have conspired to perpetuate some western food stereotypes: corn bread, beans, bacon, and a lot of grease to wash it down.

Yes, we have read of the settlers' reluctant acceptance of native fare, their suspicions concerning the piquancy of chiles and the variety of wild greens and mushrooms. Desperate conditions resulted in desperate food experiments, topped off, of course, by the fateful culinary experience of the Donner Party in 1847. But a closer inspection of the region's food traditions should offset some of the more prevalent stereotypes about what people of the West really eat these days.

Previous pages: Corn is ground the traditional way during the 1988 Festival of American Folklife. (Laurie Minor)

Defining the West, however, can be a little tricky. For many people in the East, the West begins at the Hudson River, or the Mississippi, or perhaps somewhere in the middle of the Rockies. But we are talking about food not merely as a product but as an attitude, a process, and a context. So this chapter surveys some of the products, processes, attitudes, and typical food contexts in Alaska, Washington, Oregon, California, Idaho, Nevada, Utah, Colorado, Arizona, New Mexico, Texas, and Oklahoma. Keep in mind, of course, that food is not just food. It is a way of understanding the life styles and value systems of the people who create and share it.

Like all stereotypes, food stereotypes are true — but they are not inclusive. That is why anyone who travels to the West with certain food expectations is rarely disappointed. Visitors to Alaska want — and get — king crab; in Washington they want — and get — salmon and Walla Walla onions, while Oregon is known for its wild berries, excellent cheese, and juicy pears. In Idaho, potatoes always come with the fresh rainbow trout; chiles are a mainstay in both Arizona and New Mexico. Oklahoma and Texas compete to provide barbecued beef and slow-cooked chili beans. Nevada, better known perhaps for poker chips than potato chips, provides a culinary heritage including Indian frybread and cowboy steaks. Colorado feeds its skiers roast lamb and hearty soups. And in California all tourists line up at the ubiquitous salad bar.

What you find in the West and Southwest is not a spicy purée of one easily identifiable food culture, but rather a stew pot, a smorgasbord of different cultures, traditions, and foods existing side by side, with some delicious mixing on the edges. The West, the last frontier for pioneers, can best be understood by sampling the foods and food customs that represent Steinbeck's concept of "westering." Its food is part and parcel of the land, people, traditions, and world view that surround it.

Wild, Wild Western Stereotypes

At the edge of the West, in Oklahoma, the Midwest and the South (depending on where the geographer is standing) seem to meld together in potluck and community barbecues. Take the one held in the small farming community of Morrison. Ever since the "Cherokee Outlet" was opened for settlement on September 16, 1893, a tradition of covered-dish dinners has existed. Held under the auspices of schools, churches, and farmers associations, these community-wide picnics and festivals are a way of celebrating the harvest, the Fourth of July, and the September 16 anniversary of the settlement.

In the early 1980s Calvin Pauley and Lenard James, both farmers and neighbors in the Morrison area, decided to barbecue a goat and invite a few neighbors. By the time the barbecue actually took place after the harvest in July, they had scrounged grills from half the county to barbecue two

In Oklahoma, Community Dinners

hogs, a thousand-pound steer, and a haunch of venison in addition to the original goat. More than four hundred people attended, and a tradition was born — or revived — that continues into the 1990s even after the death of Mr. Pauley. The foods served here — pit-barbecued beef, pork, venison, goat; a groaning board of covered dishes ranging from favorite casseroles to dozens of prize cakes and pies and other desserts — represent the ordinary fare of the community, for the most part, heightened by the festive event so that they come to symbolize the idealized values of the community: hard work, cooperation, communion, neighborliness, and visiting.

But the Morrison barbecue is not the only food-centered event of this small community. At the Lions Club annual stag party, a fund raiser, nearly a ton of calf testicles ("mountain oysters" or "calf fries") are deep-fat fried and served to nearly a thousand men along with beer, white bread, baked beans, french-fried potatoes, and sliced onions. The local Veterans of Foreign Wars for years held bean suppers once a month. Throughout the West, one finds similar community-based food events, often featuring the specialty foods of the area.

Other traditions also abound. Still quite common is the hearty breakfast, a leftover, perhaps, from more hearty farming days: fried ham, sausage, and bacon; fried eggs; homemade biscuits; toast; pancakes with peanut butter, butter, and syrup; strong, hot coffee; orange juice; cereal and milk. Diners and cafés along all the highways advertise chicken-fried steak and ham with red-eye gravy. People eat out to eat what they like to eat in, without having to fix it themselves, but they expect it to taste like home cooking. And it usually does. Other Oklahoma favorites include fried chicken, mashed potatoes, pot roast (a traditional Sunday dinner), and pie for dessert. It is bad manners to insist on a clean plate for the pecan pie or berry cobbler. Homebaked bread is expected for all company dinners, although it may be only biscuits, fluffy enough to float off the plate, or corn bread baked in a cast-iron skillet to give it a crunchy brown crust. Cafeterias across the country provide a menu based on this southern-midwestern-western fare, so representative of Oklahoma cooking.

But food traditions in Oklahoma reflect not only the American Midwest. As a "last frontier," Oklahoma also has its share of immigrant groups who brought and adapted their own ideas about cooking. Bohemian and Czech settlers made kolaches; African Americans grew okra; Italians, Southeast Asians, and, of course, Native Americans all added to Oklahoma's traditional food customs, creating a much more diversified food culture than stereotypes would lead us to believe. The settlement of Oklahoma by huge land runs and lotteries also contributed to the wide diversity of food customs brought from North and South.

People eat out to eat what they like to eat in, without having to fix it themselves, but they expect it to taste like home cooking.

Opposite: Practically in the Capitol's front yard, an Oklahoma cattle roundup takes place during the 1982 festival. (Dane Penland)

In Texas, Bigger and Spicier

What happens when we slip across the border into Texas? Do not expect an immediate, drastic change; it takes a few hundred miles for Texas to really become Texas. You can still get grits or hashbrowns for breakfast and cream gravy on your biscuits, and sausage drips all across the West. But Texas has a reputation to maintain. Servings are larger, and steak is available for all courses except dessert.

Although in many ways Texas food and food customs are similar to those in Oklahoma, the Midwest and the South, there are noticeable differences. Perhaps the most interesting and tasty is the so-called Tex-Mex cuisine. Mexican food crossed the Rio Grande hundreds of years ago, and its peppery flavor enhances Texas cooking. One strong tradition in Texas is the chili cookoff. At shopping centers, restaurants, schools, and churches, men, women, and children gather to produce and eat world-class chili, any way you like it. Ingredients range from the more traditional venison, beef, and pork to lamb, chicken, and turkey. Although mild vegetarian brews can be found, Texas chili is known for combinations of cumin, oregano, paprika, cayenne pepper, coriander, garlic, chili powder, and any number and kind of chiles, not to mention certain secret ingredients that often include various kinds of alcohol or even chocolate. The chili cookoff reflects many of the values of the old and new West: competition, cooperation, humor, high spirits, and a certain kind of machismo heroism based on the ability to eat chili so spicy you wonder why it does not eat away the bottom of the pot or your gullet.

But Texas is not just chili. Some of the best barbecue in the world comes from the Texas plains. One reason for the interesting flavor is the variety of things that get barbecued in Texas: not just beef and pork and chicken, but quail, wild turkey, deer, bear, buffalo, and even corn and squash are brushed with barbecue sauce. Texas also has as many fried pies, black-eyed peas, and watermelons as the states that surround it. Texans may claim, however, that theirs are better and, of course, bigger.

Any area as large as Texas has room, too, for many pockets of ethnicity — such as Polish recipes collected in San Antonio. And, yes, one can live in Texas and keep a kosher kitchen. Recipes provide a way for such groups to share their culture in a nonthreatening manner, for kitchens are more public than bedrooms or nurseries.

In the Southwest, Red or Green

Texans may use chiles with great flair and gusto, but the real culinary home of the many varieties of chile peppers is Arizona and New Mexico. Here we see the strongest influence of Native American cooking, or at least what most Americans identify as native foods. These items range from the ubiquitous Indian frybread (which is really found in nearly every state in the Union), through the expected corn and beans, to the ristras (strings of dried chile peppers) that we see hanging all over the Southwest.

But chile peppers do not make a meal by themselves, even in New Mexico. Corn and beans are the basic foodstuffs in the kitchens of New Mexico and Arizona. Hominy, posole, masa harina, chicos, atole, pinole, popcorn, corn-on-the-cob, corn bread, corn cakes, corn chips, and corn dodgers — it may be impossible to eat in New Mexico without having corn in at least one dish.

Add to the corn some beans and squash and we have the body of southwestern cooking. Add the chile peppers, fresh green or red chili sauce, and we have its soul. Although the green chili sauce is preferred for its more delicate flavor, in Santa Fe or Albuquerque the insider asks for "Christmas" and gets some of each. Squash abounds in many varieties: pumpkin, zucchini, pattypan, summer, cushaw; baked, stewed, stuffed, fried, mashed, mixed, boiled, broiled, grilled — but mostly it is eaten. Even the blossoms, a motif in silver Indian jewelry, are stuffed and fried and put in puddings.

Refried beans, handstuffed tamales, and deep-fried squash blossoms are not all that the Southwest has to offer, either. One multiethnic festival in Tucson, Arizona, has drawn as many as thirty-seven groups with culinary expressions ranging from Ukrainian stuffed cabbage and varenyky (potato dumplings) to Mexican American burritos and empanadas to Papago Indian popovers and Thai spring rolls. Northern Arizona food customs maintain ties with "mountain-man" wild food culture, including sourdough breads, chili, beans, and bacon, somewhat similar to Texas. If you visit the mountains above Flagstaff, you get great lean steak and barbecue to go with a priceless view.

Foodstuffs change as you move a little north into Utah and Nevada, but they change gradually. This is sheep country, and sheep mean good mutton, barbecued lamb, and lamb fries. In fact, the lamb and mutton culture spreads throughout the intermountain West. You can have boiled leg of mutton, lamb on a skewer, and lamb hash, in addition to delicious barbecued lamb sandwiches.

Lamb Day in a small community in central Utah features twenty to twenty-five pit-barbecued lambs. Many of the residents are Mormon. They often enjoy eating traditional midwestern dishes — similar to those encountered in Oklahoma — in a traditional family meal structure. In addition to lamb, a visitor can expect roast beef and pork, fried and baked chicken, mashed potatoes and gravy, and probably a good Jell-O salad. Molded fruit and vegetable salads serve as identification tags that say, "I'm part of a meal that features midwestern home cooking." The appearance of either side dish at a table proclaims that someone has planned the meal at least six or eight hours before it was served.

After the chiles of the Southwest, the foods of Utah and Nevada offer the tastebuds and palate a little respite. And the general characteristics of Amer-

In Utah and Nevada, Sheep Country

ican meals — large quantities, great variety, and regional specialties — are evident at every Mormon Sunday dinner. Even in Glendora, California, you will find an oven-cooked beef roast large enough to feed twelve or more, rubbed with salt and pepper, seared in a 400-degree oven for thirty minutes, then cooked slowly for hours while the family attends the three-hour church service. When they return, the roast is ready; the son prepares mashed potatoes in huge quantities; one daughter makes brown gravy from the roast drippings; the younger children set the table — it is Sunday, so the lace tablecloth, the fine china and crystal, the silverware, candles, and flowers in the center are all part of it — and the youngest may make place cards. Peas or green beans and a green salad, rolls and butter, lots of water and ice (no wine or coffee here!), and a dessert, usually pie or ice cream, complete the meal. In this family, the six children tolerate little variation; here is a meal one can count on. And, of course, it is a meal that those of us from farming country all across the Midwest and Southwest would find comfortably familiar.

Body and Soul Food

Soup is an ideal introduction to regional or even community foods. A bowl of chili soup from the Southwest, of course, but cream of cauliflower soup from Nevada or a dish of Mulligan stew from Colorado provides a quick, warm welcome to the local food culture. Because mountain climates range from cool to downright cold, this area specializes in foods that warm both body and soul. In fact, it is a little like Alaska, without the sea.

But do try the freshwater fish; pan-fried, fresh-caught trout may be a cliché, but there is nothing better. This is the land of hunters and fishers, so look for opportunities to sample fresh venison and game birds. Summers in Utah, Nevada, and Idaho produce delicious vegetables and fruits, which, thanks to modern freezing, can be eaten year-round. Try the apple-butter pie, peach ice cream, fresh blackberries with sugar and cream, and pickled prune plums from Idaho. Or try Idaho's corn oysters — a vegetarian variation on mountain oysters composed of corn, eggs, and flour and fried on a hot, buttered grill. After all, it is easy to justify a little overeating when the temperature is cold, the wind brisk, and the sky so full of white clouds they seem to move like flocks of sheep in step with the ones that roam the pastures below.

In California, Anything They Want

Then there is the ever-popular question, "What do Californians eat?," and their rather down-to-earth answer: "Anything we want to." Certainly, you can find just about any food product ever made in California's stores, restaurants, and homes. As each new ethnic group lands on the western coast, it brings with it a flood of new foods for the venturesome palate.

But everything in California is not new. In many communities, food and food preparation are just as tradition bound as in any other part of the country. For example, in Bakersfield, Chino, and Fresno you will find some of those same midwestern dinners that turned up in Oklahoma. And with good reason — chicken-fried steak with cream gravy, fried okra, fried chicken, pot roast, and well-cooked vegetables are daily fare for families whose parents and grandparents left the Dust Bowl in the 1930s.

Similarly, California's Mormon communities eat much as their Utah relatives do. So do Italian communities in the States and abroad. Members of Italian American families who live in California still make and dry their own sausage, and, in places such as Guasti, every fall the priest blesses the vineyards that provide employment, food, and wine for the communities. After the vineyards are machine picked, they are open to the community, and hundreds of families strip the vines, gathering enough grapes for jellies and jams. Spaghetti dinners also lend themselves to community celebrations.

Mexican foods, however, have had the greatest influence on California cuisine — so much so that they may indeed be the soul and center of real California cooking. Certainly, Mexican cuisine was the first. Aficionados can easily distinguish California Mexican cooking from Tex-Mex or the Indian-Mexican foods of New Mexico and Arizona, but the novice may first notice the many similarities, including tacos, refried beans, burritos, nachos with jalapeños, and lots of chunky salsa. Missing, however, is the blue-corn culture. In its place are the many southern California families who still gather together before Christmas to make homemade tamales — a gastronomic experience far removed from the canned tamales easterners may know best.

These family tamale makings sometimes resemble cottage industries, at least for a day or two. Everyone gets involved. Cheryl Garcia's family would meet at Grandma's house at seven in the morning. As many as thirty people were involved, and the work was seldom done until one or two the next morning. According to Ms. Garcia: "The uncles made the masa. Grandmother (who had already bought a whole pig and had it butchered) started cooking the meat at dawn. Grandma also roasted the chiles. The aunts peeled the skin off the roasted chiles while the children played. The uncles set up the old wood stove in the garage, preparing a fire for cooking the tamales. After the chiles were mixed with the pork meat, which had been cooked until the meat shredded off the bones, it was time to put the tamales together. It was like an assembly line: one cousin at the sink cleaned the cornhusks; about six kids spread the masa in the husks; the aunts put the meat and chile mixture on the masa; and Grandma rolled the tamales, tying the ends with strips of cornhusks. Meanwhile, the uncles in the garage tended the fire. They used ten-gallon tin cans with lids to cook the tamales in about six inches of water. The tamales were set on a steel rack away from the water, first a layer of tamales, then a towel, then a layer of tamales, then a towel, until the can

At the Center, Mexican Cuisine

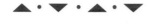

Where else would we find festivals to celebrate dates, avocados, strawberries, pumpkins, artichokes, and garlic?

Fresh Vegetables, Old Sourdough

was full. The stove would cook about three cans of tamales, which steamed for about four hours. Once all the masa was spread, which usually took four to five hours, the kids were free to play until the first batch of tamales was ready to eat. Although everyone talked and laughed and enjoyed visiting, tamale making was a lot of hard work." Cheryl Garcia is sad that her family no longer practices this tradition, so for anyone who seeks a true California culinary experience and who also has had the good fortune to be invited to eat homemade tamales, our advice is: go! eat, enjoy, and ask questions later.

Some traditional ethnic dishes are prepared only for special occasions because the ingredients can be obtained only in one of the large cities. In other cases, however, an ethnic food is still part of daily life. For instance, Basque and Portuguese families living in California both prepare dishes containing linguiça, a spicy sausage. The Portuguese include it in a kale and kidney-bean soup, which is also popular in and around Cape Cod. In Chino, California, a large Basque community serves linguiça in many forms: meat sauce for spaghetti, layered in vegetable casseroles, and especially for breakfast. One memorable Basque breakfast included eggs scrambled with linguiça, green and red peppers, onions, cheese, and potatoes; homemade biscuits; and a liter of hearty red wine. Fortunately, one could also have strong black coffee.

Homemade tamales and kale soup may not fit the image of California cuisine that the media present. However, if there is a connection, it is in the widespread use of fresh ingredients, especially vegetables and fruits. California has a large agricultural industry and a growing season that lasts year-round for most crops. Add the fact that Californians have easy access to produce grown in Mexico — it is simple to see why California cooks and eaters expect their food to be fresh. For this reason, vegetarianism is not a difficult diet to follow here.

Where else would we find festivals to celebrate dates, avocados, strawberries, pumpkins, artichokes, and garlic? Indio, the Date Capital of America, is located in the Coachella Valley and provides not just ordinary almond-stuffed dates and honey-date milkshakes, but also date butter, date breads, and date jams. Further north lie the artichoke fields that surround the small town of Castroville, affectionately known as the Artichoke Capital of the World. Naturally, artichoke cuisine has been refined in California. You may eat them boiled or steamed, french-fried or puréed in soup — even in pies and cakes. Similarly, garlic culture in Gilroy has had a distinct influence on California cooking. Putting aside the folklore of garlic (its alleged power for repelling werewolves and colds), garlic is good to eat. Around Gilroy, folks put garlic in everything: stuffed mushrooms, pesto, ravioli, spring rolls, bread, butter, escargots, steak, soups, sauces, even jelly and ice cream. Long strings of braided garlic bulbs are as common in California kitchens as ristras in New Mexico.

Just a brief note on California's breads: although it seems that every airport in the country now sells "authentic San Francisco sourdough bread," do not be misled. It tastes different in San Francisco, where in some of the commercial bakeries the tradition goes back hundreds of years. In fact, the original sourdough cultures have been cradled and coddled and kept alive in special vats from which come round and long crusty loaves of excellent bread, unmatched in the world. Sourdough cooking is, of course, not just a tradition in San Francisco; it is present in pioneer and western cooking throughout the West.

Fresh Seafood, Old Tall Tales

The West's coastal waters provide another delight — fresh seafood daily. For example, a plethora of fish and mollusks can be found in the Public Central Market in Los Angeles, at Fisherman's Wharf in San Francisco, and in almost any open-air market in numerous towns that line the coast. Try the local chowders; each reflects the uniqueness of the local ingredients. In Long Beach, if you arrive early enough, you can greet the fishermen coming in with their longboats full of freshly caught pop-eyed rockfish, flounder, sea trout, and crab. However, abalone, considered a delicacy by many, has become hard to obtain in southern California — we have to fight the otters for it. They are environmentally protected, but the abalone is not.

For more — and some say better — fish, travel north. Check out the Pike Place Market in Seattle. Both the Oregon and Washington coastlines provide an abundance of seafood, and images of fresh oysters, tuna, salmon, ling cod, halibut, clams, and Dungeness crabs mingle with the smells of fresh-baked sourdough bread, wild-berry pies, and new-pressed apple cider. Western-style cioppino and bouillabaisse are full of the bounty of the western seas. Although the salmon may no longer leap onto your plate as some of the old tall tales claim, you still can bake whole salmon with lemon, mayonnaise, and dill sauce, barbecue it, smoke it, steam it, poach it — in your automatic dishwasher, if the water is hot enough — sauté it, grill it, scramble it with eggs, or bake it in a pie. The important thing in the Northwest is that you enjoy it one way or another.

In Alaska, Wild and Warm

If you have traveled this far and are still hungry, the last stop is Alaska. Here we find many foods served in both the West and the Northwest. From the West, adapting easily to the abundant wildlife in Alaska, comes a love of wild game: venison, elk, moose, buffalo, and bear. These are roasted and barbecued just like their domestic cousins in Texas. Chili and beans, sourdough bread, and roasted beasts are basic necessities where the climate is cold. But Alaska also has summer, which brings an incredible harvest of berries and fruits. Strawberries, blueberries, blackberries, and apples all burst forth for a short, vigorous season along with tomatoes and other vegetables. Frozen and canned, these products produce jams, jellies, pies, and cobblers throughout the winter.

A great variety of fresh fish, including salmon, provide culinary delights year-round. Where else can you catch fish that are almost flash-frozen as soon as you pull them out of the water? In some ways, Alaska's culinary wonders are unmapped. The guide to its dishes is not written. Native Indian and Eskimo food has been stereotypically presented as fat, boiled, and blubbery. But delicacies and surprises are still hidden in Alaska's kitchens.

Bellying Up to the West

Napoleon is credited with saying that an army travels on its belly. If you are traveling through western parts of America, you should test his theory, bite after bite. But do not eat alone. In nearly every culture, sharing food is an intimate affair. Get to know the natives of an area by enjoying food with them. The West is especially rich in regional foodstuffs — exotic, perhaps, to some travelers, but good everyday fare to the natives, and to everyone willing to join them.

▲ · ▼ · ▲ · ▼

Recipes

Chili con Carne

Frijoles (Pinto Beans)

Danish Chicken Dumpling Soup

Janu Sier (St. Johns Cheese)

Sauerkraut

Sliced Tomato Pickle

Chili Sauce

Cowboy Frying Pan Bread

Alaska Sourdough Starter

Sourdough Hotcakes

Sourdough Bread

Sourdough Biscuits

Baking Powder Biscuits

Wheat Bread

Massa Sovada (Sweet Bread)

Pecan Bread

Cinnamon Rolls

Red Mush

Sister Cake

Sweet Soup

Chili con Carne

"This recipe may send you into shock — as you can see, it is for a large gathering! But the measurements are precise, sort of. And remember, when you serve chili, have pinto beans, but do not mix them together."

12 pounds chuck beef, cut into 1-inch cubes	2 gallons stewed tomatoes (or crushed tomatoes)	1 to 2 ounces Kitchen Bouquet
oil (or fat), for frying	2 cups Santa Cruz (Arizona) red chili powder	salt
3 pounds onions, diced		pepper
8 to 10 cloves garlic, minced	2 cups MSG (optional)	

1. In a large pan, sear meat in oil or fat. Add onions and garlic. Cook until onions are transparent and meat is thoroughly seared. Simmer until mixture dries out and more liquid is needed.

2. Add tomatoes and seasonings. Cook for at least 4 hours, adding small amounts of water when needed. Meat must be well done. Adjust seasonings. Serve hot with pinto beans on the side. Serves 80.

Stella Hughes, Clifton, Arizona. Regional America: The Pacific Southwest, 1976

Frijoles (Pinto Beans)

"A week before the opening date we headed east, towing the chuck wagon on a flat-bed trailer behind our Ford pickup, loaded to the bows with Dutch ovens, gonch hooks, fire irons, ax and shovel, tarps, 100 pounds of New Mexico–grown pinto beans, 10 pounds of Santa Cruz red chili powder grown in Arizona and a three-gallon pickle jar of sourdough starter."

Stella Hughes, "Bacon & Beans," The Western Horseman

10 pounds pinto beans, cleaned and washed	2 pounds onions, diced	1 cup MSG (optional)
3 to 4 pounds salt pork, cut into 1-inch cubes	3 to 4 cloves garlic, minced	1 cup brown sugar (optional)
	1 cup red chili powder (optional)	salt
		pepper

1. Soak beans overnight.

2. Add remaining ingredients except salt and pepper plus enough hot water to cover. Simmer on medium heat. At sea level, beans should cook about 3 hours. Add boiling (never cold) water as needed.

3. Season with salt and pepper only during the last 30 minutes of cooking. Beans should be well done and easily mashed with a fork. Serves 80 to 100.

Stella Hughes

Danish Chicken Dumpling Soup

1 stewing hen,
    cut up
water to cover
chicken bouillon
    cubes (optional)
salt
½ teaspoon whole
    peppercorns
1 bay leaf

1 large onion,
    chopped
1 piece ginger root
1 large carrot,
    peeled and
    chopped

Dumplings:
½ cup milk
½ cup water
½ cup margarine
1 slice bread, crust
    removed
¼ teaspoon salt
⅛ teaspoon nutmeg
1 cup flour
5 eggs

1. Cook chicken in water to cover until tender. Remove meat from broth; refrigerate. Set broth aside for a day.

2. Skim excess fat from broth and strain. If needed, add chicken bouillon cubes for more flavor. Stir in seasonings to taste, then add carrots. Simmer until vegetables are cooked. Add chicken.

3. To prepare dumplings, bring milk, water, margarine, bread, salt, and nutmeg to a boil. Add flour all at once. Stir, cooking until mixture sticks together and slips away from the side of the pan. Add eggs one at a time, beating after each addition.

4. With a teaspoon, shape dumplings like large almonds. (First dip teaspoon in hot broth to make the process easier). Drop dumplings in soup. When they are done, they will rise to the surface. Dumplings may be made 2 or 3 days ahead and refrigerated until ready to use.

5. Cook soup until all ingredients are thoroughly heated. Serves 4 to 6.

Nellie Jensen Doke, Ephraim, Utah. Regional America: The Great West, 1976

"Both of my parents came from Denmark before the turn of the century. Life was hard in the West at that time. It was a harsh land when the first people came to settle, but it is so beautiful to be in the mountains.

I am now eighty-two years old. My mother died when I was two years old, and I was on my own at fourteen. I knew a lot of older Danish ladies, and it was from them that I learned to cook and from them that I got the recipes that I still use today."

Janu Sier (St. Johns Cheese)

2 pounds dry cottage
  cheese
4 eggs
1 tablespoon caraway
  seeds
1 teaspoon salt
3 quarts milk
¼ pound butter, cut
  into small pieces

1. Combine cottage cheese, eggs, caraway seeds, and salt in a large bowl; set aside.

2. In a 4- to 6-quart saucepan, heat milk almost to boiling, stirring constantly. Add cottage cheese mixture and stir constantly until it appears thin and yellow green in color.

3. Hold a large, square piece of cheesecloth over a mixing bowl and strain cheese mixture, discarding the liquid. Add butter to cheese and mix thoroughly.

4. Tie cheesecloth containing cheese mixture and compress it between two cutting boards; a rock makes a good weight. Let cheese cool. Remove cheesecloth and cut cheese in ¼-inch slices.

Janina Zutis, Seattle, Washington. Regional America: The Pacific Northwest, 1976

Sauerkraut

"Our family worked together each fall to make a hundred pounds of cabbage into sauerkraut. We used it with pork roast and hot dogs. We have a recipe called bierocks that uses hamburger, sauerkraut, and onions, all wrapped in a roll of dough and baked."

1 pound cabbage
2 teaspoons salt

1. Wash cabbage, saving the large outer leaves. Slice finely and salt lightly.

2. Pound cabbage in a crock until it is covered with its own juice. Layer about 3 inches of large reserved leaves on cabbage.

3. Cover with a plate weighted down with bricks placed in a plastic bag. Set aside to cure for 3 to 6 weeks. Remove large leaves and pack sauerkraut in sterile jars. Process in a hot-water bath for 15 minutes.

Flora and Gaile Duncan, Orem, Utah. Regional America: The Great West, 1976

Sliced Tomato Pickle

1½ cups salt
1 peck (8 quarts) green tomatoes, sliced
1 large head cabbage, sliced

6 large onions, sliced
2 quarts vinegar
½ cup flour
1 cup sugar
1 teaspoon dry mustard

1 teaspoon celery seed
1 teaspoon cinnamon
1 teaspoon allspice
½ teaspoon ground cloves

1. Sprinkle salt on tomatoes, cabbage, and onions, and set aside overnight. Drain and discard liquid.

2. Bring vinegar to a boil. Mix flour with a little water and add to vinegar with sugar and spices. Add vegetables and bring to a boil.

3. Pack in sterile jars, then process in a hot-water bath for 15 minutes.

Flora and Gaile Duncan

"This recipe is more than a hundred years old. It was made by our grandmother, Flora Mae Forster Morris, and our mother, Mary Morris Miles."

Chili Sauce

½ bushel tomatoes
3 large onions, finely chopped
3 green peppers, finely chopped
5 cups vinegar
5½ cups sugar
½ cup salt
3 teaspoons cinnamon
3 teaspoons ground cloves
2 teaspoons allspice
1 teaspoon nutmeg
3 teaspoons paprika

1. Wash, scald, peel, and chop tomatoes. Cook with onions and peppers until volume is reduced by half.

2. Add vinegar, sugar, salt, and spices. Bring mixture to a boil.

3. Pack in hot jars. Process in a hot-water bath for 15 minutes.

Flora and Gaile Duncan

"We have altered this hundred-year-old recipe by adding more sugar than the original. It is used in beans, soups, and Thousand Island dressing and is delicious on warm buttered bread."

"Making bread in a frying pan goes back to the pioneers who came across the plains and the cowboys who rode the range taking care of cattle. Often you did not know where or when you were going to camp for the night. Sometimes cowboys would be gone for days or weeks at a time, traveling light so they could move with speed and ease. A cook-stove or Dutch oven is hard to pack and heavy on the pack horses, so cowboys opted to take long-handled frying pans.

When the cowboys did camp, they usually made the bread in the evening, which allowed them more time. Most cowboys could readily judge how much bread they needed for supper and the next day's lunch and snacks.

Sometimes you were in a 'dry' camp, meaning there was just enough water in a water bag or canteen for yourself, your crew, and the horses. But no water fit for cooking. If you had cooking water, the bread dough was often made right in the top of the flour sack. By forming a bowl in the flour, you had an ideal place to mix and knead the dough. And it saved getting another dish dirty.

My early ancestors fixed bread this way when they came across the plains. They passed the method on to my grand-father and my father, then to me, and now I've passed it on to my son, who will pass it on to his family.

Every year at the an-

Cowboy Frying Pan Bread

For a Steak Feed (200)
50 pounds flour
2½ pounds baking powder
1½ pounds salt
3¼ pounds sugar (or 2 pounds syrup)
3¼ pounds oil
water

For a Smaller Crowd
2 cups flour
2½ teaspoons baking powder
1½ teaspoons salt
1 teaspoon sugar (or syrup)
⅓ cup oil
water

1. Thoroughly mix dry ingredients. Gradually add oil (and syrup, if using it) while stirring well. Pour in enough water for a light dough that can be kneaded to a point where you can barely handle it.

2. Cut off enough dough to spread ⅜ to ½ inch thick in the bottom of a well-greased, long-handled 7-inch frying pan. Spread dough as evenly as possible with your hands, then poke a hole in the middle about the size of your thumb to allow steam to escape and permit the bread pone to cook evenly.

3. Place pan over a fire and cook until bottom of bread pone is light brown and pone is stiffened.

4. Set pan in a nearly vertical position close to the front of the fire. (The crust keeps the pone from sliding out of the pan and into the fire or dirt, provided you are careful. The heat hitting the top of the pone allows the bread to rise and brown on top.) Rotate the pone in the pan so that it will brown evenly. Do not flip bread to brown, as doing so will ruin the texture and flavor; it will become flat rather than light and fluffy.

5. To serve, brush off L.B.T.s (little black things) and spread hot pone with butter and jam or honey.

Dick Kirby, Baker City, Oregon. Regional America: The Great West, 1976

nual Durkee Steak Feed, we make frying pan bread to raise funds for our grange and community activities. Durkee is a small community in eastern Oregon between Baker, the county seat, and Ontario, which lies near the Idaho border and the Snake River. We hold the event outdoors in a field by the school, and it takes about two and a half hours to feed the 800 to 1,000 people who come for steak, hashbrowns, fresh-cut vegetables, beans, bread, pie, and drinks. All this we serve up with western hospitality.

With two people mixing and ten to fifteen men baking the bread in long-handled pans, we can pretty well keep the line moving. With so many pans cooking at the same time, we dig a pit eighteen feet deep, twenty-four feet wide, and twenty feet long. Railroad rails go lengthways over the fire, and we set the pans on them to start the bottoms cooking. Later, we stand the pans down in the pit, resting the handles on the edge of the pit closest to us. This catches the heat reflected from the fire under the rails and browns the top of the bread."

Dick Kirby

Alaska Sourdough Starter

1 cup distilled water
flour

1. In a nonmetal bowl or crock, mix water and enough flour to make a creamy batter with the consistency of pancake batter.

2. Cover loosely and set in a warm place for about a week. When it "sours" and bubbles a little, it is ready to use in sourdough bread and hotcake recipes.

Note: sourdough starters must be made with nonchlorinated water to avoid killing the yeast. Use distilled water for best results.

Cindy Herpst, Juno, Alaska. Alaska Program, 1984

"This is my Auntie Belle's starter recipe, which we use for making our sourdough breads and hotcakes."

Sourdough Hotcakes

"My dad, Duncan Hukill, was supposed to come to the folklife festival and make his famous Alaska hotcakes. When he was unable to attend, I went in his place and brought his starter with me (it is more than a hundred years old) and made his hotcakes and bread for the visitors."

½ cup sourdough starter
1 13-ounce can evaporated milk
1 evaporated-milk can distilled water, lukewarm
4 tablespoons sugar
3 cups flour
1 teaspoon salt
1 teaspoon baking soda

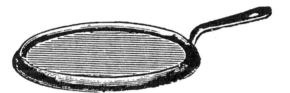

1. The night before, mix all ingredients except salt and baking soda in a large nonmetal bowl with a mixer. Allow to rise at room temperature for at least 12 hours. The next morning it will look creamy with lots of holes on the top of batter.

2. Before making hotcakes, take out ½ cup as starter for later use.

3. Add salt and baking soda to the batter.

4. Heat a griddle or frying pan, grease, and fry hotcakes. Yields 15.

Cindy Herpst, Juno, Alaska. Alaska Program, 1984

Sourdough Bread

2 cups sourdough starter
1 cup distilled water, lukewarm
3 tablespoons oil
1 tablespoon salt
1 teaspoon baking soda
1 tablespoon water, warm
4 to 6 cups flour

1. Mix starter, water, oil, and salt in a nonmetal bowl. Add 2 cups flour and let stand in a warm place overnight.

2. The next morning, dissolve soda in 1 tablespoon warm water. Add to mixture and mix well.

3. Stir in remaining flour and knead thoroughly. Form into 2 loaves and put in 2 well-greased bread pans. Grease tops. Let rise until double in size, about 2 to 4 hours.

4. Bake at 375°F for 25 to 30 minutes. Bread becomes heavy and sour as time passes.

Cindy Herpst

Sourdough Biscuits

Sourdough starter:
2½ cups flour
2 teaspoons salt
2 teaspoons sugar
1 cup milk

2 teaspoons oil
1 package dry yeast

½ cup sourdough
  starter

1 cup milk
2½ cups flour
¾ teaspoon salt
1 tablespoon sugar

1 teaspoon baking
  powder
½ teaspoon baking
  soda
bacon grease

1. To make starter, mix flour, salt, and sugar. Combine milk and oil and bring to a boil. Let cool, then dissolve yeast in milk. Blend in dry ingredients. Cover and let stand for 24 hours or until fermented. Reserve ½ cup for this recipe.

2. The night before, mix starter, milk, and 1 cup flour in a large bowl. Cover and keep in a warm place.

3. The next morning, place dough on a surface with 1 cup flour. Combine salt, sugar, baking powder, and baking soda with remaining ½ cup flour and sift over top of dough. With hands, mix dry ingredients into a soft dough, kneading lightly.

4. Roll out dough 1 inch thick. Cut biscuits with a cutter, dip in warm bacon grease, and place close together in a pan. Place in a warm place to rise for about 30 minutes.

5. Preheat oven to 375°F and bake for 20 to 25 minutes.

Stella Hughes, Clifton, Arizona. Regional America: The Pacific Southwest, 1976

Baking Powder Biscuits

1. Preheat oven to 450°F.

2. Sift flour, baking powder, salt, and sugar. Cut in shortening (not oil) or blend with fingers. Gradually pour in milk to make a soft dough.

3. Roll out dough on a floured surface to about ¾ inch thick. Do not knead. Cut with a biscuit cutter or juice can and place on a baking sheet greased with warm grease.

4. Bake for 15 to 18 minutes. Yields 12.

Stella Hughes

2 cups flour
4 teaspoons baking
  powder
1 teaspoon salt
1 tablespoon sugar
2 tablespoons
  shortening
¾ to 1 cup milk

Wheat Bread

"At the Smithsonian festival I found folks to be curious about bread and butter making, as so few people did it then and probably even fewer now. I felt bad that the butter making did not turn out because of the humidity and the commercial cream used. The big wooden butter churn brought from home was a novelty, though, and that was fun."

6 cups wheat flour
2 tablespoons dry yeast
1 tablespoon salt
½ cup brown sugar
1¼ cups dry powdered milk
½ cup oil
1 egg
1 to 2 cups apple-sauce (optional)
7 cups water, warm
7 to 8 cups flour (white or wheat)

1. Combine 6 cups wheat flour, yeast, salt, sugar, and powdered milk. (Yeast may be dissolved in warm water.)

2. Add remaining ingredients, except last flour, and beat well for 5 to 7 minutes, until shiny. Let rest for 20 to 30 minutes.

3. Add remaining flour and mix dough well. (It should not stick to fingers when touched, but should not be dry or stiff.) Knead well and place in greased bread pans; let rise until just over the pan tops, about 1 hour.

4. While bread is rising, preheat oven to 375°F. Bake for 45 minutes.

Bonnie Nielson, Ephraim, Utah. Regional America: The Great West, 1976

Massa Sovada (Sweet Bread)

"Massa sovada is a traditional Portuguese bread. It is made for many special occasions, including Easter Sunday (with Easter eggs on top) and the times we honor the Holy Ghost as well as other religious celebrations.

My family always looks forward to my special bread during Easter week. I make small buns as well as larger breads with Easter eggs hidden inside or baked on top. But sweet bread is a treat anytime."

2 packages dry yeast
2 cups water, warm
1½ cups flour

6 eggs, beaten
2 cups sugar
¼ teaspoon salt

½ pound butter
1 quart milk
5 pounds flour

1. Dissolve yeast in warm water in a large bowl and let sit for 5 minutes. Mix in 1½ cups flour to make a batter. Set aside for 30 minutes.

2. Add sugar and salt to beaten eggs. Melt butter, then warm milk in butter.

3. Combine egg and milk mixtures; add to batter.

4. Stir remaining flour into wet ingredients. Mix and knead very well, for about 30 minutes. Dough should be soft, but not too soft. Put in a 2-gallon bowl, cover with a blanket, and let rise in a warm place for 2 hours, until double in size.

5. Punch down dough and form buns in any size desired. Place on a buttered baking sheet. Cover and let rise again for 2 hours, until double.

6. Preheat oven to 325°F and bake for 30 minutes.

Mary Silva, Gustine, California. Regional America: California Heartland, 1975

Pecan Bread

2 cups milk, scalded	½ cup water,	7 cups flour
1 tablespoon salt	lukewarm	1 cup chopped pecans
½ cup brown sugar	2 tablespoons dry	
¼ cup butter	yeast	

1. Scald milk (150°F) and pour over salt, sugar (reserve 1 teaspoon), and butter in a large mixing bowl. Stir until dissolved.

2. Pour lukewarm water into a small bowl. Add remaining sugar and yeast.

3. When milk mixture has cooled slightly, add about 2½ cups flour and beat vigorously. Add dissolved yeast and mix well. Stir in pecans and enough flour to make a dough that will hold its shape.

4. Turn out on a floured surface and knead. Let dough rise. When dough is double in size, punch down and let rise again.

5. Shape dough into loaves and let rise until double and nicely rounded. Bake at 375°F for 40 minutes.

Edith Thiessen, Collinsville, Oklahoma. Regional America: The Heartland, 1976

"Homebaked bread has always been a part of my notion of homemaking. My husband, who is of German heritage, thinks that he just has to have homebaked breads. At the folklife festival, I was very disappointed to find that for some reason, probably Washington's humidity, the loaves did not rise very well, so I concentrated on the cinnamon rolls. I don't remember people's comments as well as I remember the line that would form and wait for the next pan of rolls."

Cinnamon Rolls

1½ cups milk, scalded
¼ cup sugar
1 tablespoon salt
¼ pound butter
2 packages dry yeast

1 teaspoon sugar
½ cup water, lukewarm
7 cups flour
3 eggs

Filling:
¼ pound butter, softened
1½ cups brown sugar
cinnamon

1. Dissolve ¼ cup sugar, salt, and butter in scalded milk.

2. In a small bowl, dissolve yeast in lukewarm water and 1 teaspoon sugar.

3. Add about 2½ cups flour to milk mixture and beat well. Add eggs one at a time, beating well after each addition. Add dissolved yeast and enough flour to make a soft dough.

4. Knead well and let rise until double in size. Punch down and let rise again.

5. Divide into 2 pieces and roll out into rectangles. Spread with butter and sprinkle with brown sugar and cinnamon. Roll up, pinch edges, and cut into 1¼-inch slices. Place on cookie sheets and let rise until puffy.

6. Bake at 375°F until golden brown, about 15 to 20 minutes. Yields 20.

Edith Thiessen, Collinsville, Oklahoma. Regional America: The Heartland, 1976

Red Mush

2 cups water
1 quart red fruit juice such as plum
5 tablespoons minute tapioca
⅓ cup sugar
red food coloring (optional)

1. Bring water and juice to a boil.

2. Add tapioca and cook until tapioca is clear, stirring constantly. Add sugar and red food coloring, if desired. Serve hot or cold with cream.

Nellie Jensen Doke, Ephraim, Utah. Regional America: The Great West, 1976

Sister Cake

1 quart milk, scalded
 and cooled
2 cakes yeast
2 cups sugar
1 cup shortening
 (or butter and lard
 mixed)
1 15½-ounce package
 raisins, dusted with
 flour
2 teaspoons salt
3 eggs
½ teaspoon finely
 crushed whole
 cardamom seed
7 to 9 cups flour

Topping:
whipping cream
sugar

1. When milk is cooled to lukewarm, add yeast and remaining ingredients in a large bowl. Use enough flour to make a heavy batter, but not enough to form a dough. Let batter rise.

2. Stir batter and pour into 6 individual loaf pans or muffin tins and let dough rise again. Spread cream and sugar over the tops.

3. Bake at 350°F for about 1 hour (or 30 minutes for muffins).

Nellie Jensen Doke

Sweet Soup

1 pound dried prunes
½ package raisins
2 quarts water
⅔ cup minute tapioca
4 or 5 sticks
 cinnamon
1 lemon, sliced
½ cup sugar

1. Cook prunes and raisins in water for about 5 minutes.

2. Add tapioca, cinnamon, lemon, and sugar to taste. Cook until tapioca is clear.

Nellie Jensen Doke

Hawaii

Linda Paik Moriarty

Like the Hawaiian proverb "Call to the person to enter; feed him until he can take no more," the greeting "Komo mai ai!" ("Come in, come eat!") invites friends and family to the kitchen, the heart of the traditional Hawaiian home. There, one will find the calabash, the symbol of family and unity, or a bowl of poi, the staple starch of the Hawaiians. For generations, poi and calabash have represented the integral role that food plays in Hawaii's diverse culture. While the area's roots are Polynesian, immigrant groups — Chinese, Portuguese, Japanese, Filipinos, Okinawans, Puerto Ricans, Samoans, and others — have all contributed to the unique blend of foods and food traditions that are celebrated in festivals and enjoyed in everyday meals.

Polynesian Roots

Hawaiians are farmers and fishermen by tradition. Fish and seafood provide protein, while poi from the taro or kalo plant, grown in flooded fields, provides starch. Early inhabitants of the islands often ate meals that combined such delights as taro, sweet potatoes, fish, pig, bananas, and greens from the taro top. Food was either salted, dried, boiled, or cooked in an underground oven, or imu.

Even then, the imu was reserved for special occasions, for great effort goes into preparing these underground ovens. First, a large pit is dug in the earth and filled with wood. Next, specially selected porous rocks are heaped on the wood and the fire is lit. When these rocks turn white-hot, a pig is placed on the hot rocks — its cavity filled with several more hot rocks and its outside wrapped in a basket of ti and banana leaves. The pit is then covered with dirt and left to cook for hours. When the pit is opened, the pig meat literally falls off the bones. Today, imu cooking is reserved for marriage feasts, first-year birthdays, graduations, and anniversary celebrations.

Poi can be made from either taro or kalo tubers, which are then mashed. Many Hawaiians prefer their poi slightly fermented. Kalo stems and leaf tops

Previous pages: A Hawaiian dances the traditional hula for visitors to the 1989 Festival of American Folklife. (Dane Penland)

may be cooked like spinach or stewed in coconut milk with chicken or seafood. The kalo plant is never eaten raw, as it contains oxalic acid crystals that irritate the mouth unless cooked. Despite this slight inconvenience, kalo has remained an important symbol in Hawaiian culture, in part because it is associated in lore with human origins.

When it comes to food, perhaps most visitors to Hawaii think of the luau, a celebratory feast whose origins blend native and foreign cultures, including that of early traders, missionaries from New England, and the islands' many immigrants. A typical luau includes kalua pig, poi, lomi salmon, chicken, long rice, opihi (raw limpet), raw fish, haupia (coconut pudding dessert), and a salad made of potatoes and macaroni. Sometimes the pig is replaced by laulau, a bundle of salted pork or beef wrapped in taro leaves and steamed in a package of ti leaves.

Rice from China

The Chinese were among the first groups to settle in Hawaii. They brought rice, a wide variety of vegetables, and an exotic array of spices and condiments to flavor the islands' pork, fowl, and fish. Most Chinese prepare food in a wok. Fresh foods purchased daily in Chinatown are more popular than the few foods that are preserved — usually vegetables and eggs. Typical Chinese Hawaiian foods include char siu (roasted pork marinated in a mixture of spices); manapua (a pork-filled steamed bun); beef and vegetables with oyster sauce; and steamed fish with black bean sauce.

Festival foods highlight local Chinese celebrations. Jai, or "monk's food," a vegetarian dish, is popular when people gather on the Chinese New Year. The Chinese do not believe in the killing of any living creature on the lunar New Year, so the first meal of the day is jai. Each ingredient signifies something special. The long rice denotes long life, sugar means that you will lead a sweet life, and the lily flower signifies golden purity. These meanings are attributed to Buddhists, who believe that actions in this life will affect the quality of their next life. The dish is nutritious, rich in protein and vitamins. Gin doi is another spring festival favorite. A doughnutlike dessert, gin doi is made from rice flour and filled with meat or nuts, grated coconuts, and sweetened bean paste, then rolled in sesame seeds and fried.

Spices and Bread from Portugal

The Portuguese islands of Madeira and the Azores also have contributed to Hawaii's culinary traditions. Immigrants first came from these islands in 1878 and brought with them the European love of hearty soups, sausages, baked dishes, and egg-rich pastries and breads. The Portuguese also introduced Mediterranean herbs and spices to the islands' cooking and pickling. Other Portuguese contributions include linguiça (a sausage), vinhados (pickled cod), and a variety of breads.

Bread, a staple starch among the Portuguese, traditionally was cooked in an earthen oven, called a forno. A forno is constructed of bricks and mortar and shaped like a beehive. Wood is used for fuel. In the old days, a family would bake twelve to eighteen loaves of bread and three or four main dishes each time the forno was lighted. Today, the forno is rarely used for household cooking. Instead, it is fired mostly for cultural festivities.

Many Portuguese food traditions are associated with Catholic religious feasts. Portuguese sweet bread, prepared for Easter, and malassadas (doughnuts traditionally prepared for Shrove Tuesday, just before Lent) are especially popular. The sweet bread is sold in bakeries and supermarkets. Schools and community groups also use it to raise funds for special projects. Portuguese sweet bread rivals white bread as a base for French toast, as many coffee shops offer customers this option. Malassadas are equally popular, with some bakeries specializing in this early-morning, mouth-watering treat. At the Punahou School carnival in Honolulu, the largest school carnival in the United States, the malassadas booth is extremely popular. During the 1990 carnival, 150,000 malassadas were sold in two days.

Soy from Japan

Japanese and Okinawan immigrants both have had an effect on the islands' food traditions. Traditional Japanese cooks tend to prepare fish and chicken, rather than beef; to use seaweed, soybean products, pickled vegetables, rice, and noodles; and to prepare desserts that use sweetened rice or beans. Okinawans share many of these food traditions, too, but among this group pork prevails in the everyday diet and is often highlighted by such dishes as pig's-feet soup, a delicacy traditionally served on New Year's Eve.

Both Japanese and Okinawan cooks use shoyu (soy sauce), as their main ingredient for seasoning. Shoyu is derived from the soybean. So is miso, a fermented soybean paste used for seasoning and preserving. Miso has a distinctive salty flavor and is rich in protein and digestive enzymes. Perhaps the best-known use of miso is miso soup, a traditional soup made from stock, miso paste, tofu (soybean cake), eggs, and seaweed.

Other Japanese and Okinawan dishes traditionally served in Hawaii include sashimi (raw fish, usually yellow-fin tuna caught in the islands' waters), teriyaki beef or teriyaki chicken, and musubi, a fist-size ball of rice wrapped in seaweed that contains a salted plum in the middle to prevent the rice from spoiling. Musubi is a favorite on picnics and for school lunches. Children savor the final bite into the salted plum — a treat on a hot island day!

For Japanese and Okinawans, New Year's is the most festive holiday, an occasion also to rectify financial and social debts. Much food is prepared and exchanged at this time, including mochi, a glutinous rice cake. Typically, several days before the event, a group of men with large wooden mallets pound the rice, then shape it into flat, round patties. Mochi, a symbol of long life,

Ethnic, Western, and fast foods have evolved over the years of immigration and assimilation to create today's cosmopolitan Hawaiian cuisine.

prosperity, and health, is a required ingredient in ozoni soup, eaten the morning of the new year and placed during the day on the altar of the family shrine as a special offering.

Today, few Japanese and Okinawan families living in Hawaii eat a strictly traditional diet. Instead, Western foods predominate on most days, and traditional dishes surface mainly on special occasions or holidays. This eating pattern holds true of most other ethnic groups. The one exception is new immigrants, who tend to eat a very traditional diet — and fast food.

Salt and Sour from the Philippines

The Filipinos were the last group of immigrant plantation laborers to arrive in Hawaii, most in the early 1900s. Filipino culture is a blend of Spanish, Chinese, and Malay influences, all reflected in their foods. Being the last immigrant group, Filipinos tend to live in close-knit communities. As a result, many of the traditions surrounding the everyday preparation of foods have been preserved.

Most Filipino foods are prepared in the home; in fact, few Filipino restaurants exist in Hawaii. Traditional Filipino cooks use pork and chicken in stews and soups that are heavily seasoned with onions, garlic, and tomatoes. A wide variety of unusual greens taken from pumpkin shoots, sweet potato leaves, and trees grown around their houses provide vegetables for the meal. The seasoning is generally salty or sour, and, in contrast to most other Asian food traditions, the spices seldom show much variation. Patis, a fish sauce made from brine and the clear liquid obtained from preserved fish, is to Filipino cooking what salt is to Western cuisines. Filipino desserts are generally made from rice flour, coconut milk, sugar, and bananas.

Many Filipinos are Catholic and, like the Portuguese, celebrate religious feast days. On these occasions, a pig may be roasted outdoors over an open fire. Other festival foods generally are variations on everyday fare, served with special desserts made from rice flour, coconut, and bananas, wrapped in banana leaves and steamed or fried like a doughnut, then rolled in honey. Other desserts are baked like a cupcake. Such desserts are displayed prominently in meals following the Feast of the Holy Ghost, which takes place in the fall.

A Mixed Plate

Ethnic, Western, and fast foods have evolved over the years of immigration and assimilation to create today's cosmopolitan Hawaiian cuisine. In a typical neighborhood, one can anticipate receiving malassadas from a Portuguese neighbor on Shrove Tuesday. On the Chinese New Year, you might hear a knock on the door from a Chinese neighbor bringing you a plate of jai. And when a traditional Hawaiian neighbor's child turns one year old, you may be invited to a luau, complete with a pig cooked in the backyard imu.

"E hea ike kanaka e komo maloko e hànai ai a hewa ka waha."

"Call to the person to enter; feed him until he can take no more."

"Come in, Come Eat!"

In contrast, fast-food drive-ins and lunch wagons, parked in close proximity to construction sites and office complexes, often feature a plate lunch. This is likely to be beef or chicken teriyaki, two ice cream scoops of rice, potato-macaroni salad, and a pickled vegetable. One of the more interesting dishes to evolve in these settings is the loco-moco, which consists of a scoop of rice topped with a hamburger patty, a fried egg, and brown gravy. This popular dish is a cross between the American hamburger and Japanese oyakyu donburi — truly a mixed plate to satisfy any Hawaiian's culturally diverse palate.

In the Hawaiian islands, food presentations and exchanges are such a significant part of one's family and social life that island kitchens are always stocked with pupus, or snacks. It is not uncommon for families to have an extra refrigerator in the garage filled with soft drinks and beer. Likewise, when visiting a friend, it is customary for the visitor to bring a little food gift for the household, ranging from homegrown produce to baked goods to a bag of chips. When Hawaii's residents visit other islands, it is customary to bring home some food item that is typical of that particular island. For example, Molokai is known for a white bread that is baked in a Kaunakakai bakery. Macadamia nut cookies are a specialty of Kauai. And then there is Kona coffee from the Big Island of Hawaii and mochi from the Japanese confectionery store in Kahului, Maui.

Given all of these choices, it is no surprise that one still hears the frequent call to "Come in, come eat!" This greeting echoes through the history of the islands and unites the original Hawaiians with people from the Pacific islands, Asia, and Europe. Each group has shared its food and customs with one another, creating the mixed plate of ethnic food that reflects so clearly their combined cultural traditions.

Recipes

Char Siu
(Chinese Smoked Spareribs)

Filipino Pork and Peas

Pinacbet
(Pork and Eggplant)

Laulau
(Taro Leaf Bundles)

Linguiça
(Portuguese Smoked Sausage)

Adobo Chicken

Oyster Sauce Chicken

Sakibuni No Shiru
(Okinawan Sparerib Soup)

Portuguese Bean Soup

Flavorful Favas

Fuchiba Jushime (Mugwort Rice)

Namasu
(Daikon and Carrot)

Bitso Bitso
(Sweet Potato Patties)

Pao Doce
(Portuguese Sweet Bread)

Gin Doi (Chinese Doughnuts)

Malassadas
(Portuguese Doughnuts)

Maruya
(Banana Fritters)

Poto (Steamed Coconut Cakes)

Cascarón
(Fried Coconut Cakes)

Haupia
(Coconut Pudding)

Char Siu (Chinese Smoked Spareribs)

3 pounds spareribs, cut in half lengthwise

Marinade:
1 cup sugar
½ cup soy sauce
2 tablespoons Hoi Sin sauce
½ teaspoon Chinese five spices powder
1 tablespoon coarse Hawaiian salt
⅛ teaspoon red food coloring

1. Slit the hard bone and score spareribs. Parboil, rinse, and drain well.

2. Combine marinade ingredients and marinate meat overnight in the refrigerator. Turn and mix occasionally.

3. Smoke in a kamado or smoker for 2 hours, basting occasionally with sauce.

June Tong, Honolulu, Hawaii. Hawaii Program, 1989

Filipino Pork and Peas

1 pound pork, sliced
1 teaspoon salt
pepper
1 large onion, sliced
1 clove garlic, minced
1 8-ounce can tomato sauce
1 teaspoon vinegar
1 teaspoon soy sauce
1 bay leaf
½ cup water
1 10-ounce package frozen peas
1 small can pimento (optional)

1. Brown pork. Add salt, pepper, onion, and garlic. Cook until pork is tender.

2. Add tomato sauce, vinegar, soy sauce, bay leaf, and water. Use more water if gravy is too thick.

3. Stir in peas and cook until peas are done. Add pimento. Serve on hot rice.

Connie Camarillo, Hilo, Hawaii. Hawaii Program, 1989

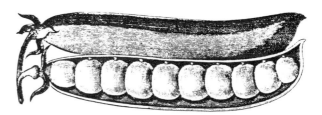

Pinacbet (Pork and Eggplant)

1 pound pork, cut
into small pieces
2 eggplants, sliced
2 bitter melons, sliced
1 large tomato,
mashed

1 medium onion,
sliced
1 clove garlic, crushed
1-inch piece ginger,
crushed
8 dried shrimp

1 tablespoon patis
(fish sauce)
½ cup water
salt (optional)

1. Sauté pork.

2. In another pot, mix together eggplant, melons, tomato, onion, garlic, ginger, shrimp, and patis. Add pork and water.

3. Simmer until eggplant is cooked. Instead of stirring with a spoon, flip pinacbet 3 times. Add salt if needed.

Connie Camarillo

Laulau (Taro Leaf Bundles)

1½ pounds pork
shoulder, cut into
cubes
1½ pounds beef
brisket or roast, cut
into cubes
1½ pounds freshly
salted cod, cut into
cubes
3 to 4 large taro
leaves (or fresh
spinach)

1. Lay 2 taro or spinach leaves crosswise to each other. Place meat and fish on leaves. Gather the corners and tie in a bundle.

2. Steam for 3 hours in a steamer.

Jane Goo, Anahola, Kauai. Hawaii Program, 1989

Linguiça (Portuguese Smoked Sausage)

5 pounds pork butt, finely chopped
½ cup wine vinegar (or cider)
½ cup white wine
1 tablespoon pepper
4 cloves garlic, minced
½ teaspoon marjoram
cayenne pepper (or crushed red pepper flakes)
15 feet hog casing
1 cup vinegar

1. Combine pork, wine vinegar, wine, pepper, garlic, marjoram, and cayenne pepper. Cover and place in the refrigerator for 2 days, turning mixture once a day.

2. When ready to make sausages, run casing through water and then soak in vinegar. Attach casing to a meat grinder sausage tube or use a handheld tube and push entire casing onto tube, allowing a few inches at the end. Stuff with meat mixture, making sure that no air remains, and tie off the lengths desired after casing is full.

3. Smoke in a smoker until sausage turns brown, about 3 to 4 hours. Yields about 5 pounds.

Note: Leftover hog casing keeps in the refrigerator for several months if covered with rock salt.

Doris and Manuel Correia, Honolulu, Hawaii. Hawaii Program, 1989

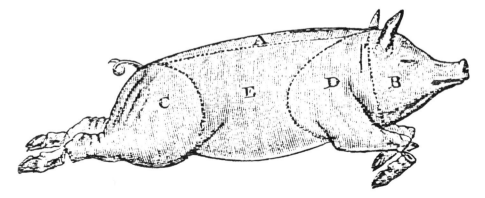

Adobo Chicken

1 3-pound stewing
   chicken (or 5
   pounds thighs),
   cut up
½ cup vinegar
1 cup water
2 cloves garlic,
   minced
1 inch ginger, grated
1 bay leaf
2 tablespoons soy
   sauce
salt
pepper

1. Chop chicken into serving-size pieces. Mix with vinegar, water, garlic, ginger, bay leaf, soy sauce, salt, and pepper.

2. Cook chicken in a pot on high heat. As the liquid thickens, turn heat to low and continue cooking until meat is tender and slightly brown. Stir chicken from time to time, cooking for about 30 to 35 minutes.

Note: To make adobo pork, follow the same procedure but add 1 teaspoon allspice.

Connie Camarillo, Hilo, Hawaii. Hawaii Program, 1989

Oyster Sauce Chicken

Marinade:
¼ cup oyster sauce
1 tablespoon soy
   sauce
1 tablespoon sugar
1 teaspoon salt
1 teaspoon Chinese
   five spices powder
1 teaspoon sesame oil
3 cloves garlic,
   minced
2 slices ginger,
   minced
1 5-pound roasting
   chicken
4 stalks green onions,
   tied in knots
Chinese parsley
   (cilantro), for
   garnish

1. Combine marinade ingredients.

2. Add chicken and marinate for 1 hour. Place onions in cavity.

3. Roast at 375°F for 1½ hours. Chop chicken and arrange on platter. Garnish with Chinese parsley.

June Tong, Honolulu, Hawaii. Hawaii Program, 1989

Sakibuni No Shiru (Okinawan Sparerib Soup)

"Many years ago, in Okinawa, sparerib soup and pig's-feet soup were a delicacy. They were served as a special dish to family and friends on New Year's Eve."

1 pound spareribs, cut into 2-inch lengths
2 30-inch pieces kobu (kelp)
2 medium daikon (turnip), cut into 2½ × 1-inch strips

11 cups water
1 tablespoon dashinomoto (shirakiku soup stock)
thumb-size piece garlic

thumb-size piece ginger, lightly pressed
2½ teaspoons miso
1 teaspoon salt
¼ pound mustard cabbage, for garnish

1. Parboil spareribs for 5 to 10 minutes. Drain and rinse.

2. Wash and rinse kobu. Tie knots every 5 inches, then cut between the knots.

3. Bring 3 cups water to a boil in a saucepan. Boil kobu for 5 minutes; add pinch of salt. Add daikon and cook for another 5 minutes. Drain and rinse in cold water.

4. Put 8 cups water in a saucepan and bring to a boil, adding dashinomoto. Add spareribs, garlic, and ginger; remove scum and bubbles as they appear on the surface of the water. Continue cooking on medium heat for 1 hour. Add kobu and daikon, and cook until kobu is soft, about 45 minutes. Add miso and salt to taste.

5. Parboil mustard cabbage in salt water, drain, rinse in cold water, and lightly squeeze out water. Use as garnish. Serves 6.

Kay Kimie Hokama, Honolulu, Hawaii. Hawaii Program, 1989

Portuguese Bean Soup

2 pounds ham hocks
water
2 8-ounce cans
    tomato sauce
1 large onion,
    chopped

2 to 3 large white
    potatoes, chopped
2 pounds linguiça
    (Portuguese
    smoked sausage)
1 bunch flat Italian
    parsley

1 small head cabbage,
    sliced
4 15-ounce cans
    kidney beans,
    drained

1. Cook ham hocks in water to cover until tender. Add remaining ingredients, except beans.

2. Cook soup until vegetables are tender. Stir in beans and simmer for 15 minutes. Serves 4 to 6.

Doris and Manuel Correia, Honolulu, Hawaii. Hawaii Program, 1989

Flavorful Favas

1 4-ounce package
    dried fava beans
    (horse or broad
    beans)
3 quarts water
½ cup chopped
    onions
2 tablespoons
    chopped parsley
1 red chile pepper,
    chopped
3 cloves garlic,
    chopped
⅓ cup vinegar
5 tablespoons oil
2 teaspoons coarse
    Hawaiian salt

1. Wash and soak beans overnight. Cook in simmering water for 2½ hours. Drain, saving 1 cup liquid.

2. In a saucepan, combine beans, reserved liquid, and remaining ingredients. Cover and simmer for 30 minutes or longer. Serve hot or chilled.

Doris Correia

Fuchiba Jushime (Mugwort Rice)

"Mugwort is an herb that makes good tea and is a refreshing drink."

3 cups rice
3½ cups water
¼ pound pork belly, parboiled, drained, and thinly sliced
1 teaspoon dashinomoto (shi-rakiku soup stock)
1½ cups mugwort leaves, parboiled, drained, and chopped
2 teaspoons soy sauce
3 tablespoons oil
1 clove garlic, minced
½ teaspoon rock salt (or miso)

1. Wash rice in a saucepan or rice cooker. Add water to cover and soak for 1 to 2 hours. Drain and set aside.

2. In another saucepan, bring 3½ cups water to a boil. Add dashinomoto, pork belly, mugwort leaves, rice, and soy sauce. Stir in oil, garlic, and salt, to taste.

3. Cook until rice is tender, about 20 minutes. Stir lightly and let rest for a while before serving. Serves 6.

Kay Kimie Hokama, Honolulu, Hawaii. Hawaii Program, 1989

"When I was six years old, my grandfather took my brother and me to Okinawa, where my grandmother was waiting for grandfather to return from Hawaii. I lived in Okinawa for many years. In those days, the 1920s and 1930s, young girls were expected to learn to cook and sew as well as help on the farm. My grandmother started to teach me to do these things at the age of eight. I learned the original way of preparing Okinawan dishes just using salt or soy sauce to provide the seasoning and taste. After World War II, many different people came to Okinawa, and the original way of preparing dishes and the tastes have now been lost."

Namasu (Daikon and Carrot)

1 medium daikon (turnip), pared and shredded
¼ medium carrot, peeled and shredded
salt
½ cup rice vinegar
½ cup sugar
1 teaspoon slivered ginger root
½ teaspoon salt
½ teaspoon lemon salt

1. Put daikon in a bowl and salt lightly. Mix and let stand for 3 minutes.

2. Place carrots in another bowl and salt lightly. Mix and let stand for 2 minutes. Rinse daikon and carrots and squeeze well.

3. Make a sauce with remaining ingredients. Stir in daikon and carrots. Refrigerate and serve chilled.

Kay Kimie Hokama

Bitso Bitso (Sweet Potato Patties)

2 cups raw yellow-flesh sweet potato, grated
¼ cup sugar
¼ cup flour

1. Wash, peel, and grate sweet potatoes. Add enough sugar and flour to hold shape.

2. Form into ½-inch thick patties 2 inches in diameter. Fry until golden brown. Serve with adobo chicken or meat.

Connie Camarillo, Hilo, Hawaii. Hawaii Program, 1989

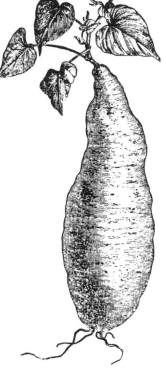

Pao Doce (Portuguese Sweet Bread)

2 packages dry yeast
1 cup warm water
2 tablespoons sugar
handful of flour
1 package dry powdered milk
1 quart water
5 pounds flour
1½ pounds sugar
2 teaspoons salt
¼ pound butter (or margarine)
½ cup shortening
12 eggs, beaten
1 tablespoon lemon extract

1. Dissolve yeast in warm water with 2 tablespoons sugar and handful of flour. Cover and let rise for 10 to 15 minutes.

2. Mix powdered milk with 1 quart water.

3. In a large bowl, mix dry ingredients. Cut in butter and shortening. Add eggs, then pour in yeast mixture and milk; mix well. Knead for 10 to 15 minutes; if mixture is too wet, add a little flour. Let rise in a covered bowl for 5 to 6 hours or overnight.

4. Punch down dough and let rise for another 2 to 3 hours. Punch down again and let rest for 10 minutes. Flour hands and cut dough into equal parts. Shape, then let rise in pans for 1 to 2 hours. Yields 6 to 7 loaves.

5. Bake at 350°F for 45 to 60 minutes.

Doris and Manuel Correia, Honolulu, Hawaii. Hawaii Program, 1989

Gin Doi (Chinese Doughnuts)

1½ cups brown sugar
1¼ cups cold water
⅛ cup yams, cooked and mashed
1 teaspoon whiskey
1 pound mochi (rice) flour
½ cup sesame seeds
1 quart oil, for frying

Filling:
½ cup roasted pork, minced
½ cup char siu (Chinese barbecued pork), minced
¼ cup dried baby shrimps, soaked and minced

¼ cup chopped green onions
¼ cup chopped Chinese parsley (cilantro)
1 tablespoon oyster sauce

1. Combine sugar, water, and yams. Beat until sugar is dissolved. Add whiskey and stir lightly.

2. Place flour in a large bowl. Pour in sugar mixture and stir until dough can be handled, adding more flour or water if needed.

3. In a separate bowl, mix ingredients for filling.

4. Pinch dough into golfball-size pieces and flatten with fingers. Place a small amount of filling in center, seal edges, and form into a round ball. Roll each doughnut in sesame seeds.

5. In a wok heat oil until very hot on medium heat. Oil is ready if it sizzles when a small piece of dough is dropped in. Reduce heat to low, and place about 5 doughnuts, one at a time, in oil. Roll each until it becomes light brown. Turn heat to high or medium-high. Using a wire mesh spatula, flatten doughnuts against side of wok; they will double in size. Remove from oil when doughnuts are light and not oily. Repeat procedure with remaining doughnuts. Drain on paper towels.

June Tong, Honolulu, Hawaii. Hawaii Program, 1989

"Gin doi is an exotic dessert eaten during the spring festival. It is round, which symbolizes family get-togethers, and it is rolled in sesame seeds, which signifies the bearing of fruit. Notice how the dough doubles in size while it is cooking. This illustrates how gin doi will double your richness in health and wealth and prosperity."

Malassadas (Portuguese Doughnuts)

2 packages dry yeast
1 cup warm water
5 pounds flour
3 cups sugar
1 teaspoon salt
1 cup milk
1 dozen eggs
½ pound butter or
   margarine
1 gallon oil, for frying
sugar

1. Dissolve yeast in warm water with 1 tablespoon sugar and 1 tablespoon flour.

2. Combine flour, sugar, salt, milk, eggs, and butter. Add yeast mixture and mix. Knead, then let dough rise until double in size.

3. Pinch off small pieces of dough and deep fry in hot oil; drain and roll in sugar.

Doris Correia, Honolulu, Hawaii. Hawaii Program, 1989

Maruya (Banana Fritters)

1 cup flour
2 teaspoons baking
   powder
4 tablespoons sugar
¾ cup milk
4 bananas, sliced
oil, for frying

1. Mix dry ingredients. Stir in milk, then add bananas.

2. Heat oil in a frying pan. Pour in rounds of about 2 tablespoons batter and fry until brown on both sides.

Connie Camarillo, Hilo, Hawaii. Hawaii Program, 1989

Poto (Steamed Coconut Cakes)

2 cups quick biscuit
   mix
⅓ cup sugar
½ teaspoon baking
   powder

2 eggs
1 cup coconut milk
food coloring
   (optional)

1. Mix dry ingredients. Add eggs, coconut milk, and food coloring if desired.

2. Pour batter into a greased pie pan or 2½-inch foil-lined cupcake or muffin pans.

3. Steam for 15 minutes.

Connie Camarillo, Hilo, Hawaii. Hawaii Program, 1989

Cascarón (Fried Coconut Cakes)

1 10-ounce package
   mochiko (sweet
   rice flour)
¾ cup sugar
2 cups shredded
   coconut
1 cup coconut milk
1 quart oil, for frying

1. Combine mochiko, sugar, and coconut. Add coconut milk and mix just to moisten dry ingredients.

2. Form dough into 1-inch balls and flatten slightly.

3. Heat oil and deep fry until golden brown.

Connie Camarillo

Haupia (Coconut Pudding)

3 cups frozen coconut
  milk, thawed
  (or 2 cups fresh
  coconut milk
  mixed with 1 cup
  water)

½ cup sugar
½ cup cornstarch
½ teaspoon vanilla
pinch of salt

1. In a saucepan, combine coconut milk and sugar. Gradually mix in cornstarch. Add vanilla and salt. Stir and cook on medium heat until thickened.

2. Pour into an oiled 9-inch square pan. Chill for at least 1 hour. Cut into 36 squares.

Jane Goo, Anahola, Kauai. Hawaii Program, 1989

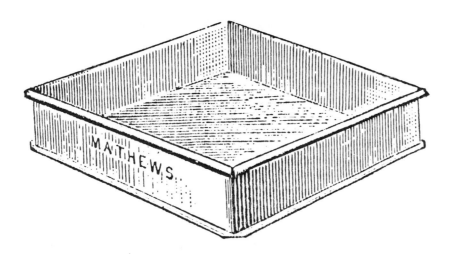

Puerto Rico

✤ · ✤ · ✤ · ✤

Nydia A. Ríos Colón

A small countryside party, a jolgorio, or even the mourning of a deceased family member or community friend — it does not take much to start Puerto Ricans eating. And if the occasion is a wake, it may start with tears, but more often than not the mourners will retire to a nearby home or restaurant to share food and laughter. Food has always occupied a place of honor in our island's culture, especially during public celebrations. That is why, even today, the yard around a country home is called "el batey," the diminutive of batey — the plaza or public square — where our native ancestors, called Indians, gathered to celebrate in the early days. Back then, the island was called Borinquen, and frugality was a way of life. However, even during pre-Columbian times, the people of Puerto Rico enjoyed tropical fruits, vegetables, seafood, honey, and yucca, processed as cassava. Rice was brought from Asia to the Caribbean via the Bering Strait well before the first Spaniard touched foot on the island on November 19, 1493. Unfortunately, the first rice plants did not survive, so rice was reintroduced by the Spaniards. Today, rice is a staple on everyone's table, often served with beans or chicken.

Privilege for Cooks

Within ten or fifteen years after the Spanish landed, the first African slaves and craftsmen began to arrive, bringing with them a variety of new foods. Smugglers also had an effect on the island's foods, as did slaves who escaped from other European settlements on surrounding islands or from the South American continent. During the years of slavery, cooks were considered privileged. Some slave owners granted them freedom in their old age, and descendants of cooks sometimes also benefited from these personal exemptions.

People from the Lesser Antilles also have had some impact on Puerto Rico's foods. Before the arrival of the Spanish, and in the years just after they came, Carib Indians from the Islas Inútiles (Idle Islands) periodically fled their drought-stricken islands and landed on Puerto Rico in search of food

Previous pages: A Puerto Rican cook grates cassava. (Raisaac G. Colón)

and the spoils of war. More than warriors came from these islands, however. These same islands produced the English-speaking cooks who sometimes gained their freedom after living in Puerto Rico. People from the Lesser Antilles modified many of Puerto Rico's folk or Creole foods.

The era of slavery extended almost until the end of the nineteenth century. Throughout this period, olla podrida (porridge pot) was the main dish. Other popular dishes included viandas (root vegetables) and bacalao (cod and viandas), vegetables, rice and beans, roast pork, and carrao (turkey). Beef also was served, but not often. Criollos, the local people, and jíbaros, country people, tended to eat chicken with rice and pasteles (vegetable, root, and meat pies wrapped in plantain leaves). Blacks and others who lived near the coastline grew batatas (sweet potatoes), taniards (yautías), maíz (corn), ñames (yams), malangas (taros), white potatoes, and a wide variety of produce. Food was exchanged freely with surrounding islands and imported from Spain, Africa, and elsewhere.

The nineteenth century saw several other additions to the island's larder and food traditions. Early in the century, King Ferdinand VII announced his Cedula de Gracia, a royal decree that permitted people from around the world to emigrate legally to the island. Previously, one had to be Cristianos Viejos, old faithful Christians. Later in the century, Hindus and Chinese arrived, and, at the very end of the century, people from North America.

But Puerto Rico is not simply a repository of the foods of other nations. We have exported foods as well. Perhaps our most famous export is the piña colada, but there are others. During the Korean and Vietnam wars, for example, U.S. and Oriental soldiers ate our native yucca. Today, the salsa used in our kitchens has become a popular Caribbean dance, complete with folk roots and rhythm.

In Puerto Rico, even the pots and pans and kitchen utensils reveal the island's ancient food customs. The árbol de higuera (totumo tree) has provided rural and local artisans a medium for carving elaborate decorations for centuries. Called ditas, these decorated items come in different shapes and sizes, ranging from cups and spoons to dishes and bowls. The coconut shell was and still is carved into cocas (cups) and used to drink coffee, tea, or other hot drinks. Some of the larger coconut shells have handles and are used to serve food. Over time, these decorative cups and dishes develop a particular taste that enhances the flavor of their contents. For buffets and other large gatherings, ditas are used with bateas (wooden trays), lebrillos (wooden tubs and pans), and artesas (troughs or wooden bowls). Trays, carved from bullet wood or guayacán (holy tree), are also used at these traditional gatherings, as are trays carved from ausubo or caoba (mahogany) — provided that you can afford them.

Foods have played such a vital role in Puerto Rico's identity that, years ago, people gave a special name — correcostas — to the person who traveled from town to town, carrying recipes, gossip, and stories.

Pots and Pans with Taste

During the Christmas holidays and on other festive occasions, trullas (carol-singing troupes) carry food in these special trays to the houses of friends and neighbors. In Puerto Rico, the period from Christmas to Three Kings Day (January 6) is followed by twenty-four extra party days to accommodate the endless exchange of social gifts and visits. Preserves, drinks, meats, sausages, and other dishes are prepared and exchanged during this social season. People drink, eat, dance, and visit with one another for days. These periods of time are called Octavas, Octavitas, and Octavón.

Festivals from Crab to Coffee

Religious holidays, patron-saint days, and local craft or food festivals also provide Puerto Ricans with other reasons to display their many food traditions. Certain foods, in fact, are now associated with certain islands, cities, and regions. For example, each year a coffee festival is held in Yauco, and the Big Head Pineapple Festival is held in Lajas. But that is not all. We also have a Crab-Festi Mardi Gras in Maunabo, the Setí Fish Festival in Arecibo, the Griddle Cake Festival in Vieques, the Cofre, Trunk, or Chest Fish Festival in Naguabo, the Shark Festival in Maunabo, the Devil Crab Festival in Fajardo, and the Breadfruit Festival in Ceiba, to name a few.

Not every city or region has a festival, but even those that do not are known by the foods, drinks, and fruits they grow or prepare. To name just a few, Bayamón is known for its chicharrón volao (fried pork skin), Vega Baja for its melao (molasses), Loíza for its empanadillas de jueyes (crab-filled patties), Ponce for its quenepas (fruits), Mayagüez for its mangoes, Isabela for its queso de hoja (flaky cheese), Peñuelas for its oranges, Yabucoa for its granos almojábanas (rice patties), Jayuya for its tomatoes, Corozal for its plátanos (green plantains), and Patillas for its gandules (green pigeon peas) and ausubas (bullet-wood fruits).

Recipes on the Road

Foods have played such a vital role in Puerto Rico's identity that, years ago, people gave a special name — correcostas — to the person who traveled from town to town, carrying recipes, gossip, and stories. The correcostas sang and danced at festivals and just had a good time. In the process, he spread information about folk behavior, history, and food. A variety of social circumstances conspired to do away with the correcostas by the middle of this century, but their contributions are well remembered.

Visitors to the island today often appreciate our Creole and other local foods. They can sample the island's variety in a friquitín (small fritters shop), a fonda (small restaurant or cafeteria), and the more formal restaurants found in business hotels. Whatever the setting, Puerto Ricans are likely to share with you their fondness for food. As Luis A. Becerril, a politician from the old school, was famous for saying, "In Puerto Rico, everything is a question of food."

Recipes

Pastelón de Yucca

Escabeche con Yucca

Tembleque (Coconut Custard)

Pan de Maíz Dulce

**Agualoja de Jengibre
(Ginger Liqueur)**

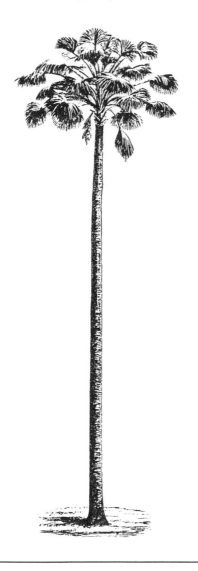

Pastelón de Yucca

1 pound ground beef
½ cup olive oil
1 large onion, sliced
1 clove garlic, minced
2 cups tomato paste
2 green peppers,
    sliced
1 cup petit pois
    (small peas)
recao
salt
pepper
2 pounds cassava
    (yucca)
½ cup stuffed green
    olives
1 cup red peppers,
    roasted and cut
    into strips

1. Preheat oven to 400°F. Grease and flour a large baking pan.

2. In a heavy frying pan, sauté beef in ¼ cup oil with onion and garlic.

3. Combine meat mixture in a large mixing bowl with tomato paste, peppers, peas, and seasonings.

4. Peel, boil, mash, and squeeze dry yucca. Combine with remaining olive oil in another bowl.

5. Alternate layers of meat and cassava mixtures in baking pan. On top form strips of cassava in a lattice shape to decorate the dish.

6. Bake uncovered in the center of the oven for about 1 hour. Garnish with olives and pepper strips. Serves 8.

Collected by Nydia A. Ríos Colón, San Juan, Puerto Rico. Caribbean Program, 1989

Escabeche con Yucca

2 pounds cassava
    (yucca)
1 teaspoon salt
2 tablespoons
    chopped stuffed
    green olives
1 tablespoon capers
1 red bell pepper,
    diced

Marinade:
1 medium onion,
    sliced
1 cup olive oil
1 clove garlic,
    minced
2 bay leaves
½ teaspoon pepper
juice of 1 lemon
2 ounces vinegar

1. Peel cassava and cut into chunks. Boil in salted water until soft, but still firm, about 20 minutes. Drain and set aside to cool.

2. To make marinade, sauté onion in ¼ cup oil until transparent. Add another ½ cup oil, garlic, bay leaves, and pepper. Cook on high heat for 1 minute. Remove from stove, place in a glass or ceramic mixing bowl, and set aside to cool. Add lemon juice and vinegar.

3. Sauté cassava in remaining oil, stirring frequently, for 5 minutes. Add to marinade and stir in olives, capers, and red bell pepper.

Note: To substitute papaya for cassava, peel and seed 2 pounds unripe papaya, then cut into large chunks. Dissolve 1 tablespoon baking soda in 2 quarts water and soak papaya for 10 minutes. Drain and rinse several times under running water. Sauté before mixing with marinade and condiments.

Collected by Nydia A. Ríos Colón

Tembleque (Coconut Custard)

½ cup cornstarch
1 cup water
2 cups coconut milk, canned or fresh
½ teaspoon vinegar (if canned milk used)
¼ cup orange-blossom water
¼ cup sugar
pinch of salt
¼ teaspoon ground cloves
grated lemon peel (or melted chocolate or cinnamon)

1. In a heavy 2-quart saucepan, dissolve cornstarch in water. Add coconut milk (and vinegar, if canned milk is used), orange-blossom water, sugar to taste, and salt. Cook on medium heat, stirring constantly to keep cornstarch from lumping. Stir in cloves and continue on medium heat until mixture comes to a slow boil.

2. Test ½ teaspoon of the custard by dropping it into ½ cup cold water; if it forms a soft ball, or at least holds together, it is done.

3. Remove from heat and spoon into dessert dishes. Sprinkle with lemon peel, cinnamon, or melted chocolate. Serves 8.

Note: To make a variation called marmoleado, layer the custard parfait fashion with melted chocolate in individual dessert or beverage glasses.

Collected by Nydia A. Ríos Colón

Pan de Maíz Dulce

4 banana leaves
2 cups cornmeal
2 cups corn kernels
  (4 ears corn),
  mashed
1 cup flour
2 cups coconut milk,
  canned or fresh
½ teaspoon ground
  cloves
½ teaspoon
  cinnamon
½ cup brown sugar

1. Preheat oven to 400°F. Generously grease and flour 2 loaf pans, 7 × 4 × 3 inches.

2. Prepare banana leaves by immersing them in hot water to soften; then trim to pan size. Place 1 banana leaf on the bottom of each pan.

3. In a large mixing bowl, combine cornmeal, corn, flour, coconut milk, cloves, cinnamon, and sugar to taste. Beat with a wooden spoon until a smooth, heavy batter is formed.

4. Pour batter into prepared pans and cover each with another banana leaf. Place pans on a rack in the center of the oven and bake for about 1 hour or until a knife blade inserted in the center comes out clean.

5. Remove from oven and let stand at room temperature for about 5 minutes. Invert onto wire racks, remove bread from pans, and cool. Take off banana leaves and slice to serve. Yields 2 loaves.

Note: The traditional recipe uses 4 cups cornmeal rather than cornmeal and corn kernels.

Collected by Nydia A. Ríos Colón, San Juan, Puerto Rico. Caribbean Program, 1989

Agualoja de Jengibre (Ginger Liqueur)

6 cloves
6 anise florets
2 sticks cinnamon
½ pound ginger root,
   grated
2 cups water
2 liters dark rum
1 cup molasses
   (or honey)

1. With a mortar and pestle, pound to a powder cloves, anise, and cinnamon (or grind in a blender). Add ginger and continue pounding (or blending) until mixture is grayish white.

2. Put ginger mixture in water and bring to a boil. Lower heat and simmer for about 20 minutes. Cool.

3. Pour into a ½-gallon bottle or jar. Add rum and molasses.

4. Cover and let stand for 48 hours. Serve with ice and water or as an after-dinner drink. Yields ½ gallon.

Collected by Nydia A. Ríos Colón

Virgin Islands

✳ · ✳ · ✳ · ✳

Violet A. Bough

The history and culture of the U.S. Virgin Islands are exceptionally diverse. Archaeological digs have unearthed jewelry, pottery, and utensils at the burial sites of the Carib and Arawak Indians who lived on the islands from 300 B.C. until A.D. 1500. Evidence that Africans also predate Columbus's arrival at Salt River, St. Croix, in 1493 is less detailed but quite convincing. And, by the 1600s, the French, Danish, Dutch, and English all had followed the Spanish to the three islands known today as the U.S. Virgin Islands: St. Croix, St. Thomas, and St. John. France ruled St. Croix from 1674 to 1733, then sold it to Denmark. Denmark also ruled St. Thomas, from 1666 to 1917, and St. John, from 1717 to 1917. In 1733, after having provided most of the labor on all three islands, the Africans on St. John revolted; however, it was the uprising on St. Croix on July 3, 1848, that caused slaves on these three "Danish West Indies" islands to be freed. Finally, in 1878, Africans rebelled against their economic status on St. Croix and somewhat improved their living conditions.

For all of their influence on architecture, religion, manners, street names, and titles, the Europeans had a surprisingly small impact on Virgin Islands foods. Private homes may serve such European items as rolla pilsa, liver postoi, herring gundy, croustades, and rodgrod (red grout), a Danish dessert, but today most African, Hispanic, and Continental eateries feature native dishes — boiled fish with slippery okra fungi (cornmeal mush) and sweet potatoes or plantains on the side; fried fish and johnnycakes or hareper (pumpkin or banana fritters); salt fish and dumplings; souse (pig's feet) and potato salad; roast or stewed goat or roast pork with seasoned rice and potato stuffing; red peas soup; conch and rice; arroz con pollo (chicken and rice); kallaloo (greens soup) and fungi; benye or beignet (a fried, lightly sugared doughnut); and meat pâtés.

American cuisine officially joined that of the Amerindians, Africans, and

Previous pages: Ingredients for Virgin Islands foods are readied for the 1990 Smithsonian Folklife Festival. (Betty Honzik)

Europeans on March 31, 1917, when the United States purchased the Danish Virgin Islands for $25 million. By the late 1920s, Puerto Rican laborers and a number of Hispanics from the nearby islands of Culebra and Vieques had moved to the Virgin Islands. Those who stayed added another dimension to the islands' food customs. Arroz con pollo y habituelas, bolsillo, roast pig, and many other tasty, well-seasoned dishes come from their food traditions.

Centuries before this, however, Old World recipes were already adapting to New World ingredients. For example, in Denmark, red grout is made with strawberries. In the Virgin Islands, strawberries were replaced by sago or tapioca, either of which can be colored red with the juice of a prickly-pear cactus. Similarly, the bushes used to make kallaloo may not be like the West African originals, but our New World substitutes work just as well.

If It's Monday, Kallaloo and Fungi

Until the 1930s or early 1940s, most Virgin Islanders cooked their meals at home. Special dishes were served each day of the week. For example, kallaloo and fungi were served on Monday, red peas soup on Tuesday, and fish and fungi on Saturday. Popular dishes for Sunday included heartslit (liver) and rice or mashed yams, dove pork and rice, or either beef, tripe, or bull-foot soup. On Sunday mornings the aroma from island kitchens filled the air — and hearts — with thoughts of delicious after-church dining.

Back then, life was more easygoing. Fresh fish was easily obtained from the boats of fishermen, seines along the seashore, or open-air vendors. Vegetable markets provided an abundance of produce for side dishes or seasoning. Virgin Islanders disdain the use of salt and pepper alone — herb seasoning is much more popular. Even the blandest meat gains a distinctive flavor when a cook uses a mortar and pestle to blend rock salt, chible (chives), thyme, onion, garlic, cardamom, mace, cloves, allspice, and hot pepper. In the 1960s fast-food outlets displaced some home cooking and home dining, but soon even these restaurant menus included native cuisine.

Each of our islands is like a cook — the same dish tastes slightly different, depending on where you eat it. Take kallaloo and fungi. Crucians, people from St. Croix, prepare the liquid using a bush called popololo; in dry weather, they may substitute chopped spinach. Other ingredients include whitey Mary, pussley (purslane), bower, and bata bata (all local bushes), okra, pieces of hot pepper, conch, pig's tail, ham, fish, salt beef, crabs, and plain cornmeal fungi. However, Crucians never add onion, chives, or sweet pepper, ingredients used by cooks on some other islands.

Festival Fare

The most elaborate dishes are prepared for festivals, religious holidays, and major wedding anniversaries. In past years, family members and close friends would prepare the food in sufficient amounts to feed a hundred or more guests. Today, these events tend to be catered. Nevertheless, certain tra-

Opposite: Fruit preserves and rum fill the many-layered and elaborately iced Vienna cake made in the Virgin Islands. (Sallie Sprague)

"All ah, we share our foods and should be one."

ditions still persist. Vienna cake or black cake, topped with boiled icing, is the highlight of many of these meals. Certain ingredients used to make black cake are soaked for months or more in spirits, while the stewed guavaberry and green lime skins (green gage) used in Vienna cake are obtained months in advance. Guava, guavaberry, and coconut open-faced tarts also are prepared for these festive occasions. Typical beverages include Brow sodas (a carbonated soft drink produced on St. Croix), maubi (a spicy homemade beverage), ginger beer, Miss Blyden (sorrel), and guavaberry or guava liqueurs.

Christmas sweet breads also have survived through the ages. These breads are served with a slice of ham and glass of wine to holiday visitors and groups of Christmas serenaders. Unfortunately, caroling has not survived as well as the sweet breads. Times change — these days, tall wedding cakes are no longer placed on the head or carried on foot.

On the other hand, candy making and fruit preservation traditions continue. Mangoes, coco plums, tamarinds, marmee apples, guavas, guavaberries, and green lime skins are preserved for cake and tart fillings, while lasinger (jawbone candy), dondusla (glazed hard candy filled with peanuts), and coconut, almond, peanut, ginger, and peppermint sugar cakes sate the sweet tooth of adults and children alike.

Good Friday is another special day in the lives of Virgin Islanders, who celebrate it by abstaining from meat and vinegar. All kinds of fish are prepared for this holy day — grouper, snapper, smoked herring, shad, mackerel, and salt fish — but they are cooked in oil or a butter sauce with no vinegar. On this day of reverence and mourning, quiet is observed from noon until three in the afternoon.

Changing Ingredients, Unchanging Tastes

At Thanksgiving and Christmas, the traditional duck or turkey is prepared differently today from the way it was before the advent of modern kitchen appliances. No longer is it necessary to reserve the fowl a month or two before the event and dress it after it is delivered live. Nor do modern cooks fire up the brick oven in the yard in the early morning hours to roast the bird, bake stuffing, and make tarts, pound cake, or bread. Island cooking has progressed from coal pot and brick oven to kerosene stove to electric and gas ranges to microwave ovens. But no matter how much the equipment changes, the ingredients and taste remain the same.

Virgin Islanders do not change easily, either. No matter how far they travel, their requests for food are the same: Do you have salt fish and dumplings, or maybe fried fish and johnnycakes? How about kallaloo and fungi or souse and potato salad? Where's the roast goat with stuffing and all the trimmings, or red peas soup? Do you have any boiled fish and slippery okra fungi? Where's the arroz con pollo con habituelas or the lechón

(roast pork) with plenty of skin? Mon, I don't know when I last had a dove pork and okra fungi!

It is true that many people from the Caribbean, United States, Europe, Middle East, and Far East have come to the Virgin Islands. Certain restaurant menus reflect this fact. But another trend also is evident. Here, whether you dine on Trinidadian curry, Greek shish kebab, Chinese chow mein, or Italian pasta, variety is the spice of life. That is why, in the Virgin Islands, we say, "All ah, we share our foods and should be one."

✳ · ✳ · ✳ · ✳

Recipes

Pasteles (Pork Pasties)

Meat Pâtés

Fried Fish

Fish Stew

**Empanadillas
(Crab and Cassava Pies)**

Kallaloo and Fungi

Red Peas Soup with Dumplings

Souse and Potato Salad

Fungi with Okra

Johnnycakes

Horseshoes

Vienna Cake

Tropical Tarts

Virgin Islands Ginger Beer

**Agua Pirringa and Agua Coquito
(Coconut Drinks)**

Pasteles (Pork Pasties)

Sofrito:
1 bunch cilantro,
    stems removed
6 cloves garlic
1 large onion, roughly
    chopped
20 tiny ajices (sweet
    peppers), cored
3 green peppers,
    seeded and roughly
    chopped
¼ cup oil
2 teaspoons salt

Filling:
2 tablespoons
    shortening
1 pound pork loin,
    cut into 1-inch
    pieces
½ pound ham,
    chopped into
    small cubes
3 tablespoons
    chopped stuffed
    green olives
3 tablespoons tomato
    paste, diluted in 2
    tablespoons water
¼ cup sofrito

Dough:
2 medium purple
    yautías (Spanish
    root)
1 large cassava
    (yucca)
2 green bananas
¼ pound pumpkin
    (or butternut
    squash)
1 teaspoon paprika
1 tablespoon
    shortening

10 to 12 banana
    leaves

1. To make sofrito, blend cilantro, garlic, onion, peppers, oil, and salt in a blender until smooth. Reserve ¼ cup for this recipe and refrigerate or freeze the remainder in a tightly covered container (it will keep for several months).

2. For filling, fry meat in hot shortening until brown. Add olives, tomato paste, and ¼ cup sofrito. Cook on low heat for almost 1 hour, then set aside to cool slightly. If all liquid has evaporated from meat, add a few more spoonfuls oil.

3. While meat is cooking, prepare dough. Peel yautías and cassava with a small, sharp knife. Grate with bananas and pumpkin or squash into a bowl. Add paprika and shortening and mix to form a soft dough.

4. To form pasteles, lay a banana leaf flat and cover with a little oil from meat mixture to soften the surface. Place ⅓ cup dough on leaf and spread into a rectangular shape about ¼ inch thick. Put 2 to 3 tablespoons meat mixture on the left side of dough, then fold over the right side to enclose dough. Continue folding the leaf, tucking under the ends to make a neat, rectangular package. With kitchen string tie together 2 banana-leaf packets like a present.

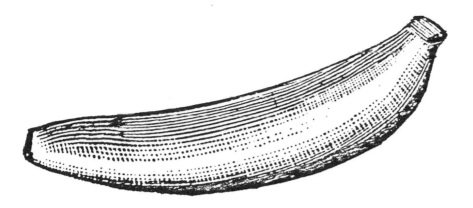

5. Boil packages in a large pot of salted water for 45 minutes, making sure that they are always covered by water. Pasteles are done when the leaf peels easily from the dough inside. Serves 10 to 12.

Evarista Santiago, St. Croix, U.S. Virgin Islands. U.S. Virgin Islands Program, 1990

Meat Pâtés

Filling:
1 pound ground beef
1 4-ounce can tomato
  paste
2 tablespoons
  chopped pimento
2 cloves garlic
salt
pepper

Dough:
See johnnycakes
  recipe, page 305

oil, for frying

1. Brown meat for filling. Add remaining ingredients and cook on low heat for 20 minutes. Cool slightly.

2. Make johnnycake dough. Pinch off pieces, forming dough into circles 5 inches in diameter.

3. To make pâtés, place a small amount of meat filling on one side of dough. Fold over the other side to form a half circle. Tightly seal the edges by pressing dough between your fingers and crimping edges.

4. Fry pâtés in hot oil, turning once so that both sides are golden brown.

Helmie Leonard, St. Thomas, U.S. Virgin Islands. U.S. Virgin Islands Program, 1990

Fried Fish

2 pounds grouper (or
    red snapper), cut
    into 2-inch pieces
juice of 2 limes
oil, for frying

Seasoning salt:
¼ cup salt
1 tablespoon pepper
2 cloves garlic
1 medium onion,
    sliced
2 stalks celery,
    chopped
2 tablespoons
    chopped parsley

1. Cover fish with lime juice and enough water to cover and let sit for about 1 hour.

2. To make seasoning salt, process salt, pepper, garlic, onion, celery, and parsley in a blender until mixture becomes a fine grain. Extra seasoning salt may be stored in a tightly covered container.

3. Remove fish from water, pat dry, and rub with seasoning salt.

4. Fry fish in sizzling hot oil for about 4 minutes on each side, until golden brown on all sides. Serve with johnnycakes. Serves 6.

Helmie Leonard, St. Thomas, U.S. Virgin Islands. U.S. Virgin Islands Program, 1990

Fish Stew

3 pounds firm-fleshed
    fish fillets (grouper,
    red snapper, or
    yellow tail), cut
    into chunks
juice of 2 limes
salt
pepper

2 medium onions,
    sliced
½ green pepper, cut
    into thin strips
½ red bell pepper, cut
    into thin strips
½ small hot pepper,
    minced

4 large cloves garlic,
    mashed into a
    paste
3 sprigs fresh thyme
3 green onions, cut
    into ¼-inch slices
1 cup water
6 tablespoons butter

1. Season fish by rubbing each piece with a mixture of lime juice, salt, and pepper.

2. Line the bottom of a heavy frying pan with onions. Lay the fish on onions and scatter remaining vegetables on top. Pour in water and cover fish with small pats of butter.

3. Cover pan and cook on medium to low heat until fish is cooked through, about 10 to 15 minutes. Serve with fungi (see kallaloo and fungi recipe, page 302) or fungi with okra (page 305). Serves 6 to 8.

Helmie Leonard

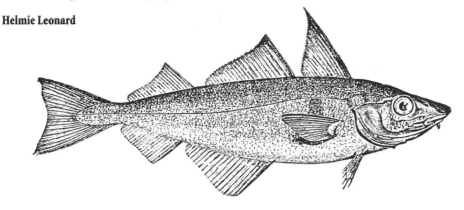

Empanadillas (Crab and Cassava Pies)

Filling:
½ pound crab meat
3 tablespoons sofrito
(see pasteles recipe,
page 298)
1 teaspoon paprika
⅓ cup oil

Dough:
2 large cassavas
(yucca)
2 tablespoons flour
1 teaspoon salt
water

oil, for frying

1. Place crab meat, sofrito, and paprika in a medium frying pan and add oil, stirring mixture to form a thick paste. Cook on low heat for 30 minutes. Set aside to cool slightly.

2. Make dough by peeling cassavas and grating them into a large bowl. Add flour and salt and a few spoonfuls of water to make the mixture into a soft dough.

3. To form empanadillas, cut freezer paper into 8-inch squares. Put ½ cup dough on a square and spread into a rectangle about 4 × 6 inches. Place 2 tablespoons crab mixture on the left side of the dough and fold over the right side to enclose crab. Seal by pressing the edges through the paper.

4. Refrigerate empanadillas for at least 1 hour. Remove from their paper wrappings and fry them in hot oil. Serves 4.

Evarista Santiago, St. Croix, U.S. Virgin Islands. U.S. Virgin Islands Program, 1990

Kallaloo and Fungi

1 pound salt beef
1 small hot pepper
1 pound pickled pig's tail
1 pound pickled pig's snout
6 quarts water
1 pound smoked ham butt, chopped
2 pounds fish, cut into bite-size pieces
1 pound conch, cubed
2 small eggplants, finely chopped
2 pounds frozen chopped spinach
2 pounds okra, chopped

Fungi:
3 quarts water
salt
1 pound cornmeal

1. Soak beef, pepper, pig's tail, and pig's snout in water for 3 to 4 hours or overnight. Rinse, then cut up meat. Cook in water until tender, about 1 hour.

2. Either the night before or 3 to 4 hours before cooking kallaloo, bone the fish and fry it. Also cook conch in boiling water until tender. Set aside.

3. Add chopped vegetables, fish, conch, and ham butt to meat mixture and simmer for 1 hour.

4. Prepare fungi 20 minutes before serving kallaloo. Boil salted water and pour in cornmeal; stir constantly, preferably with a wooden fungi stick, for approximately 15 minutes. Cornmeal will absorb water as mixture becomes stiffer, resembling a thick porridge. Serves 8.

Louise Petersen Samuel, St. Croix, U.S. Virgin Islands. U.S. Virgin Islands, 1990

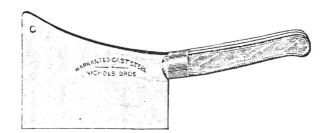

"Kallaloo is a favorite dish for parties and picnics. It is very nutritious because it contains a variety of greens, such as tannin leaf, bower, popo-lolo, bata bata, whitey Mary, pussley, and kallaloo bush. Spinach may be substituted for greens. In the old days, our people would cook this pot and eat it on Old Year's Night, searching for good luck in the new year. Now, the younger generation doesn't seem to do this as much."

Red Peas Soup with Dumplings

1 pound salted pig's
  tail
6 quarts water
2 16-ounce cans red
  beans
1 pound sweet
  potatoes, peeled
  and cubed
½ pound pumpkin
  (or butternut
  squash), peeled
  and cubed
1 medium onion,
  chopped
3 cloves garlic,
  minced
1 tablespoon finely
  chopped chives
1 teaspoon finely
  chopped fresh
  thyme
1-inch fresh ginger,
  finely chopped
pepper
¼ cup tomato sauce
  (optional)

Dumplings:
2 cups flour
½ teaspoon salt
2 tablespoons butter,
  softened
¾ to 1 cup water

1. Soak pig's tail in water for at least 3 to 4 hours to remove most of the salt. Rinse and cut up, then cook in water for almost 1 hour, until meat is tender.

2. While pig's tail is cooking, prepare dumpling dough. Mix flour and salt. Add butter and enough water to make a firm dough that does not stick to your hands. Knead until smooth, then cut dough into golfball-size pieces and flatten into a circle 3 to 4 inches in diameter. Set aside on a lightly floured surface.

3. Add remaining ingredients to soup and simmer for 1 hour. Drop in dumplings 15 minutes before serving. Serves 6.

Louise Petersen Samuel

Souse and Potato Salad

Souse:
6 pounds pig's feet, cut up
2 pounds pig's ears
1 to 2 hot peppers, whole
3 cloves garlic, minced
1 onion, chopped
2 stalks celery, finely chopped
salt
juice of 6 limes

Potato salad:
3 pounds potatoes
1 medium jar mayonnaise
1 tablespoon mustard
3 or 4 tablespoons relish
4 stalks celery, finely chopped
1 large onion, finely chopped
1 green pepper, finely chopped

2 or 3 hard-boiled eggs, diced (optional)

1. To prepare souse, boil pig's feet and ears in salted water until tender; remove ears in about 1 hour and feet in 1½ hours. Wash off grease.

2. In a separate pot, bring several quarts of salted water to a boil and add peppers. Remove from heat and add garlic, onion, celery, and lime juice to taste. Add degreased pig parts to pot, cover, and marinate until cool.

3. To make potato salad, boil potatoes in salted water, cool, peel, and dice.

4. In a bowl mix mayonnaise, mustard, relish, vegetables, and chopped eggs until blended. Reserve 1 celery stalk, 2 rings of green pepper, and 1 egg for garnish.

5. Combine potatoes with mayonnaise mixture and serve chilled with souse. Serves 8.

Louise Petersen Samuel, St. Croix, U.S. Virgin Islands. U.S. Virgin Islands, 1990

Fungi with Okra

1½ quarts water
salt
¼ pound okra, sliced
1 pound cornmeal
¼ pound shortening
¼ pound butter

1. Bring salted water to a boil. Add okra and boil for 10 minutes.

2. Mix in cornmeal and stir with a fungi stick, adding shortening as cornmeal begins to absorb water. Stir in butter when fungi is almost done, or a smooth mush.

Helmie Leonard, St. Thomas, U.S. Virgin Islands. U.S. Virgin Islands Program, 1990

Johnnycakes

4 cups flour
2 teaspoons baking
    powder
1 teaspoon salt
1 tablespoon lard (or
    shortening)
4 tablespoons butter,
    softened
water
oil, for frying

1. Mix flour, baking powder, and salt in a large bowl. Add lard or shortening and butter with enough water to make a firm dough.

2. Knead on a lightly floured surface until smooth. Divide dough into golfball-size pieces and gently flatten with the palm of your hand into a circle about ⅜ inch thick.

3. Prick the cakes several times with a fork. Fry in hot oil. As they cook, the cakes should puff up slightly and will become golden all over. Serves 6.

Helmie Leonard

Horseshoes

½ pound butter
½ pound shortening
1 pound brown sugar
1 teaspoon grated orange peel
1 teaspoon vanilla extract
1 teaspoon almond extract
1 teaspoon lemon extract
1 teaspoon cinnamon
½ teaspoon mace
½ teaspoon nutmeg
1 teaspoon salt
3 teaspoons baking soda
1½ cups water
3½ to 4 pounds flour

1. Cream butter and shortening with sugar, adding orange peel, extracts, and spices as mixture becomes light and fluffy.

2. Add salt and baking soda to water. Alternately mix flour and water with the butter and sugar mixture until the dough comes together. Leave some flour for rolling dough.

3. Turn dough out onto a lightly floured surface and roll a portion of dough to an 8 × 12-inch rectangle. With a pastry cutter, cut ½-inch strips, making ribbons of dough ½ × 8 inches. Shape into horseshoes on a cookie sheet.

4. Bake at 350°F for 15 to 20 minutes, until the edges turn light brown. Carefully remove with a spatula and put on a flat surface to cool.

Louise Petersen Samuel, St. Croix, U.S. Virgin Islands. U.S. Virgin Islands, 1990

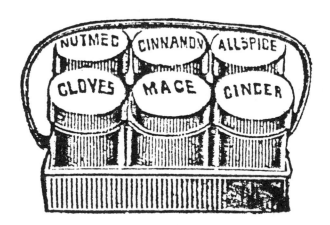

Vienna Cake

½ pound butter
1 pound sugar
3 large eggs
4 cups cake flour
3 teaspoons baking
   powder
pinch of mace (or
   nutmeg)
1½ cups milk
1 teaspoon vanilla
   extract
1 teaspoon almond
   extract

⅛ teaspoon yellow
   food coloring

Icing:
3 pounds powdered
   sugar
1 pound shortening
1 cup water
1 tablespoon white
   vanilla (or almond)
   extract (or juice of
   1 lime)

Fillings:
strawberry preserves
raspberry preserves
blackberry preserves
guava jelly
pineapple preserves
lime marmalade
rum

1. Grease and flour 2 9-inch cake pans. Preheat oven to 350°F.

2. Cream butter and sugar. Add eggs, 1 at a time, beating well after each addition. Sift dry ingredients. Mix milk with extracts and food coloring.

3. Add dry ingredients alternately with milk to butter mixture, stirring just until each addition is mixed in. Pour into prepared pans and bake for 45 minutes to 1 hour. Let cool, then unmold and finish cooling on racks.

4. To make icing, whip shortening and gradually add powdered sugar. Add enough water to reach a consistency to pipe on cake, then add flavoring.

5. To assemble, slice each cooled cake into 2 or 3 layers. Each layer should be filled with a different flavor of preserves, about ⅔ cup each. Mix choice of preserves with 3 tablespoons rum for each layer. Fill and assemble layers, then ice and decorate cake.

Louise Petersen Samuel

"As a little girl growing up, I remember my mother baking bread in the old brick oven. The bread couldn't bake fast enough — it was gone in a minute. When I got in my teens, she would send me into the streets with my basket to sell pastries. Now I make many large bridal cakes. Once, the bride didn't cut it for days, saying it was too pretty to cut. Maybe tomorrow, she would say, but there were a whole bunch of tomorrows before she finally cut it and by then it had spoiled.

Originally, this cake was from Vienna. For the liqueur, we substitute Cruzan rum, guavaberry, or cherry heering. We also use our native homemade jams, such as green gage (green lime), guava jelly, or guavaberry chopped fine and stewed like a preserve. The cake tastes best after it has aged four or five days. Remember to keep it cool and covered."

Tropical Tarts

Dough:
¼ pound margarine (or butter)
¼ pound shortening
1 pound sugar
½ teaspoon vanilla extract
½ teaspoon almond extract
½ teaspoon cinnamon
10 cups flour
3 teaspoons baking powder
½ cup milk
water

Coconut filling:
3 cups grated coconut, preferably canned
1½ cups sugar
2 teaspoons almond extract

Guava filling:
1 16-ounce can guava shells
1 teaspoon vanilla extract
1 teaspoon cinnamon

Pineapple filling:
3 pounds canned pineapple
½ pound sugar
1 teaspoon vanilla extract
1 teaspoon cinnamon

1. To make dough, cream margarine and shortening with sugar in a mixer. Add vanilla, almond extract, and cinnamon; beat until light and fluffy. Mix flour and baking powder; add all at once to creamed ingredients. Pour in milk and enough water to make mixture come together as a soft dough.

2. Place dough on a lightly floured surface and gently knead for a few turns. Divide into 4 pieces and roll out each tart shell. Put dough in aluminum pie pans and crimp the edges. Refrigerate while preparing choice of fillings.

3. For the coconut filling, mix ingredients and cook for 40 minutes on low heat.

4. For the guava filling, mix guava shells with vanilla and cinnamon, and cook on low heat for 30 to 40 minutes.

5. For the pineapple filling, mix pineapple with sugar and flavorings and cook for almost 1 hour on low heat.

6. Let cooked fillings cool slightly, then pour into unbaked tart shells. Use extra dough for lattice work or other decorative trimmings. Extra dough also may be used to make individual turnovers using the same fillings.

7. Bake tarts at 350°F for 45 minutes, rotating them in the oven for even baking.

Helmie Leonard, St. Thomas, U.S. Virgin Islands. U.S. Virgin Islands Program, 1990

Virgin Islands Ginger Beer

½ pound ginger
1 gallon water
½ to 1 cup sugar
few drops almond
    extract (optional)

1. The day before serving, peel and finely chop ginger. Put in a blender with a small amount of water and purée until smooth. Soak overnight in water in the refrigerator.

2. The next day, pour ginger through a cheesecloth. Add sugar to taste and a few drops almond extract, if desired.

Helmie Leonard

Agua Pirringa and Agua Coquito (Coconut Drinks)

Agua pirringa:
3 whole coconuts
sugar
3 quarts water

Agua coquito:
agua pirringa
rum (optional)
1 can condensed milk
1 can evaporated milk

1. To make agua pirringa, break open coconuts and cut into small pieces, peeling off the outer shell with a small, sharp knife. Grate coconut meat and soak in water, or put coconut pieces in a blender with 1 quart water and purée thoroughly.

2. Strain coconut mixture through a fine sieve, squeezing it dry by wringing it in your hands or a dish towel. Add sugar to taste plus remaining 2 quarts water, depending on consistency desired. Serve chilled, with ice.

3. To make agua coquito, add rum to taste, condensed milk, and evaporated milk to prepared agua pirringa.

Evarista Santiago, St. Croix, U.S. Virgin Islands. U.S. Virgin Islands Program, 1990

"Agua coquito is traditionally served as part of the feast celebrating the ninth and final day of the Day of the Cross ceremony."

Violet A. Bough was born in Frederiksted, St. Croix, and received a master's degree in education from Columbia University. She taught and supervised social studies and Virgin Islands history and culture in the Department of Education. Now retired, she works frequently on community and cultural projects.

Charles Camp has been the Maryland state folklorist since 1976 and is president of the National Council for the Traditional Arts. For the Smithsonian's folklife festival in 1975 and 1976, he served as the regional field research coordinator. In 1985 he produced the film *Fish Market* for the Maryland Folklife Program. More recently he wrote the book *American Foodways.*

Contributors

Linda R. Crawford is author of *The Catfish Book* (1991) and is at work on a book about watermelon. She attended the University of Texas and the Cooperstown Graduate Program in New York and is director of the South Delta (Mississippi) Library Services.

Rayna Green, a Cherokee, directs the American Indian Program at the Smithsonian's National Museum of American History. After completing her doctorate in folklore and American studies at Indiana University, she taught at several universities and worked with public service institutions. She is author of several books and numerous articles on Native Americans and American food customs, including "Wasting Away in Margaritaville: The Cult of Nachismo and the New American Cuisine."

Lin T. Humphrey teaches English and folklore at Citrus College in Glendora, California. She lives in nearby Claremont, where she and her husband created "soup night" on Thursdays for friends. She earned a master of arts degree in English at the University of Arkansas and has been a fellow of the National Endowment for the Humanities. She is coeditor with her husband of *"We Gather Together": Food and Festival in American Life* (1988), a collection of food-centered essays.

Theodore C. Humphrey chairs the Department of English and Foreign Languages at California State Polytechnic University in Pomona, where he teaches folklore, writing, and eighteenth-century English literature. Also a fellow of the National Endowment for the Humanities, he holds a doctorate from the University of Arkansas and is coeditor with his wife of *"We Gather Together."*

Lynne Ireland is acting director, Museum of Nebraska History, Nebraska State Historical Society. She is author of *The Neligh Mills Cook Book* (1990) and has published essays on food traditions in the *Center for Southern Folk-*

lore Magazine and *Foodways and Eating Habits: Directions for Research* (1983). She received her master of arts degree in American folk culture from the Cooperstown Graduate Program in New York.

Anne R. Kaplan is an editor with the Minnesota Historical Society Press. She has written articles on regional foodways and was coauthor of *The Minnesota Ethnic Food Book* (1986) and a contributor to *The Digest: A Review for the Interdisciplinary Study of Food*. She received her doctorate in folklore and folklife from the University of Pennsylvania.

Yvonne R. Lockwood is the Michigan folklife extension specialist with the Michigan Traditional Arts Program, Michigan State University Museum. In addition to her ethnographic work in the Upper Great Lakes region, she has researched and written extensively on the Croats in the Burgenland, Austria, and the Moslems in Bosnia, Yugoslavia. She holds degrees in folklore from the University of California, Berkeley, and in history from the University of Michigan.

Linda Paik Moriarty coordinated the Hawaii program at the 1989 Festival of American Folklife. For the past fourteen years she has imported and traded a wide range of South Pacific traditional arts and handicrafts. A graduate of the University of Hawaii, she is author of *Ni'ihau Shell Leis* (1986).

Kathy Neustadt specializes in New England folklife as well as American food customs and festivities. Her doctoral work at the University of Pennsylvania culminated in a dissertation on the clambake held annually in Allen's Neck, Massachusetts.

Maida Owens directs the Louisiana Folklife Program, where she surveys and documents folklife in Louisiana. She was an assistant editor of *Folklife in the Florida Parishes* (1989) and editor of *Fait à la Main: A Source Book of Louisiana Crafts* (1988). She earned a master of arts degree in anthropology from Louisiana State University.

Ralph Rinzler was the founding director of the Smithsonian's Office of Folklife Programs. He directed the Festival of American Folklife from its inception, in 1967, until his appointment as assistant secretary for public service, in 1983. He retired from that position in 1990.

Nydia A. Ríos Colón worked for thirty years for the government of Puerto Rico on various projects involving food customs and culture, particularly folk dancing. Now retired, she is completing her doctoral dissertation at the Advanced Studies Center for Puerto Rico and the Caribbean.

Illustration Sources

Drawings used with the recipes are reproduced from the following sources:

Animals: A Pictorial Archive from Nineteenth-Century Sources. Jim Harter, ed. New York: Dover Publications, 1979.

Pages 27, 54, 55, 95, 142, 145, 301

Book of Animals. Helen Iranyi, ed. A Main Street Press Book. New York: Mayflower Books, 1979.

Pages 118, 191

Burpee's Farm Annual. 1888. Reprint. Warminster, Pennsylvania: W. Atlee Burpee and Company, 1975.

Pages 60, 101, 109, 152, 153, 190, 194, 268, 269, 303

Food and Drink: A Pictorial Archive from Nineteenth-Century Sources. Jim Harter, ed. 3rd rev. ed. New York: Dover Publications, 1983.

Pages 23, 29, 30, 33, 34,

47, 49, 58, 59, 85, 87, 91, 113, 116, 150, 151, 154, 155, 157, 161, 163, 165, 166, 187, 204, 221, 227, 229, 232, 233, 249, 251, 270, 275, 279, 286, 299, 308, 309, 318, 319

Goods and Merchandise: A Cornucopia of Nineteenth-Century Cuts. William Rowe, ed. New York: Dover Publications, 1982.

Pages iv, v, 56, 62, 112, 158, 207, 209, 288, 306, 312, 314, 317

Handbook of Early Advertising Art: Pictorial Volume. Clarence P. Hornung, ed. 1947. 3rd ed. New York: Dover Publications, 1956.

Page 206

The Illustrator's Handbook. Harold H. Hart, ed. New York: A and W Visual Library, 1978.

Pages 28, 31, 45, 52, 64, 66, 73, 93, 97, 98, 104, 105, 123, 159, 208, 219, 224, 226, 247, 267, 273, 285, 302, 304

Montgomery Ward and Company: Catalogue and Buyers' Guide. No. 57, Spring and Summer, 1895. Reprint. New York: Dover Publications, 1969.

Pages 69, 70, 103, 111, 162, 167, 169, 193, 195, 196, 200, 202, 223, 250, 253, 254, 257, 272, 277, 278, 289, 297, 305

Sears, Roebuck and Company. Catalogue No. 117, 1908. Reprint. Northfield, Illinois: Digest Books, 1971.

Pages 65, 94, 141, 149, 258, 259

Treasury of Animal Illustrations from Eighteenth-Century Sources. Carol Belanger Grafton, ed. New York: Dover Publications, 1988.

Pages 25, 147

Index

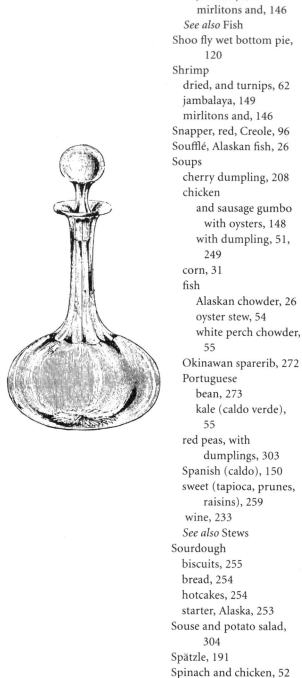

Katherine S. Kirlin is a public affairs and media relations professional at the Smithsonian Institution. An eighth-generation native of Natchez, Mississippi, she finds that her abilities as a raconteur and food enthusiast come naturally.

Thomas M. Kirlin, a writer and poet, was raised on a farm in Iowa and earned his doctorate in English from the University of Iowa. The Kirlins and their daughter live in Washington, D.C.

The text of this book was composed in Minion, created by Robert Slimbach for Adobe Systems, Inc., in 1990, with display typography in Bauer Bodoni, a typeface designed by Bauersche Gießerei in 1926. The book was designed and digitally composed by Marc Alain Meadows of Archetype Press, Inc., Washington, D.C., on an Apple Macintosh IIcx computer. Output of the type was performed by General Typographers, Inc., Washington, D.C., on a Linotronic L-300 processor. The book was printed on Penn Supreme by R. R. Donnelley and Sons Company, Crawfordsville, Indiana.

The Authors

The Book

Dedicated to Annie and the festival participants

© 1991 by the Smithsonian Institution. All rights reserved.

Library of Congress Cataloging-in-Publication Data

Kirlin, Katherine S.

  Smithsonian folklife cookbook / by Katherine S. Kirlin and Thomas M. Kirlin.
      p.   cm.
    Includes index.
    ISBN 1-56098-091-5 (alk. paper). — ISBN 1-56098-089-3 (pbk. alk. paper)
    1. Cookery, American. I. Kirlin, Thomas M. II. Title.
TX715.K5895 1991
641.5973 — dc20   91-268

British Library Cataloguing-in-Publication Data is available

Manufactured in the United States of America
98 97 96 95 94 93 92 91   5   4   3   2   1

∞ The paper used in this publication meets the minimum requirements of the American National Standard for Permanence of Paper for Printed Library Materials Z39.48-1984

Grateful acknowledgment is made to reprint the following copyrighted material: Page 22: Poem "Good Grease" from *There Is No Word for Goodbye* by Mary Tallmountain (Blue Cloud Quarterly Press, 1982). Copyright © 1982 by Mary Tallmountain. Reprinted by permission of the author. Page 192: Karjalanpiirakat recipe from *The Great Scandinavian Baking Book* by Beatrice Ojakangas (Little, Brown and Company, 1988). Page 215: Quotation from *My Antonia* by Willa Cather. Copyright © 1918 by Willa Cather, renewed 1977 by Bertha Handlan. Reprinted by permission of Houghton Mifflin Company.

Smithsonian Institution Press
Editors: Amy Pastan and Duke Johns
Production Manager: Kathleen Brown

Produced by Archetype Press, Inc.
Editor: Diane Maddex
Art Director: Marc Alain Meadows
Production Assistants: Rebecca S. Neimark and Mary McCoy

Cover illustration: Tapestry of the 1976 Festival of American Folklife embroidered by Ethel Mohamed, a traditional needleworker from Belzoni, Mississippi. (Eric Long, Office of Folklife Programs, Smithsonian Institution)

For permission to reproduce photographs appearing in this book, please correspond directly with the owners of the photographs, as listed in individual captions. The Smithsonian Institution Press does not retain reproduction rights for these illustrations individually or maintain a file of addresses for photo sources.